HUMILIATION

William Ian Miller

Cornell University Press
Ithaca and London

HUMILIATION

And Other Essays on Honor, Social Discomfort, and Violence

First published 1993 by Cornell University Press.

International Standard Book Number 0-8014-2881-5
Library of Congress Catalog Card Number 93-1273
Printed in the United States of America
Librarians: Library of Congress cataloging information
appears on the last page of the book.

⊗ The paper in this book meets the minimum requirements
of the American National Standard for Information Sciences—
Permanence of Paper for Printed Library Materials, ANSI Z39.48-1984.

For my mother and father

Contents

Preface

Most of us are familiar with the unpleasant emotions that attend losing face in social interaction; we know only too well the sick feeling of being exposed as thinking we are more than we really are and the humiliation of having our poses of competence undercut by our own ineptitude. This book is about the anxieties of self-presentation, the strategies we adopt to avoid loss of face in our routine social encounters, and the emotions—namely, humiliation, shame, and embarrassment—which maintain us as self-respecting and respectable social actors. I approach these themes in a variety of ways so that this book is less one argument than a series of arguments, suggestions, and observations.

The themes emerged from my years of studying the heroic society of saga Iceland. The sagas generated my consuming interest in the discomfitures that plague us in even the most conventional of social encounters. They reveal, with unusual astuteness, the behaviors of a people who cared with the totality of their being about the public figure they cut and about the respect they elicited. These people could not contemplate self-esteem independent of the esteem of others.

We, in contrast, allow ourselves the possibility of self-esteem in the face of the contempt of others. But even though we can envisage self-esteem without independent confirmation, it is hard to achieve and not always a virtue if achieved, for it can be as easily the defining trait of the sociopath as of the saint, of the self-centered boor as of the self-confident person of great inner strength. In short, although we may think of ourselves as interesting and entertaining, that is not our call to make. So we, like the saga people, are not strangers to the nervousness and tensions that necessarily accompany caring about what others think about us. Like those ancient heroes, we care about honor, about how we stack up against all those with whom we are competing for approbation.

This concern is one of the central themes of this book. Honor is not dead with us. It has hidden its face, moved to the back regions of consciousness, been kicked out of most public discourse regarding individuals (though it remains available for use by nation-states to justify hostility); it can no longer be offered as a justification for action in many settings where once it would have constituted the only legitimate motive. But in spite of its back-alley existence, honor still looms large in many areas of our social life, especially in those, I would bet, that occupy most of our psychic energy. Honor is intimately tied to the idea of reciprocity. Much of the substance of honor is still rooted in a desire to pay back what we owe, both the good and the evil. The failure to reciprocate, unless convincingly excused, draws down our accounts of esteem and self-esteem.

It has long been noted that, in honor-based cultures, shame is the flipside of honor. But in our complex modern culture the domain of shame has contracted as the domains of humiliation and embarrassment have expanded. Humiliation (or the fear of it) is perhaps the key emotion that supports our self-esteem and self-respect. Humiliation is the price we pay for not knowing how others see us. Humiliation (and the fear of it) is in fact the very "power the giftie gie us" that Robert Burns prayed for. It is perhaps our most powerful socially oriented emotion of self-assessment. Humiliation cannot be avoided, having made itself, or at least the threat of it, a normal feature of most routine social interaction. Routine interaction is thus a risky and complicated business, requiring competence if we are to survive with our honor and self-esteem intact. I do not mean to deny that the routine can be routine and thus easily negotiated. Surely the person who always feels panicked in the presence of others has started to develop the strangenesses of a Dostoyevskian character. Nevertheless, most socially competent people are also routinely aware of these risks as necessary features of the monitoring systems that maintain their social competence—and at times painfully so.

The emotions of humiliation and shame construct, destroy, and recreate volatile hierarchies of moral and social rank. Shame and humiliation do not work in quite the same ways in their relation to rank (we shall see that shame requires groups of rough equals, while humiliation can work within and across stable hierarchies), but they carry out the same kind of rough work of punishing moral and social failure. Thus not infrequently honor, humiliation, and the obligation to pay back what one owes find themselves inextricably bound up with violence. Violence is the focus of Chapter 2, but it also figures insistently in the discussions of gift exchange and reciprocity in Chapter 1 and especially in the treatment of the emotional economy of the heroic in Chapter 3.

Throughout this book I am concerned to get at the extent it is possible to talk about emotions across time and across culture. The precise experience of many of our richest emotions—among which I include, of course, humiliation—is in various ways influenced by and dependent on the social arrangements that elicit them and the vocabulary used to express them. I shall thus give some attention to how the emotion we indicate by the word *humiliation* was referenced, if at all, in other times and places. We will thus make incursions, even if only briefly, into the emotional worlds represented in the sagas, in *Sir Gawain and the Green Knight,* and in some works of Shakespeare and Dostoyevsky, among others.

One of the common strategies of humiliation-avoidance which we all use is to claim narrow limits of competence for ourselves. By doing so, we narrow our range of accountability; writers, academics especially, beg indulgence from the reader when they venture outside their special domains of competence. Let me make a few gestures in that direction. By training I am a literary critic and philologist, by profession I have become a historian of medieval Iceland, for which, however, most of the sources are literary. By employment I am a law professor and teach traditional courses in law in addition to courses in line with the themes of this book. But this book ranges beyond my areas of formal expertise, mainly into psychological and anthropological matters, but also implicitly into cultural sociology and a kind of concretely situated social theory which I associate with the work of Erving Goffman and through him to Georg Simmel. I am clearly indebted to them. That I give the impression that humiliation and other related unpleasant emotions generated by normal social interaction are the central emotions of everyday social existence may seem to impart an ironical misanthropy to some of the discussions. I can't say I disown the irony, but I do wish to disown at least some of the misanthropy.

A word about pronouns: because of the small crisis in third-person singular narration I have tried to resolve certain awkwardnesses by third-person-plural "theys" that clearly then behave as if they were singular. At times I have simply moved to *you*, which may strike some as too familiar. At other times I vary between *he* and *she*. In Chapter 2, where the topic is violence, it would be a cruel joke to pretend to gender equality by typing violators as *she*. And it would, of course, not do at all to maintain the present regime by typing victims as *she* either. The easiest strategy seemed to be to make my victims and violators and even most of my observers *he* when a more noncommittal third-person plural would have appeared awkward.

Parts of Chapters 2 and 3 were given as papers or as lectures at various venues over the past few years. All of the chapters have been read by various colleagues, students, and friends. Shared lunches with Don Herzog revealed our surprisingly consistent take on many things and generated several points developed here; exchanges of voluminous electronic mail with Carol Clover forced me to face up to many of my complacencies or at least to feel guilty about those I am too wedded to to forgo, such as my attachment to a too-good-to-be-true view of the grandness of the heroic ethic. She is, after all, one of the few people who needn't accept what I say about the Viking world on faith. I benefited greatly from my colleague Phoebe Ellsworth's expertise in the psychology of emotions and her good sense in many other matters. Others whose readings and comments deserve mention: Elizabeth Anderson, Robert Bartlett, Guyora Binder, David Cohen, Heidi Feldman, Robert Geline, Anna Headly, Leo Katz, Richard Pildes, Christina Whitman, and two anonymous reviewers whose careful readings produced detailed suggestions for improvement. Rachel Godsil and Larry Kramer deserve special mention for subjecting portions of the book to a detailed edit and doing their best to curb the excesses of my free-associational mode of argumentation. As is the case with anything I have written, my wife, Kathy Koehler, has criticized, suggested, and encouraged; she is my muse.

William Ian Miller

Ann Arbor, Michigan

HUMILIATION

Introduction:
Burning a Witch

What follows is an account of an incident that took place many years ago. It touches on the main themes of this book: violence, reciprocity, and the emotions such as humiliation and shame that do the work of self-assessment and self-maintenance in the drama of social interaction.

I will begin by anticipating the conclusion and then follow with a more circumstantial account. Imagine hosting a get-together for a group of twelve. You have stocked up on food and drink, and because not a few of the members of the group are lusty drinkers, the drink alone represents a considerable expenditure. The time comes for the guests to arrive. No one appears. But no one is ever quite on time. More time passes; finally, one person shows. It is your friend in the group, the person who had introduced you into it, and the only person in it who up until then had not been an utter stranger to you. Now you both sit and wait. Did you forget to tell them the right time, the right day? The lateness passes beyond fashionableness, heading toward inconsiderateness and beyond into something more ominously disconcerting. At last a phone call. It is from a woman in the group, a lawyer, a toughminded, no-nonsense person. She tells you simply that people have decided not to come (they preferred watching the regional finals of the NCAA basketball tournament, she says, at her house; sorry for the inconvenience; you can come over if you like; good-bye). How would you feel? What did you ever do to deserve that?

Or imagine how you would feel if you were one of the people who as part of a concerted action decided not to show up? What brought you to such drastic action? It is one thing to think someone deserves such treatment and quite another actually to treat a person that way.

Let me start this story again. For a year or so our group of faculty, spouses, and students interested in reading Old Norse would get together every two or three weeks at a different member's place to translate a portion of an Icelandic saga assigned to us at the previous meeting. The host was charged with providing beer, wine, and food. Translating would begin after several beers and continue through more, so that by the time the last person translated no one was in much of a condition to tell or care about the result. Although we seriously intended to carry out the group responsibility of acquiring competence in Old Norse, Seriousness, with a capital **S**, was bad form, for we imagined that the Vikings we were studying would be disgusted if they chanced upon us talking "academically." So serious ideas had to be carefully packaged as off-hand comments that just seemed natural to the moment. And somehow, almost unconsciously, we also banished from our little group all notions of status—professor, spouse, student, lawyer—that were imported from without.

Remarkably, several of the group members became rather proficient within a year's time. Some never did, but that fact didn't prevent the group's membership from staying constant and everyone from developing an attachment to the enterprise and to one another too, even though the group had drawn together people who otherwise had little in common. There was, however, one slightly pompous person who—how shall I say it?—was not as well liked as the others. Yet even he was accepted, if not loved. But he introduced a thirteenth member, a professor who did not fit in very well and who was to become the object of our correction. His initial incompatibility was not all his doing. We had clearly accorded him less of a welcome than we would have if he had been introduced by one of the better-liked members of the group. Nevertheless, he soon so distinguished himself as an offensive personality in his own right that we came to see him as completely emancipated from his patron. Being somewhat older than the others and more established in his career, he held himself out as an authority on everything. He had the socially and academically suicidal habit of lecturing to people about their own subject matter on which he was usually woefully misinformed. We found him physically unappealing also, yet he fancied himself a ladies' man and repeatedly importuned the women in the group with his advances. Their brush-offs led him to observe to the other male members that the women were a rather unattractive lot, their pulchritude varying directly, in his view, with their willingness to entertain his advances. The men, not averse to tale-bearing, did not withhold these opinions from the women.

After six months the thirteenth member volunteered to host the group. The idea to shame him arose as an unintended conclusion to rather aimless complaints about going to X's house which were aired by group members as we arranged rides and planned how we could delay going until the basketball game was over *without offending X.* Finally, the lawyer suggested that we meet at her house and forget going to X's altogether. (She had suffered the most from X's advances.) I remember a rush of adrenaline as I agreed, which both assisted and suppressed the assaults of conscience I assumed were also playing themselves out among the others. When assembled at her place, we were all rather too easily given to hilarity. We drank quickly and a lot and occasionally had doubts, leading some to suggest that we should call X and tell him we would be right over. The lawyer treated such vacillations as cowardly: we had embarked and we must see it through.

We felt a strange mix of excitement, even exhilaration, vindication, satisfaction, but also guilt, shame, embarrassment, and uncertainty. Was this how people who burned witches felt? We made jokes about the situation, drawing the connection between our own actions and the kind of ostracism and social disciplining that might have taken place in saga society. And we laughed harder than the jokes deserved. We constructed self-congratulatory justifications for our behavior: we hyperintellectualized souls had shown ourselves worthy of our subject matter and were wonderfully preindustrial in the best Viking manner. We told ourselves that X had had fair notice of what awaited him, not only from the contents of the material we read and talked about in the group but also from all the little sanctions of social control that we'd meted out to him all along—ignoring, eye-aversion, verbal put-downs, interruptions, dismissively short answers to his questions, using his name in direct address excessively or not at all—but to which he had of course remained densely oblivious.

Could it have been worse for Mr. X? If his friend had not shown up he could have suffered his humiliation without having to pretend to the continued health of his social being in front of someone else. And what prompted the lawyer's call to him some two hours into the shaming ritual? Given the forcefulness of her character, it seemed motivated mostly by her desire to show that she, for one, was not afraid to take responsibility for the events. She had borne down those members who felt that we just shouldn't do what we had ended up doing; if she hadn't quite organized the ostracism, she was the catalyst who allowed everyone else's vague hostilities to coalesce into concerted group action. Did it also dawn on her that the call prevented him from constructing for himself a face-saving story along the lines that he had gotten the night wrong, that the slight was unintended? Her call let him know not only that we were not at his house but that we were at her house *together*. Or was her motivation also partly a way of showing herself and ourselves that we could, even in the midst of this action, maintain the *forms* of decency and thus accord him an explanation? After all, she did coldly invite him to join us if he wished to attend. But that "decency" was for our benefit alone: thus did our consciences increase his suffering. We had burned a witch. The thirteenth person got the message at last and never joined us again.

Embedded within this perhaps unsettling narrative are many of the themes that make up the substance of the chapters that follow. First, consider the matter of reciprocity. Every good turn deserves another, as the old saw would have it. On the positive side, the group engaged in convivial exchanges; some of these were formalized, as when we determined whose turn it was to host, but most were left to those social practices about which, like language, we know more than we know we know. We know how to act right, so that when we don't we feel awkward and embarrassed; we know how to read social signals and to remedy a glitch when it occurs; in short, we know how to act as properly socialized beings act. But one person did not have this kind of competence. It is one of the essential features of such incompetence that the person so afflicted is incapable of knowing that he is incompetent. To have such knowledge would already be to remedy a good portion of the offense. Yes, we have willful violators of norms who might also have to be disciplined, but they are not properly described as incompetent. In fact, the willful violator, who might range anywhere from clown, to ironist, to curmudgeon, even, in some instances, to criminal, often has a more acute awareness of the norms as norms than the person who is "naturally" pleasant.

On the negative side, too, one good turn also deserves another, but here "good" drips with sarcasm. Nevertheless, we were not simply following the law of the talion, not simply repaying X's good with good, his evil with evil. Our responses had been modulated. We mostly suffered his offenses, restricting ourselves to small sanctions that he was incapable of perceiving. It is not uncommon that the socially incompetent prey off the amiability and the mannerliness of others. The incompetent are the direct beneficiaries of the reluctance of the people they offend to make scenes. The bore can thus continue to bore, the boor continue to be boorish, because it is excruciatingly painful for us to violate the norms that maintain noncontentious smooth and respectful social interaction by confronting them with their boringness or boorishness. Have you ever noticed that the person who reprimands another's misbehavior often embarrasses us much more than the offense that provoked the reprimand in the first place? It was only by the chance convergence of several fortuities that X was so aggressively sanctioned. If it had not been for the peculiar circumstances of the basketball game, X's hosting, and the presence of the indomitable lawyer, we would have continued to suffer X, gossiping about him among ourselves and persisting in the ineffectual coldnesses that he was never sensible of. Without the challenge of the lawyer, without her stepping beyond the bounds and taking the responsibility for being bold and courageous in her vindictiveness, the rest of us—was it our cowardice or our virtue?—would have continued to muddle along politely and painfully. Humankind seems more inclined by "nature" to be *homo pullus* (man the chicken) than *homo lupus* (man the wolf).[1] And probably it is not a bad thing that we are.

But we felt or were made to feel by the lawyer that we had incurred an obligation to X stronger than the one to accept the invitation to meet at his house: the obligation to pay him back for all the offenses he had done us. Accepting X's hospitality would have made us beholden to him or, if not quite that, would at least have allowed him to discharge his debts of hospitality, to improve his moral claim to being a member in good standing in the positive and sociable cycles of exchange we had created. X was treated to the rude truth that not only hospitality engenders obligations to reciprocate, but that offenses and assaults do too. Both the good and the ill received oblige the other to make a return.

The first chapter in this book deals directly with the obliging force of gifts and hospitality. It seeks to demonstrate the continuing tyranny of a norm of reciprocity whose force we officially deny.[2] The official view is that gifts are free, that they are windfalls to receive and kindnesses to confer. They are contrasted with mercantile exchanges, in which everything is calculated and cash is the only tie that binds. I suggest in conclusion that there may be an intimate connection between our official denial of the dark, obliging, and importuning side of gifts and the official illegitimacy of revenge. Once, when people understood that whatever else gifts may do, they create obligations first, people also understood that obligation arose any time one received something gratuitously. Thus an insult or any other wrong was a kind of negative gift, which, like a positive gift, demanded repayment. Among rough equals, repaying one's debts, whether those incurred by receiving gifts or those incurred by receiving insults or offense, was what the honorable person had to do.[3] Honor demanded the punctilious concern to pay back what one owed. The high position honor held in this system of values was directly sustained by the force of the norm of reciprocity.[4] That norm weakened its hold when the assault on honor—by Christianity and later by commerce, which claimed that it was foolish, irrational, sinful, and promoted disorder—began to bear fruit.[5] In the new public order, debts that arose by gift were redefined away by the ideology of the free gift that created no debt, only joy in both giver and receiver. Vengeance became illegal and the emotions that supported vengeance were devalued morally. Even mercantile debt in this now honorless public order held the debtor in less of a grip, thanks to the creation of a new law of bankruptcy, founded on the idea that the vagaries of the market, not moral failure, created debtors. There is indeed a big truth in that idea, but it is funded in part by weakening the grip of the norm of reciprocity. A world in which debts can be discharged at something less than what was bargained for is a world in which honor has been badly trumped.

The official discourse of commerce and the ideology of the free gift are two sides of the same anti-honor coin.[6] Yet the norm of reciprocity persists, almost with a vengeance. We still *feel*, even as we refuse to understand it or admit it, that gifts oblige us and that wrongs oblige us to make return and even up accounts. We still feel bound to return kindness and we feel frustrated when we are prevented from returning wrongs. Not even X was so utterly unsocialized as to think that he could avoid taking his turn as host. And I suppose that it was some time before he left off fantasizing revenge for the pain we had caused him. This is the grander stuff that emerges from more homely matters I deal with in Chapter 1, where it is the intrusiveness of the norm of reciprocity as it plays itself out in the relatively small-stakes world of dinner invitations and valentines that provides our immediate subject, for in this world we feel most intensely the grip it still holds on us. The chapter discusses with particularity the gift's ability to impose obligation and thus its power to importune and annoy; it discusses some of the strategies and costs of adept avoidance of obligation and the anxieties and discomforts attendant on convivial exchange. Some of these strategies we enter upon fully consciously, others are grooved by habit or by an almost unconscious feel for what the situation calls for. My account, then, is partial, intentionally taking the point of view of the person on whom the obligation is imposed rather than of the person imposing it. Given the vastness of the topic, my decision was to be monocular and specific, rather than binocular and general, to give the readers their own opportunity to flesh out the implications for the other side of the equation. What emerges, in any event, is a wondrous sense of the psychological and social complexity that informs the content of our competence at handling these "simple" practices.

Violence is the subject of Chapter 2. Was what we did to X violent? Or was it just cruel? Or was it simply justice? These are some of the questions that will occupy us. I try to uncover what we mean when we speak about violence, the implicit claims that are encompassed within the concept—all with the goal of discerning whether it is possible to make cross-cultural and trans-temporal comparisons about levels of violence. A certain romanticism and an implicit moralism creep in when we seek to know whether it was better then or is better now, whether the grass is greener on the other side or whether there is no place like home. If answers to such questions are forthcoming, one of the chief criteria informing them will have to do with the relative quantity and quality of violence in the cultures, the relative security of the body, and the relative freedom from fear about these things. I assume that much of what drives historical inquiry is the desire to make moral claims about the virtues and vices of various customs, values, social formations, and political arrangements. Just because one believes, as I do, that values and norms are socially constructed, one is not required to forgo making moral judgments about various social regimes.

Violence is a highly contested category. Although everyone thinks that they know it when they see it, in many settings its presence or absence is often the very issue in dispute. People tend to think that violence is an attribute of things they oppose; they thus metaphorize it and make it stand for other concepts such as dominance, difference, silence, even constraint. I argue for an incontestable core to violence—when fist meets face—that shades by degrees into more and more contestable claims of violence in which political and normative agendas predominate. But these kinds of claims are not random; they follow certain culturally predictable patterns that I attempt to uncover.

From our point of view nothing we did to shame X was violent, yet we cannot be so sure that he would concur. We feel that violence is more than just physical intrusion, for as we all know, and in spite of the silly saying taught us as children, a few well-chosen words hurt a lot more than most sticks or stones. Some people may think that our group members, who knowingly caused so much psychic pain, must have been rather violent people. Because we acted in concert, because we intended his humiliation, there is a sense of the event as being more violent than if it had resulted from independent decisions not to go. That is, we could be perceived as having been violent but no one would agree that violence was done. I think finally that our intuitions are more likely to confirm here a distinction between the cruelty or callousness of our behavior and any claim that we were violent. Would that change if X had killed himself for shame?

But I cannot be sure that the reader isn't likely to privilege X's view of the event because this particular narration invites people to imagine themselves more easily in the position of the person being shamed than with the vigilantes who shamed him. He was one and we were many. He thus invites more focused attention, more sympathetic energy than the lot of us would. To the observer, he thus appears as the victim in the account, not as the victimizer. And with his victim status comes a certain power to define his victimizers as violent, as people, that is, who made him a victim. We are also more likely to identify with the person whose emotions we can most easily experience vicariously. In this account it is easier for the observer to feel X's shame than to feel whatever the multiplicity of possible motivations the shamers and humiliators may have been.

Given my particular special knowledges, I could not help but think about the connections between honor and violence, since as a historical matter and even a contemporary sociological one, a culture of honor is often perceived by both insiders and outsiders to be a culture of threat and violence. Chapter 3, "Emotions, Honor, and the Affective Life of the Heroic," deals directly with the emotions that sustain a culture of honor. The chapter begins with a discussion of some of the problems that face the historian trying to uncover the emotional life of another culture across barriers of time, space, language, and culture. In spite of the hurdles, if the sources are circumstantial enough, we should be able to do reasonably well uncovering that life, even if, obviously, we cannot reexperience the precise experience of the other. (For that matter, we cannot precisely reexperience our own experience either.) I try then to give an account of the behaviors of shame and envy within the context of a bloodfeuding culture, because these, more than any others, appear to be the emotions that give the most characteristic color to the heroic. Shame maintains the ethic of courage and face, envy the ethic of competitiveness. The shame of heroic society looks much like our shame, except it is a broader notion, encompassing more of its people's emotional life than our shame does of ours. It is also triggered more easily, and by failings different from those that elicit shame in us. Yet there is a recognizable core of shared features between their shame and ours. Their envy is our envy in the sense that their word for it meant, like ours, the pain suffered at the contemplation of another's pleasure and achievement. But their envy played a very different social role; in a society grounded on heroic assumptions it was quite literally the way of the world.

As I mentioned in the Preface, a recurrent theme of this book is that we are more familiar with the culture of honor than we may like to admit. This familiarity partially explains why stories of revenge play so well, whether read as the *Iliad*, an Icelandic saga, *Hamlet*, many novels, or seen as so many gangland, intergalactic, horror, or Clint Eastwood movies. Honor is not our official ideology, but its ethic survives in pockets of most all our lives. In some ethnic (sub)cultures it still is the official ideology, or at least so we are told about the cultures of some urban black males, Mafiosi, Chicano barrios, and so on. And even among the suburban middle class the honor ethic is lived in high school or in the competitive rat race of certain professional cultures.

It is surprising how much certain styles of honor and the heroic are recognizable if not exactly translatable across cultures. The rough structure of honor, perhaps more than any other ethical system, travels well, although the exact content of honor varies greatly across cultures. Achilles and my colleagues and I all seek prestige, and all envy the attainment of it by our competitors. All of us care about maintaining face. Achilles has to be ready to kill and to act without fear of being killed himself to maintain his honor. Should he fail, his entire being suffers. His most effective strategy for regaining face is to avenge himself on the person who caused his failure or to reduce others to his own lamentable state. For us the stakes are lower. We can separate our professional and private lives; we can even have more than one professional life. We can fail here and still be honored there. Above all, honor does not require us to put our physical lives on the line, although, as we shall have occasion to wonder in Chapter 5, I am not sure that the emotional consequences of playing for professional prestige are all that less intense than those of playing for honor in the *Iliad*. We all thrill in our honor, and we sicken in the shame of our failures. Achilles is utterly recognizable.

The final and longest essay in this book is an anatomy of humiliation, which I have divided into two chapters, 4 and 5. Chapter 4 seeks to carve out a domain for humiliation which is distinct from shame on one side and embarrassment on the other. I distinguish a state of humiliation from the emotion. X, for instance, humiliated himself in our eyes every time he bothered the women, every time he lectured about things we knew more about than he did, but he did not feel humiliated for doing so. Had he been self-aware enough to *feel* humiliated, he probably would not have engaged in the behavior that humiliated him. It was the goal of our shaming ritual to make him feel humiliated, even if the ritual could not succeed in informing him of the precise ways in which he had been humiliating himself all along. A more sensitive soul would never have been the object of a ritual that operates crudely by saying "we don't want you in our sight," but also more subtly by saying "we want you to see yourself as you have appeared in our sight."

There is an intimate connection between pretension and humiliation. Humiliation is the emotion we feel when our pretensions are discovered. By taking this view of humiliation, I reject masochism or torture as providing the paradigm for humiliation, as some have done. Humiliation inheres in every nook and cranny of the normal. We know it in the myriad of little humiliations we frequently suffer or risk suffering in every face-to-face interaction. The humiliation of the perverse, of extremis, of death camps and interrogation rooms is parasitical on the usual and familiar, not the other way around. I claim that humiliation's genre is the comic and that this comedy plays itself out in various complex ways in the morality of social control.[7]

In pretension lies the possibility of feeling humiliated and the near certainty of being seen as humiliating oneself. But not all pretension is a vice of the pompous buffoon, the person who pretends to more than he is. Some pretension arises when you are exactly what you purport to be, but are in the wrong setting. This "structural pretension," my pretentious coinage for a common social fact, is the risk you incur of being seen to be putting on airs by simply being out of place, by being on the other's turf, when the status you occupy in the world is one that is perceived to be ranked above those with whom you now find yourself: thus the corporate lawyer at a Harley rally, the tweedy academic in the working-class bar, the adult among teenagers, among any number of readily available examples. The risk of this kind of structural humiliation is one of the costs of being higher in some hierarchy than the people judging you. But humiliation in general is not just a risk of the high. It is a normal risk of most all normal social interaction.

Chapter 4 is also concerned with the fear of ridicule and the strategies, mostly self-defeating, we use to avoid being laughed at when we do not mean to be laughed at. The strategy of being humble often leads to pride in one's humility, thus leaving one open to being exposed and humiliated as a hypocrite. To be "cool" is to sport an air that supposes some amount of pretense and self-satisfaction, again leaving one open to deflation. Even the naturally cool (if such a condition is possible) occupy by their very coolness a position that makes a fall possible. The unhumiliatable are those unenviable souls of whom it could be said that "when you got nothing, you got nothing to lose."

One might hazard the strong claim (with some amount of irony) that our world is divided into two types of people: those who humiliate themselves but who are too insentient to know it, and those who feel each social interaction as a minefield in which one's esteem and self-esteem can be blown into a million foolish little shards. These latter are in the mold of the characters who crowd the pages of Dostoyevsky's novels; they find that the best strategy for avoiding humiliation is to become expert at enduring it, even to self-inflict it in order to have it on their own terms. These are the souls who accept that humiliation is a fact of social life, who make sure never to be caught being seen as foolish without knowing that they are playing the fool," and who never let others see them without first seeing themselves as others would, while presuming these others to be as expert in discerning a fool as they themselves are. They can then satisfy themselves on their greater perspicacity, their greater self-awareness, and on their ability to manipulate the audience that condemns them.

In Chapter 5, "Humiliation Historicized," I take up in more detail an issue raised in Chapter 3: the extent to which the vocabulary of the emotions affects the quality and sensibility of our emotional life. If we lacked the words or the simple concepts of embarrassment and humiliation, would our emotional experience be less rich or subtle? These concerns force us to confront directly the applicability of my claims to other times and other places. I tackle this problem by closely examining the superb Middle English poem *Sir Gawain and the Green Knight*. When *Gawain* was written, English had no word for the emotions of embarrassment and humiliation, yet I can demonstrate that the poem depends on the reader's ability to perceive within the large domain of shame certain subsets of affect which behave differently from plain old shame. And these subsets mark out domains that would later acquire the names humiliation and embarrassment. But I make no strong claims about the relation of vocabulary to the richness of emotional life, concluding instead with a kind of inconclusiveness. Yes, there is a connection between how we talk about the emotions and the precise quality of our emotional life, and yes, there is an intimate connection between the dominant cultural values and the quality of emotional life, especially if one of those values says that talking about your inner states is bad form. Nevertheless, *Gawain* shows, and the Icelandic sagas do not disconfirm, that even in the absence of a specifically dedicated vocabulary the capacity to lead a very rich emotional life exists. Some people (we usually call them poets) express these feelings via circumlocution, metaphor, and circumstance. And if these emotions are not completely congruent with ours, they nonetheless bear sufficient points in common so that comparison, recognition, and rough mutual understanding are achievable.

All the chapters in this book raise the question of the general applicability of the claims I am making. Are my takes on violence simply those of an academic who has had a two-decade love affair with the heroic culture depicted in old books? Are my claims about the emotional life of Nordic heroes utterly infected by the emotional categories of English? Are my views on humiliation and the aggravation of unwanted invitations to dinner more a betrayal of my own misanthropy than insights into emotions and the social practices they inform? Are my views on gift exchange too idiosyncratic? As a historian I am aware of change through time, of the effects of social and political arrangements on so-called human nature, of the riskiness involved in making general claims that purport to cover more than the local and the familiar, and, above all, of the peculiar twist the social and cultural setting and individual psychology of the researcher bring to the truth of his or her subject matter. But I am ambivalent. My discussion of violence attempts to discover the local and particularist claims that people blithely ignore when using the concept even as I hint at some trans-local claims of my own. The gifts chapter focuses mainly on practices I am intimately familiar with and thus its claims should be held to obtain only for the narrow American academic or educated white communities I am immersed in. Yet I also claim to find the driving force for the essay in the tale of a somewhat psychotic Viking. Even though I make the conventional scholarly hedge that I can claim to accept responsibility only for the narrowest applicability of my claims, I note a desire to claim a little more than that. I bet that I would not have to change all that much in the gifts chapter to make it comprehensible to a Viking or a Maori. Details would change, of course, but the grip of the norm of reciprocity, the annoyance of the gift—these are things they would understand. How could they not? It was from reading about their cultures that I came to be conscious of the emotional setting of our own practices. I am thus not claiming that you necessarily will have had the experiences I describe, but you will surely have no trouble in recognizing them either. They will be within your contemplation of the predictable, the possible, the comprehensible, and the experienceable.

Chapter 3, focusing on heroic culture, suggests, as indeed I have noted, that certain aspects of honor-based culture are still with us. And half of the essay on humiliation (Chapter 5) pays particular attention to the problem of the translatability of emotional life across time (and by implication, space). So where am I in this localist versus universalist debate? I do not want to repeat here what I expound more fully in the book. Suffice it to say that if the Vikings or any other Other are not just like us, and they are not, they are not centipedes either. I suppose I am a chastened particularist. I now doubt interpretations that claim to demonstrate difference almost (the qualifier is important) as much as I have heretofore questioned the complacency of our willingness to see sameness. If we choose to locate sameness in the eye of the beholder, then difference belongs there too. If our blindness to difference is an aspect of the imperialism of our own cultural categories, might it not be that we have overcorrected by constructing some pretty marvelous chimeras of difference in order to compensate? Might it be that those same categories send us false positives of difference as well as of sameness?

Yes, language and culture have a way of cabining the thinkable, and differences in language and culture necessarily produce differences in thinking, even in perceiving and feeling. But the differences are not themselves unpredictable, nor are they unrecognizable. No, we cannot think just like others unless we become them, but we can learn to imagine quite well how they will act and what thoughts they must be having to justify and give coherence to their actions. It is surprising indeed how close we can come, if we are observant and do our homework. So I am left with interpretivism (what else do we have?), but without the religion of mandatory difference or the dogma of the inscrutable diversity of cultural and social experience.

Perhaps I trouble myself about this because I fear the trendinistas who will suspect my credentials as a social constructionist. With them, I too think it admirable to stand against those who purport to explain social and cultural phenomena by easy recourse to that lazy tautology, human nature. But to say something is socially constructed is no explanation either unless it is seen as a promise to provide a complicated story about just how the particular practice is indeed constructed. I believe that no culture is so purely coherent that competing views are not available within it and that all cultures are riddled with internal contradictions and competing claims. And because cultures are not coherent, because they are riddled with contradiction, because they do not exist without some knowledge of the practices of other cultures, because they are always impinged upon from without and subject to locally originating change from within, we should not be surprised to find some fairly widespread practices and many vaguely similar styles across cultures and through time. Thus it is that many of us have had experience with the norms of honor and may have participated in activities not unlike burning a witch.

1

Requiting the Unwanted Gift

To have received from one, to whom we think our selves equall,
greater benefits than there is hope to Requite, disposeth to
counterfeit love; but really secret hatred; and puts a man into the
estate of a desperate debtor, than in declining the sight of his
creditor, tacitely wishes him there, where he might never see him
more. For benefits oblige; and obligation is thraldome; and
unrequitable obligation, perpetuall thraldome, which is to one
equall, hatefull.

—Thomas Hobbes, *Leviathan*

Introduction to the Dark Side of Gifts

There once was a man named Egil, a rather obstreperous character,
well known for his ruthless Viking adventures and also for his great
talent for poetic composition. In his later years he settled down for
good in Iceland.[1] A younger poet named Einar, not unwarlike himself, made Egil's acquaintance. They would talk about the fine points
of poetry and trade stories about their exploits abroad. They became
good friends. On one occasion when Einar was in Norway he was
given a shield, adorned with gold and precious stones, by Jarl Hakon
as a reward for a poem Einar had composed in his honor. When Einar
returned to Iceland he went to visit Egil, but Egil was away. Einar
waited three days "for it was not the custom to stay any longer than
three days on a visit." But before leaving, Einar hung the shield above
Egil's place and told the servants to tell Egil it was a gift. Egil returned home, saw the shield, and asked who owned such a treasure.
He was told that Einar had visited and given it to him. "Then Egil
said, 'To hell with him! Does he think I'm going to stay up all night
and compose a poem about his shield? Get my horse. I'm going to

ride after him and kill him'"(chap. 78). As Einar's luck would have it he had left early enough to put sufficient distance between himself and Egil. So Egil resigned himself to composing a poem about Einar's gift.

How are we supposed to take the tone of Egil's curse and his intention to kill Einar? Was he serious? We do know that Egil had a reputation for being persnickety in matters of hospitality and exchange. When at others' houses he did not especially like being served buttermilk if beer was available. He killed one man for such inhospitality, while he contented himself with gouging out the eye of another who tried the same trick (chaps. 43–44, 71–72). Egil was also one of those people who make hyperbole converge with reality to the great vexation of those around him. This style of his means we cannot be too quick to assume that Egil was only joking about killing Einar. But seriousness comes in all manners of intensity. If Einar had been a short ride away there may well have been trouble. Whatever the immediate intensity of Egil's murderous designs he was not sufficiently committed to them to invest much time in seeing them through. At times, even Egil could give prudence a chance. It was now simply easier to sit down and compose a poem praising the gift and Einar's generosity.[2]

Ever since Mauss's *The Gift* it has been a commonplace among anthropologists that gift exchange is serious business.[3] In the honor-based culture of saga Iceland the world of gifts corresponded point for point with the universe of honor and blood. Just as an assault or an insult had to be repaid, so did a gift. Just as an honorable man could not avoid giving insult if he were to show himself honorable, so he could not avoid the demands of giving gifts. Men who gave gifts were men of honor. Those who did not give were not part of the honor group. In the saga world, as I have written elsewhere, the idiom of gifts, of repayment and requital, served also as the idiom of honor and feud.[4] Insults and injuries were understood to be gifts, of negative moral value to be sure, but gifts nonetheless, and as such they demanded repayment. And Egil shows us that the correspondences ran equally well in the other direction: gifts could be understood as insults.

Egil also reveals the normative underpinning of gifts which created their capacity to insult. The foundational norm is that every gift demands a return. In the words of Norse wisdom literature and straight from the mouth of Odinn: "a gift always looks for repayment" and "repay a gift with a gift, gift against gift."[5] Gifts are obligation-creating, more viscerally so than contracts. It was precisely the obligation to make a return that annoyed Egil. By giving someone something you unilaterally bound that person to make repayment. You made the recipient your debtor, thereby constraining him, until repayment was made, to make petty shows of gratitude and deference. You put the person to the trouble of having to make return. And most important, you reduced the other person's status relative to you. In the paradigmatic contractual debt relation, it is the debtor who wills his lower status. He seeks out the creditor and formally agrees to discharge the obligation. Everything is spelled out, how much is to be paid over in the first place and when it is to be paid back later. In the gift setting, it is the giver, the person corresponding to the creditor in the contractual paradigm, who wills the debtor's status.

Obviously, not all gifts were insults. People enjoyed giving and receiving, and they gave to those they wished to honor and to those they liked and loved. But inherent in the gift is the power to annoy as well as to please, the capacity to challenge as well as to comfort. To give a gift well (so that it did not offend) took social competence. It took practical knowledge about when to give, to whom to give, what to give, how costly the gift, what to say when handing it over, the posture to assume, and so forth. By knowing how to negotiate the maze of possible meanings, the astute giver could disarm the gift of hostile potential, because it was absolutely clear that gifts had hostile potential. The duty to make return meant that each gift was also a challenge, a challenge to repay. Thus a gift so costly that it could never be adequately repaid had the capacity to shame the recipient in the same way that someone was shamed by an insult that he was unable to avenge properly. A gift not costly enough might harbor an insult as to the recipient's status or his capacity to repay. A gift given to one person might cheapen the gift given to other more meritorious recipients or might insult those who felt entitled to receive but who were not given the opportunity to accept. A gift given at the wrong time raised suspicion as to its motive. Gifts were thus to be given at conventional times when the recipient would be ready to receive.

We can guess three reasons why Einar may have offended Egil. First, the gift was so costly that with it was also transferred a considerable risk of inadequate repayment; second, the gift, it seems, was made out of season. In the saga world people rarely went to another's farm to give a gift. It happened the other way around. One got a gift when one went to another's farm, a gift of hospitality and oftentimes a parting gift as well. Third, the shield, given originally to honor Einar as a poet, might well have been construed by Egil as a challenge to match Einar's poetic skills. Whether he meant to or not, Einar had initiated a kind of dueling banjos. Even if his intention was to honor Egil, there was no way to separate the shield from the fact that it was an emblem of Einar's reputation as a poet. And it is not unlikely that Egil would begrudge Einar, even envy him, his successes in a field once dominated by himself. But Einar was also offering Egil an opportunity to reaffirm his own poetic greatness, for Egil's poem would memorialize his own poetic talents as well as Einar's generosity.[6] In the end, it was no mean compliment to Egil that Einar thought him the man he most wanted to record the exchange. Egil understood this and acquiesced, but he was still annoyed.

The power to make another your debtor, however, did not mean that all the power to humiliate lay with the giver. The moral and social risk of nonreciprocity is not the recipient's alone. At the moment of handing over the gift the giver took a very big risk, the insult of having his gift refused. And once it was accepted he still risked the insult of humiliating returns. Too hasty a return of like for like was very close to a refusal to accept in the first place. Too slow a return might signal contempt for the giver as a person not being of quality sufficient to merit repayment.[7] Whether a particular act shamed the giver or receiver depended on a multiplicity of variables. Relative status was probably the most important of these. A gift to a person of very high rank could be repaid simply by its acceptance.[8] Very large gifts, such as gifts of land, were themselves markers of and often perceived as the officialization of the ranked subservience of the recipient. As such they could be regarded with suspicion or even rejected out of hand.[9] Yet a large gift to someone too impoverished to be within the honor group could be a source of honor to the giver, especially once Christian notions of almsgiving and charity gained general currency.[10]

If all went well, gifts honored the giver as a man of means and generosity and the donee as someone worthy of being involved in exchanges with such a man. Much exchange of gifts was regularized by people who had long established the ground rules between themselves as to the time, place, and manner of giving. In such settings gifts were above all signs of continuing friendship. They were accompanied with the emotional displays that indicated positive sociability and morality: joy, gratitude, pride. But gifts were really more than just the signs of some deeper emotional and moral state of affairs, they were the state of affairs itself. Friendship meant gift exchange, and even the bonds of kinship needed to be recemented and reaffirmed with gifts. Without gifts there was no friendship, and without gifts kinship thinned into a mere hypothesis of common blood or affinity. In short, kin and friends were those people with whom one exchanged gifts.

Then why the edginess, why the hostility? The short answer is that friends and kin were a large category, some of whose members did not always have your interests at heart. These were the people, after all, who were competing with you for honor, "with" here having the sense of both accompaniment and opposition. The excess of nervous competitiveness which informed the game of honor meant that convivial gatherings were also times of anxiety. A smooth and regularized gift-exchange relationship between two individuals could elicit envy from third parties, from those who felt that they had a claim to be recipients but were passed over or given less than they thought would do them honor. Who would get the seat of honor, who would get the most distinguished gifts, whose words would be greeted with attentiveness and whose would be interrupted or ignored? The host who tried to treat everyone equally probably insulted more people than he did when he made the unavoidable distinctions people would discern anyway in the quality of gifts and in seating arrangements.[11] Gifts were not just things you gave to friends. You also gave them to people who were not yet friends but with whom you wanted to establish a positive exchange relation. These people were usually your enemies, that is, those with whom you were already exchanging corpses and insults. Thus it was that if friendship and kinship meant gifts, gifts did not necessarily mean friendship and kinship.

In honor-based societies such as saga Iceland, gift exchange was no small change. Much of the economic work of distribution and provisioning took place under the rubric of gifting. Among people in the honor game it would have been insulting, rude, or declassé to seek to buy and sell rather than to give and take.[12] And because this was the class that controlled most of the resources, social and material, the economic function of gifts took on an importance it does not have in industrial and postindustrial societies. This has led some to suppose that much gift-exchange behavior in preindustrial societies was economically interested, in spite of its mandatory external form of being free and disinterested. Pierre Bourdieu, one of the most astute writers on gift exchange since Mauss, supposes that people repress or, in his words, "misrecognize" the interested aspects of gift exchange because the time gap between gift and return and the language and emotions of gift giving allow them the leeway to do so.[13] The form of the gift, in effect, allows for certain styles of domination and economic exploitation to take place under the guise that there is no domination at all, only beneficence and amicability. Bourdieu does not appear to be arguing for a kind of universal cynicism. It would, after all, be hard to see how such a system could be maintained, because if everyone is behaving cynically there is no advantage in being a cynic. The richness of Bourdieu's account would seem to indicate his commitment to a much more problematic relation between the types of knowledge people have and the motivations and intentions underpinning particular actions. Bourdieu's actors seem to be adepts in a kind of doublethink. People give because they are supposed to in certain settings; they also give because they want to and they want to for a variety of reasons: to gain honor, to do something for people they like, to humiliate people they don't like, to manipulate both people they do and do not like, to do the things proper members of their culture do, and to get gifts in return, all with an awareness that certain advantages accrue to the skillful giver and receiver of gifts. Even if we allow for some people to be purely self-interested and cynical, only motivated by the prospect of getting back more than they give or by gains enabled by the manipulation of others, they still must acquire within the constraints imposed by the idiom of gift exchange if they are to succeed in their purpose. This surely must limit the kinds of economically rational calculations they can make, even if it does not limit to the same extent the kinds of social calculations they must make in order to be an honorable giver and receiver of gifts.

I have presented this very quickly painted sketch of a wonderfully rich arena of social action because it helps provide the groundwork for an examination of educated middle-class American gift exchange practices, which are similarly rich if somewhat less important.[14] As in saga Iceland, the richness of our practices is a function not only of the multiplicity of possible social meanings of the moves in the game but also of the dense emotional accompaniment of the action. Social richness has a way of provoking psychological richness, which in turn raises the stakes in the social game. Do not understand me to be making the claim that nothing has changed. Much has changed and surely almost everything has at the macro level. That is, the relation between gift exchange as a system and the meaning and import of that system within the network of other fundamental social systems has changed utterly. Economically, gift exchange plays an insignificant role in our lives.[15] This does not mean that Christmas is not important economically. Without it many retailers would go out of business. But the people to whom Christmas is economically crucial—the retailers—are not the intended beneficiaries of the gifting process. Socially, unlike saga people, we can do quite well in a variety of roles and settings without being especially good at giving gifts or receiving them. In the saga world one's skill in the gift game was inseparable from one's skill in feud and in the politics of honor preservation and acquisition.[16]

But at the micro level of face-to-face interaction the changes between us and them are less noticeable, and similarities often strike us as more salient than do differences. Gifts still have their dark side. They still threaten, humiliate, annoy, manipulate, and vex. They can connect us with as well as cut us off from others. Welchers will eventually be sanctioned among us as they would have been among the Icelanders. Like them, we rarely fail to keep a mental accounting of who owes what to whom. Even in the noise and bustle of the conventional turn taking among group members treating the rest of the table to pitchers of beer, we tend to notice if, time and again, the same person seems to be last to volunteer in hopes that people will have had their fill before it comes to him to have to pay. Eventually that person will be saddled with a reputation for being cheap, or shamed by pointed teasing into shelling out, or even, finally, uninvited. This last sanction becomes inevitable for those souls who are immune to the repayment obligation, having by a quirk of character an absolute preference for bearing the cost of being thought cheap than for bearing the cost of a pitcher of beer. What is different most clearly between us and the Icelanders are the stakes, the styles of ostracism. We won't kill the welcher or even seriously entertain the thought. We have the luxury of being able to spread our being thinly among a multitude of different social roles, none of which impinges very greatly on the others, and we have the benefit of a milder range of sanctions for our breaches within each role.

There are other important differences too. In saga Iceland the gift game, like the honor game, was mostly a man's game. Men gave and men received. Many gifts superficially appearing as gifts to a woman were just as often gifts to men connected to her, such as fathers and brothers.[17] Among us the styles of gifting are also gendered. Men (I assume a heterosexual norm) are less likely to shop to buy gifts for men than women are to buy gifts for women.[18] The world of male-to-male gifting tends to revolve mostly around barroom etiquette of exchanging rounds of drinks, although professional norms may dictate circulation of harder goods. Male academics might, for instance, occasionally treat another male colleague to a book (often one of their own, since these can be purchased directly from the press at an author's discounted price). But gift exchange between men generally takes the form of exchanges of consumables, of food and drink, rather than of durables.[19] If a man does shop to buy a durable it is much more likely to be a gift for a woman, and often signals a period of courtship. Once they become a couple their gifting practices toward each other get subsumed into even more predictable cultural scenarios, and the exchanges they have with others will undergo a change too. I include drinks and meals in the world of gifts, for like any durable gift that to some might seem the more archetypal gift, such transfers demand gratitude and repayment. In fact, it seems that the obligation to reciprocate is even more keenly felt in gifts of food and drink than in gifts of durables.[20]

Couples generally exchange consumables in the form of dinner invitations. Exchanges are transfers of food, drink, and the thin entertainment of predictable conversation. When couples give durable gifts on selected occasions such as birthdays and holidays it is usually women who make the purchases. Women, however, are equally at home with consumables and durables. They also are more likely than men to exchange one particular nondurable: revelations of self. One reveals her inner feelings to her friend and her friend is to understand that that revelation demands a similar commitment on her part.* But do we wish to think of this exchange as a gift? Or are we now vastly extending the notion of gift to areas where it is more

---

*Gossiping raises different obligations. There is a difference in the obligation raised by telling someone your own secrets and by telling them someone else's. Nevertheless gossip-exchange networks have elaborate mechanisms for distinguishing who gets told what kinds of things and what their obligations are as to confidentiality and reciprocation. There is also a difference between revealing secrets among equals and in confessing wrongs to a superior. And then too the act of revealing takes on different meanings depending on the social situation. Men frequently "confess" to women as part of a strategy, only vaguely conscious, of absolution via seduction.

metaphor than the thing itself? We could imagine, by such extension, any social practice demanding reciprocity as a kind of gift.

The mere ability to raise an obligation of reciprocity does not alone make a gift. Mercantile exchanges involve reciprocity and no one considers them gifts. Central to the notion of a gift is the way in which reciprocity is effected and enforced. A gift leaves the exact return unspecified. The timing, the quality, the amount of the exchange are all left to the recipient. And although the recipient's freedom is restricted by patterns of past practice, by norms that suggest the whens, wheres, whats, and hows of the return, the nature of these restrictions is not like those of the world of contract and mercantile exchange. In that world the nature and timing of exchange is specified or impliedly specified with much greater particularity and, ultimately, it can be enforced legally. Yet we run a risk if our notion of gift is too closely tied to the absence of legal sanctions enforcing a return. The archetypal gift-exchange economies of primitive peoples often do not recognize an autonomous group of rules known as laws which are distinguishable from any other norms of proper social behavior, and yet they often have a notion of gifts distinguishable from other types of exchanges.

It seems that at least two crucial criteria distinguish gifts from contracts or purchases. In loans and purchases not only is the return specified but the terms are set *before* the first exchange. And second, people talk and act differently when they are making gifts than when they are lending or selling. Needless to say, disputes can arise on this score. Many borrowers thought they were getting a gift, but by and large when people say gift they mean gift. Then there is Bourdieu's insight that thinking in terms of gifts means misrecognizing their obligatory aspect, even (or especially) in cultures that openly recognize the overriding claims of a norm of reciprocity. When we give gifts and when we make return, a good part of our consciousness believes itself free and disinterested. At the moment of giving we suspend the notion that repayment is being demanded in a way we do not when we deal mercantilely. Gift exchange supposes a commitment to sociable forms, to continuing relations, even if the gift is one of the ways we exact deference and achieve dominance among those with whom we relate. So it is that unlike a commodity, a gift cares precisely who receives it. Gifts are destined for particular people in a way that commodities are not.[21]

Are we any closer to deciding whether exchanges of verbal inti-
macies are gifts? We gain nothing by considering the linguistic demands of response in conversation as a gift.[22] The formal exchange of
words is not a gift independent of the particular content of the message. But if gifts are understood as bits of oneself, of one's person
being handed over, then communicated self-revelation or those messages classified as "secrets" should bear all the aspects of a gift.
Usually those people who engage in the game of mutual exchange of
secrets are also those who will soon be exchanging food and drink,
invitations, and visits, engaging in the collection of behaviors and
actions that constitute intimacy and friendship, the very types of relations which are constituted as well as indicated by gift exchange.

In saga Iceland the class of likely recipients of durable gifts was
coextensive with the class of people one would invite to share food
and drink. This is clearly not the case among us. Recipients of durables are more likely to be kin,[23] whereas gifts of consumables are
intended for friends, workmates, and neighbors.[24] These likelihoods
tend to track certain norms. Imagine, for instance, that a workmate
and spouse invite you to dinner. The dinner invitation is, by itself,
independent of any other anxieties the particular people doing the
inviting might cause you, no breach of a norm; in fact it is in accord
with norms of sociability. Now suppose the same workmate gives you
a durable gift independent of any holiday or occasion warranting it.
You are immediately suspicious. You think that that person wants
something he or she is not entitled to expect. Even a gift on a holiday
or birthday is suspect unless the workmate is more than just a workmate and a pattern of exchanges has already been embarked on which
effectively normalizes the gift. The style of gift then seems to be a
marker of the type of relation. Kin get durables. Friends get invited in
or treated to food and drink. We also treat kin like friends, but we
treat only a very few special friends like kin in these matters.

Exchanges of durables may involve practices different from those of
consumables, even if for the most part many of the strategies of
exchange are quite similar. For example, mutually consumed food and
drink usually requires greater coordination between giver and receiver than do exchanges of durables. The very purpose of the exchange of consumables requires a commitment of bodies to particular
places for particular lengths of time. Exchanges of durables, on the
other hand, do not involve much preexchange negotiation and coordination of times and places. The timing of these exchanges tends to

follow well-grooved expectations. Durables are to be transferred at birthdays, certain holidays, weddings, or at occasions already coordinated for the purpose of sharing consumables. In this last instance, durable gifts are often thought of as being "brought along." A gift that is brought along does not prompt the suspicions that a gift made independent of normalizing occasions does. Durables can also show up by mail independent of any spatial commitment on the part of the giver. We should also observe that the burden of coordination attending the exchange of consumables allows for the greater possibility of polite refusal. To refuse a durable is a much harsher matter indeed, for the refusal can be understood only hostilely and not as a part of an ongoing negotiation whose perceived end is to enable an eventual exchange. Durables could be further broken down into types, each with its own particular sociology. Gifts of money, of which more below, have their own rules.

But it is not my purpose to give a comprehensive presentation of the whole range of practices in American gift exchange. My narrower goal is to discuss closely the micropolitical and social problems raised by several well-known cultural scenarios: the unwanted dinner invitation, the exchange of valentines by young children, gifts of money, and the decision to buy a gift at a gift shop. These are rather homely topics and not much to encourage any reader to continue who has made it this far. Yet in spite of their homeliness these topics are rich with problems of strategy, the intersection of social norms and rational choice, the quandaries of coordinating expectations and behavior when conflicting norms are called into play by the same situation, and the anxiety of face (honor) which inheres even in our unheroic social interactions. Above all, the homeliness of the topics suggests that the problems inherent in these types of exchanges are not a deviation from some normal ideal smooth-running exchange but are the problems inherent in normality itself.

An Invitation to Dinner

Invitations to dinner have a logic of their own. I first sketch out some of the more general aspects of this logic before we get to specific strategies of negotiating unwanted invitations. In the meantime you might keep in mind an idea of the small panic of being called and invited over by someone you have no wish to socialize with. The norms governing the sharing of food at someone else's behest are sensitive to a number of variables. Stage of life cycle, for instance, tends to be reflected in the relative formality of the occasion. Spontaneity, a virtue among the young, becomes a vice in maturity or, at best, a kind of strategy to salvage the effects of poor planning and procrastination. The hedonization of the American palette that began in the 1970s and has pretty much continued unabated since and the consequent developing sophistication in culinary matters raise the stakes of the decision of what to serve guests.[25] There are surely elements of potlatch or competitive gift exchange here.[26] Among those who care about such things, being known as a good cook is not quite enough. One needs to be recognized as a better cook than the guest, if, that is, the guest pretends to a similar competence. An invitation to dinner from serious cooks has then something of the aspect of a challenge. But the challenge has different consequences depending on the guest. To guests who like playing that game, the chance to reciprocate is simply a part of the game, and the only anxieties generated are the usual ones in a clearly bounded contest. For those guests, however, who recognize a good meal when they see it but who also do not care to spend time on such things, the invitation generates real anxieties, the anxieties associated with how to reciprocate adequately. How in the world can one reciprocate and still not feel beholden? Whatever one serves will be plebian fare as far as they are concerned. Nor can one solve the problem by taking them out to a good restaurant, for to take that course is an admission of moral failure, a blatant attempt to do with money what should have been done with the soul. One either must remain forever beholden or find some adequate way to excuse the inadequacy of the return.[27]

Let me quickly suggest some fertile grounds for excusing reciprocity before returning to this problem in greater detail below. The expectations of what constitutes adequacy in reciprocity depends on the family configuration of the guest. If the guest is a single male, reciprocity by return invite is excused; even a single female might get some consideration on this account, but only some.[28] A couple with young children can find in their little ones a source of excuse, but a couple with no children or with self-sufficient children, that is, with children who prefer the absence of adults and who are more dangerous to others than to themselves when adults are absent, are virtually without excuse unless lingering or chronic illnesses come to the rescue. Age and status differences also excuse a return invitation. In fact they often demand no return beyond forms of deference. It is thus perceived to be well within the order of things for the employer to have the employee to dinner, the tenured professor her untenured colleague, the professor (*en famille*) the grad student,[29] but not for the invitation to go the other way around without presuming against the normal presumptions.

What is clear is that invitations to dinner, if status, age, or familial condition do not prevent it, raise the obligation to reciprocate as clearly as such an obligation can be raised in the world of gifts. And the reciprocation must be by return invitation unless one is able to do some very fancy maneuvering. Now let us recall Egil. There is cause for irritation in these invitations precisely because they are capable of imposing obligation, of unilaterally making another a debtor. In this sense they are acts of petty aggression. The first invitation comes as an offer of closer relations and has the capacity to force those relations by imposing an obligation to make a return of the same type.[30] It forces a person to have to be *with* the other. This is why an invitation can be so annoying. It puts the recipients to continuing a relation they might not have otherwise wished to embark on at the cost of looking ill-mannered or cheap. Of course, not all first invitations carry this meaning. When host and guest are self-defined as friends in other fields of interaction, some of the edge is taken off the request. Some first invitations are themselves issued out of a sense of obligation in obedience to other norms. These give rise to a weaker claim for reciprocation by return invitation and, in fact, are often fully repaid by a simple warm show of gratitude by the guest. Such are the invitations of welcome given to people new to town or new to the workplace. Such also are the invitations issued to people who form a group independent of the inviter's decision to assemble them. Here the obligatoriness binding the inviter resides in a desire to avoid the excessive significance born by your exclusion of any particular member of the group. Imagine, for instance, the significance of inviting every colleague or classmate but one. If you are going to have your officemates over you must have all of them over, but each one of them incurs less of an obligation to reciprocate than the obligation you had not to exclude any particular one of them in the first place.

The strength of the obligation to reciprocate also varies inversely with the number of people on the guest list: the bigger the gathering, the weaker the obligation. As a related matter, most feel that invitations to very formal gatherings make considerably less of a moral claim on the invitee than invitations to small and informal gatherings.

This is only a superficial paradox. Formality in dining as in other areas of face-to-face interaction is a kind of distancing device varying inversely with intimacy and the strength of the claim on another's moral being. Thus the dinners that fill social calendars at Christmas time impose lesser burdens to reciprocate than meals given at other times of the year. The giver's gift is more to the season than to the guests, and the sense on the giver's part is less one of initiating an intimacy than in fulfilling the obligations of the holiday season. But invitations by people of similar standing unmotivated by demands of the calendar demand full reciprocity.

I mentioned earlier that givers take a risk that their gifts will be refused. We all know that refusals are humiliations and insults, and we must suspend all kinds of disbelief to accept with good humor the excuses that are proffered for why the other somehow cannot accept our invitation. We also are not completely unaware of the imposition inherent in such offers. This is why we seek indications of the recipient's willingness to accept *before* we give a gift or issue an invitation. We believe, clearly, that surprises should never really be all that surprising to be in good taste.[31] With gifts of durables, consent can be inferred in a number of settings and between a number of sorts of people. Sometimes they are the fruit of a smooth and pleasant history of gift exchanges with the other. Now one, now the other gives or has repayment to make and repayments are made, both seasonably and adequately. Timing is regulated fairly closely by well-established conventions. Birthdays, weddings, births, Christmas are occasions not only when gifts are expected to be given but also, crucially, when they are expected to be received. Children can be assumed to be ever-willing recipients of gifts from adults, and their return need only be signs of joy at the receipt, as well as gratitude and deference. Sexism supposes (incorrectly) that women are like children in this regard: willing recipients of suitor's gifts for which repayment is to be made by various postures of the body as in the tilt of the head and torso in unconscious displays of deference and, more crudely, as in the conscious if passive adoption of the postures of sexual coupling. Even in more equal distributions of power, courtship presumes an intimate connection between gifts and bodies. Women, I would bet, must feel most keenly the intrusiveness, the aggressive aspect of gifts, every time they are the recipients of gifts from men with whom they have not already regularized relations to their own satisfaction.

But the conventions by which a willingness to accept dinner invitations can be inferred are not quite so clear. There has to be improvisation, feeling out, and guesswork. As a result, the risks of imposing and the risks of refusal are greater because there is so much more room for glitch and misfiring. Like gifts of durables, the willingness of the lower-status party to accept the invitations of the higher-status party is presumed. Refusal carries a stiff price, not only because to do so might elicit reprisal by the insulted inviter but because the status difference itself makes the refusal an even greater insult than a refusal between equals.

One of the costs of reciprocating fully is that it does not end the interaction unless it is coupled with other indications that no further intimacy is desired. A return gift, as anthropologists have noted, is understood not only as a requital of the initial gift but as a new gift raising its own obligation to reciprocate.[32] The danger is, in other words, that once you exchange invitations the subsequent refusal to continue exchanges has moral consequences. Lurking in the first invitation is the horror that after one acceptance there is no easy way out of an eternal recurrence of gift and countergift. Now we all know that each invitation doesn't lock us into perpetual enforced intimacy. It doesn't because both sides have ways of signaling their more limited intentions and desires. Some of these signals, as already noted, are implicit in the status of the parties, the timing of the invitation, the identity and number of the invitees, and whether the invitation is to satisfy norms of hospitality independent of the actual identity of the invitee. But more often than not the setting does not give us our easy out; we have to do the signaling work ourselves. The strategies of avoidance, the styles of distancing oneself, come in all sizes and shapes and it takes a great amount of social competence to select or improvise styles and strategies that accomplish the goal of preventing intimacy while at the same time preserving cordiality. The problem is to save yourself without giving offense. And it is no easy matter to carry off well.

Culture provides us with various sorts of rules which regulate the minutiae of social interaction. Some of these rules we think of as manners, others are less consciously codified or codifiable as a body of rules to aspire to and thought of simply as the way normal people act naturally.[33] It is a trait of this latter kind of "rule" that we are usually conscious of them only when they are violated, and even then we are less conscious of a rule that has been violated than of a vaguer sense that something isn't quite right. It is often in the set of those rules we call manners that we find the raw matter for constructing successful strategies of avoidance. Although manners are not just something to be taken on or put off at whim, they certainly allow for much more conscious manipulation than, for example, the "rules" governing voice volume, eye contact, facial expression, the appropriate speed of speech, the number of hesitation sounds like ah and um, and so on. I do not mean to launch forth on a discourse about what distinguishes manners from the rest of ruled behaviors that do similar work beyond the brief observations I have just made. I will make only a few quick points about manners, some of which may also apply to more inarticulatable norms of smooth social practice. Manners help us negotiate social encounter without giving offense; they include practices that allow others to maintain their self-respect even as we deny them what they want, or means of remedy that undo the effects of our trespasses on others' boundaries of self.[34] They provide us with ways of signaling respect and inclusion even as they are used to distance us from others. Consider what it means to treat others in a way that they will recognize as "mannerly." People whom we treat with good manners are granted at the very least that degree of dignity which types them as people entitled to mannerly treatment. The existence of manners as conventions of practice saves us the costs of having to negotiate anew a significant portion of the ground rules of interaction. Manners provide us with lines to say and even with entire roles to play in certain selected settings. As a result they can keep the psychological cost of a lot of social interaction lower than it would otherwise be, the cost often being no more than the occasional blush and awkwardness of embarrassment. For the most part manners facilitate the maintenance of uneventful social interaction quite well. But manners, as most of us ill-mannered sorts feel in our bones, often force us into precisely those activities and interactions we wish to avoid. We feel that they compel small but annoying compromises with our "true" selves. Manners have the power to make us feel cowardly for adhering to them, as in those situations in which we feel inhibited by them from assaulting those who are ill-mannered to us.

But as with all rules, there is a lot of play in the joints of manners. They leave room for considerable individual maneuver and style, strategy, and improvisation. We even recognize that certain character types are defined almost entirely by their orientation to manners as manners.* There is, for example, the person of impeccable manners,

---

*These character types are different from those we recognize for having a strange manner, rather than bad manners. These strange-mannered souls are defined by their inadequate competence in those more inarticulatable practices that are the

the person who makes one aware of manners as an articulatable code in which people are ranked according to their expertise. Impeccability requires that manners never be felt as "natural," that they never be allowed to sink into the morass of norms unconsciously adhered to, but that they be seen to require breeding, training, conscious attention, and, above all, talent. Impeccability means the ability to disconcert others ever so slightly as to the quality of their own manners. Impeccability comes in variant versions: there is the hauteur of certain classes of servants of the aristocrat and of some aristocrats themselves, which is not the same style as the fussiness and lack of equity in a certain style of middle-class schoolmarmism. Graciousness, on the other hand, is a kind of softened impeccability that is really of an entirely different order. The gracious person sets people at ease and manages to do so without making them feel painfully inadequate for the quality of their manners. Still she is able, as a result, to create in others a most compelling obligation to defer and to admire, such admiration and deference themselves being a kind of recompensing graciousness in the others. There is the curmudgeonly or blunt soul whose charm is a function of knowing which manners can be infringed upon as long as sufficient signs of decent sentiment accompany the infringement. This kind of gruffness is a remarkably appealing style as a relief from impeccability, but it wears thin unless it has the expectation of impeccability to play off against. A universe of curmudgeons would grow quickly tiring and drive the curmudgeon motivated by true contrarian tendencies into, God forbid, impeccability. There is another nontrivial point being made here too: it is not as if manners or other norms stand above or outside our real selves. They are part of the muck from which we constitute our real selves. They make it possible to have stances, to have postures, to have personalities, to have identity, to be people who can be fussy, curmudgeonly, gracious, and weird. They do not just squelch some pristine presocial self and soul.

Let us get to particulars and look more closely at how to deal with an undesired invitation to dinner and the various strategies available to save yourself from an eternal cycle of exchanges while at the same time giving the minimum amount of offense possible. Consider first the refusal. Refusals come in all varieties. Some are genuine: you

---

substance of acting normally, not by their relation to the code of manners. Vernacular usage defines more precise modes of such incompetence. We thus distinguish among nerds, dorks, turkeys, nudnicks, pains-in-the-ass, jerks, etc.

cannot attend because you really do have a prior engagement; you really are picking up your mother at the airport; you really will be out of town that weekend. The problem here is that if the excuse really does excuse your nonacceptance you get no advantage from it, for another invitation will inevitably be forthcoming.° To discourage another attempt the excuse must convey that your priorities are such that they do not adequately value the honor of the invitation. I'd love to come but I just can't miss *Casablanca*. In the age of VCRs such excuses are perhaps little short of abrupt and rude refusals. People have done better with this: I'd love to but our regular baby sitter is out of town and we do not feel comfortable about leaving the kids with someone they are not used to. You are written off as a somewhat overprotective parent, but not as rude. There are those who feel the best strategy is not to be specific, but to be cool and general: sorry, but we have a prior engagement. With no further explanation this is about as direct a refusal as is possible unless the invitation is given on very short notice. But the softer souls, who feel lies must be specific to be believable, may tip off the feebleness of their excuse if the specificity is somewhat too circumstantial. Some inviters make excuses very hard to come up with by shifting the date to counteract your first excuse or by calling you six weeks in advance. Such people have left themselves very little margin indeed to excuse others' excuses, and this in the end drives most of us to say yes to such requests even when we do not want to go.

So we usually end up going, even though we do not want to, unless we are so firm of purpose that we do not care how much the inviter is humiliated. It is the rare person who will answer an invitation with a direct, "Sorry, but I really have no interest in attending." How often we wish we had the nerve or courage to say such things, but even if we had the courage we might not wish to make use of it. Word would get out and we would be sanctioned. As in the world of honor, but writ smaller, inadequately excused refusals of gifts are insults. In Iceland they could easily lead to violence. Among us they lead to what

---

°At some point even real excuses will fail to excuse. Consider the case in which the first legitimate refusal of an invitation is followed by another invitation which again conflicts with something that would be perceived as providing a legitimate excuse if it had been offered the first time. Even a not-too-sensitive inviter will by the second or third time start to doubt the veracity of the excuse, or if not doubting its veracity, expect that the invitee should make the gesture of coordinating the get-together by inviting the inviter over.

theorists of disputes call avoidance. The inviter, if at all sensitive, writes the person out of his or her social circle. Some may consider this result no sanction at all, but an inducement to say no. But the fact remains that we do not usually say no without providing adequate excuse. Why? The real sanction is not the fear of being ostracized by the inviter or by third parties for having mistreated the inviter, it is that we need to see ourselves as people who allow other people their self-respect when we have no great reason to deny them that. Our own self-respect seems to hinge on it. We need to see ourselves as properly socialized, unless we have cultivated styles that let us play at being improperly socialized in certain restricted settings. Recall again the curmudgeon or the needler who amuses as much as he annoys. This need to see ourselves as respectful of others' self-respect is not so much undertaken rationally as it is borne on a suffusion of empathy, an emotion that in this instance makes us more sociable than cold reason might wish us to be.

The second best world is to make sure that we have to get together only once. There is a third best world that eventually requires one return invitation before closure can be achieved. Several strategies are available in the second best world. Once at the event, the guest may quickly see that the host couple wants no more intimacy with the guest couple than the guests with them. Such information is deduced not from any failures of attention or rudenesses on the part of the hosts. The identity of the other guests may indicate how the hosts peg you in the world, and on how they do may absolve a return in kind. If you are invited to a small gathering with one other low-status couple from the workplace you may discern that the invitation was not an offer of intimacy at all but an offer of charity. The makeup of the grouping may also show that you are there in a limited capacity, because, for instance, the real guest of honor likes the Icelandic sagas and the host wants you to entertain him. But this is tricky turf. If the hosts explicitly tell you that you are invited to help them out by entertaining their guest with strange tastes, reciprocity is made by accepting the invitation. If, however, it is only your own discernment that notes you are there to do some of the real work of entertaining, an obligation to reciprocate in kind is clearly not excused.

Bringing a nice bottle of wine might insulate you from charges of cheapness for failure to make a return invitation, but the wine does not adequately discharge the obligation, no matter how expensive it may be. This is so because eating and drinking in one's home is a special specie that raises debts that in most instances can be discharged only by the same specie. The problem is not expense incurred, but of hospitality extended. The bottle of wine may work for the single male invited by a couple but not for a couple. They too must open their home.

How do you have the others back and let them know at the same time that this reciprocation ends the matter? You win if you get their social selves to admit that you have behaved properly and sociably, even if their psychological selves know that they have been turned away. Timing, perhaps, bears the biggest burden in determining the significance of the return. One signals the message of reluctance to get intimate or to socialize further by delaying the return. What constitutes tardiness or slowness will vary with the particular circumstance, but the cost of delaying is that one must feel that slight twinge of awkwardness, that mild urge to offer excuses, to provide explanations (false of course) in the presence of the other. So strong is the power of the obligation to reciprocate that it engenders guilt and shame with regard to people you ultimately do not consider worth your time, but who extract their time from you nonetheless.

There is a rich capacity to signal coolness by the manner of reciprocation as well as by its timing. I have already mentioned that the guest list is an easily disownable, but quite effective, way of letting others know how you rank them in your estimation. People who have had you over by yourself can be invited for a return with others. Even in the fare itself there can be messages, as was suggested above, and never once do you have to act as anything but amiable and entertaining hosts. But these are hardly foolproof ways of getting the other off your back. People who aren't sensitive enough to see that you do not care to be intimate with them from the beginning are also not as likely to pick up on subtly graded distancing signals. The denser the soul, the more unsubtle the message has to be. Yet we often suffer such obtuseness rather than suffer our own bluntness. Bluntness, we feel, is cruel in a way that the subtler indications are not. We believe that the subtler signs operate almost unconsciously, that they suggest vague feelings and rough senses, that even if operating consciously they allow the other some option of self-deception and allow all to avoid the pain of acute embarrassment. Bluntness can make a scene; it clubs the other's consciousness and makes us feel that we have behaved disrespectfully, indecorously, almost violently, and makes us feel like the violator of norms of a higher order than those violated by the person whose attentions bother us. Above all, we like to avoid confrontations that prevent us from maintaining the fiction of decorous if distant amiability. And so we suffer the boring souls who turn out, in the end and by default, to be our friends.

Bess's Valentine

One Valentine's Day the doorbell rang around six in the evening. At the door were the four-year-old boy who lived around the corner and his mother. My wife answered the door, and seeing that they had a valentine for Bess, my three-year-old daughter, got the valentine she had had Bess make for the boy that afternoon. I marveled at my wife's skill in handling this. How in the world did she know to be ready for this exchange? The boy, a year older than our daughter, was not a very frequent playmate of Bess's and we were only on cordial but stand-offishly neighborly terms with his parents. What luck, I thought, that she had thought to have something ready for the boy. Then the glitch occurred. What Bobby handed over to Bess was an expensive doll, some twenty dollars' worth, clearly bought for this occasion. What Bess handed Bobby was some scribbling, representing an attempt to draw a heart, and a cookie that my wife, with Bess's indispensable assistance, had baked that afternoon. The visit broke up quickly after the exchange. We had been fixing dinner when they appeared, and Bobby and his mother only got far enough beyond the threshold so that we could close the storm door on the cold air outside. There was an undeniable look of disappointment on the boy's face when he left, and Bess, though hardly disappointed, was mildly bewildered at having gotten such a nice gift out of the blue. As soon as the door closed my wife expressed her embarrassment and acute discomfort. What could we do? How could we repay them? How could we rectify the situation? I too felt embarrassed although not quite to the same extent as Kathy, for it was not me who was going to have to have future dealings with Bobby and his mother. It is also true that both Kathy and I felt some amusement with our embarrassment. Discomfitures of this sort are funny even at the cost of your own pain. And of course, academic that I am, I started immediately wondering why we felt acutely embarrassed and maybe even shamed and Bobby's mother did not, because she did not manifest any sense that something had not been quite right in the exchange.

The structure of the valentine exchange can be described as a simple game. The players each have one move and each must make that move (in this instance the move is giving a gift to the other) without knowledge of what the other has given. The object of the game is to match the value of the other's move. Both players lose if there is great discrepancy between their moves.[35] Both win if there is a small increment between their moves. Normal social interaction presents various versions of this game fairly frequently. Christmas-gift exchanges and choosing how to dress for a party or other social function in which it is not totally clear that there is one correct way of attiring oneself follow this pattern. (Birthday-gift exchanges, however, follow a different structure unless the players celebrate their birthdays on the same day.) This game requires certain broad skills no matter what its particular setting may be. Adept players must understand the norms that govern the situation; they must also have the ability to judge the other party's understanding of those norms and his or her willingness to adhere to them even if understood, and they must make reasonably accurate assessments of the other party's assessments of themselves in these same matters.

Winning in the gift exchange does not mean getting the best present. That is what Kathy and I understood to be a loss. Winning is guessing what the other will give and giving a gift adequate to requite it. Social norms do the work of coordinating people's behavior so that most of the time these interactions pass without glitch. We know what to give and how much to spend and we reasonably expect that others know what we know and that they will act accordingly. Small variations can be tolerated; they are even desired to some extent. If, for instance, you want to dress at a level of formality that will accord with that of everyone else, you might still want to wear something more tasteful or nicer than what others have on. If I give you a gift costing twelve dollars and you give me one costing ten dollars, no one is embarrassed, and I might even exact a very small amount of greater gratitude than the gratitude I have to give to you to make up the difference. But when my gift to you cost a dime and your gift to me cost twenty dollars we should, if we are properly socialized, feel awkward and embarrassed. The embarrassment, however, will not be equally distributed. The person who spent the most will feel the least embarrassed, generally speaking. Why? We can even make the question a little harder by referring back to Bess's valentine. Why was it that my wife and I felt greater unpleasant feelings, when we followed the norms governing the situation, than I am supposing Bobby's mother did, who clearly broke the rules by vastly exceeding the appropriate amount of expenditure for little kids on Valentine's Day?

Just what are the sources of embarrassment, shame, humiliation, and even guilt (perhaps) that were provoked by this situation? The lowrollers cannot feel embarrassed that they broke the rules of the Valentine game, because they did not. By one account the highrollers, if embarrassed, are embarrassed more because they caused the lowrollers' embarrassment than because they exceeded the norms of propriety governing the game. No doubt there is a causal connection between the highrollers' embarrassment and their failure to adhere to the norms of the Valentine game inasmuch as that was what caused the lowrollers' embarrassment, but that would be getting the psychology of it wrong. Their experience is one of second-order embarrassment, the embarrassment of witnessing another's embarrassment, not the primary embarrassment of having done something embarrassing. It seems that what is going on here is that there is more than one game being played and that there are more than one set of norms governing the transaction. The true source of the lowrollers' embarrassment is that they have also been shamed by being bested in the much more primitive game of gift exchange that Einar and Egil were playing at the beginning of this chapter. The simple fact remains that a gift demands an adequate return even if that gift, by its size, breaks the rules governing the particular exchange. The norms of adequate reciprocity trumped the norms of Valentine's Day. Yet there is a cost here born by the highrollers. Because the highrollers defied the normal expectation they do not acquire honor to the extent that they caused shame. Their action, in effect, has made the whole transaction less than zero-sum.

A somewhat different account also suggests itself. I have been supposing the giver's lack of primary embarrassment. But it might be that Bobby's mother was more than embarrassed by embarrassing us, she might have felt humiliated, not by breaking the rules of the Valentine's Day game but by having to realize how much more greatly she valued us than we valued her. Her pain then, if pain she felt, was not really a function of misplaying the Valentine game in the same way ours was. To be sure, the game provided the setting for her humiliation but it needn't have. Her pain, in other words, was not caused because she violated the norms of Valentine's Day, but because she overvalued us. In contrast, our pain was solely a function of the Valentine's Day glitch. Yet I suspect that she felt no humiliation whatsoever, for the situation provided her with an adequate nondemeaning explanation for the smallness of our gift. Our gift, she would know, was exactly what the situation called for. The normal expectations of the situation thus shielded her from more painful knowledge.

The peculiar facts of Bess's gift show us also that who ends up bearing the costs of norm transgression will depend on the makeup of the opposing sides. The discussion above assumed highroller and lowroller to be individual actors in a one-on-one game, but in our Valentine situation there were mother and son on one side and mother and daughter on the other. If we look now only at the emotions engendered by the exchange, Bobby's mother felt no shame and only a little embarrassment. Bess's mother felt much embarrassment. Bess felt quite pleased. But Bobby, alas poor Bobby. Here was the true bearer of the cost of his mother's indiscretion. Bobby, one can reasonably suppose, was deeply envious of the gift Bess was to receive and had been sick with desire for a similar gift. Recall, when you were little, the painful experience of being the guest watching the birthday child open the presents. But Bobby can console himself that this Valentine gift will lead to an immediate return and not be miserably deferred as with birthday gifts. And what has Bobby's mother led him to believe he will be receiving? I would guess it was a little more exciting than Bess's scribblings and one chocolate chip cookie (made according to a health-food recipe no less).

Our discomfort was utterly unassuaged by the knowledge that our gifts involved our own efforts (or at least Bess's and Kathy's). Our personalized efforts did not match the larger money expenditure of the other party. The issue wasn't just the money, because if Bobby had handed Bess a twenty-dollar bill we would have refused the gift without much anxiety. Here a breach of norms governing the form of the gift (e.g., no money unless under very certain conditions) is not as capable of embarrassing the receiver, if at all, as are breaches of norms governing the value of the gift. But we need to be more specific. The failure to abide by the norms governing the value of a gift only embarrasses the receiver if it exceeds the value of a normal gift; embarrassment is the lot of the giver if the gift's value is less than the norm. It seems in the end that our judgments are also quite particularized, taking into account not only the money spent but time and energy expended, the uniqueness of the gift, the seriousness of it, how individualized it is, how much such things mean to the giver, how much they mean to the receiver, the state of relations between the parties, and so on. Our cookie and Bess's scribbling were not going to balance the money and the time Bobby's mother took in picking out a gift for Bess. Our cookies were promiscuous, meant to be eaten by us and by anyone who stumbled by when we were eating them. When it is not clear that the personalized effort of one party was significant, when the labors engaged in could also be interpreted as an attempt to avoid spending money or were not engaged in specifically for the recipient, then monetary value will probably trump mere expenditures of effort. Obviously these rankings can undergo readjustment. If Bess were a recognized art prodigy, if Kathy were a professional cook, then our gifts would carry other meanings, as they would, too, if Bobby were the Cookie Monster.

One of the immediate moves that the embarrassed recipient makes is desperately to try to reconstruct a plausible account for the breach, to attempt to interpret it away by supposing legitimizing or justifying states of mind for the giver. Perhaps she was playing a different game. Could the value of the gift be partially excused because Bobby was a year older than Bess, or because Bobby was a boy, or because his mother had a warm spot for Kathy, or a warm spot for Bess? Was this really a gift initiating a youthful courtship in which gifts do not demand returns in the same specie? Was it simply that Bobby's mother never stinted in buying Bobby anything and that the toy she bought Bess had a much lower value to her than it did to us? Was she known to be inept in these kinds of things and hence each subsequent ineptitude bore a diminishing power to humiliate and embarrass? Or was the embarrassment that we thought she might be making a pitiable attempt to buy our friendship, in which case our very palpable embarrassment at our own failings would be compounded with our embarrassment for her as well. Whatever, no amount of such explanation for her action made us feel any less embarrassed. And we had played by the rules! But, as it turns out, only by the rules of the Valentine game. This game, as we discovered, was nested within a larger game of honor that demanded that each gift be requited with an adequate return, and that game we had lost.

The cost of our losing was our minor humiliation and shame and our great embarrassment. In our culture in that particular setting it was a cost we could bear. In other settings we may have had to suffer the sanction of being reputed cheap and even ostracized on account of it. In other cultures humiliation and shame exact a greater toll. Reuters recently published the following story picked up by papers as column filler:

> *Monday June 10, 1991:* **Scorn over gift leads to double suicide**. Beijing: A couple from northern China committed suicide on their nephew's wedding day after relatives scoffed at the value of their gift to him, a Shanghai newspaper said.
>
> Following custom, the couple from the province of Shanxi wrote in a gift book that they were giving a total of $3.70 as a wedding gift, less than half the $8.50 other relatives gave, said the Xinmin Evening News.
>
> Unable to bear their relatives' scorn and worried about future wedding gifts for their other nephews and nieces, husband Yang Baosheng hanged himself after his wife, Qu Junmei, drowned herself in a vat, the newspaper said.

For Reuters and the newspapers that printed it, the story was clearly intended to be comical in a black way, an example of the strange behavior of people with strange names (note that giving the names of the suicides is part of the process of ridicule). The story is told as one of silly people who kill themselves for trifles. Any possibility of tragedy is skillfully prevented by several devices. There are the strange names already mentioned. There is the detail of drowning in a vat, which carries with it all the indignities of pure farce. Above all, there are the money amounts involved: these people committed suicide because of $4.80. And therein lies the real comedy of the presentation. Such levels of poverty and economic underdevelopment are so unthinkable for us as to be a source of amusement and wonder. But anyone who has gotten this far in this book should be able to discern the unfathomable shame and the desperate reassertion of dignity which these people tried to accomplish with their suicides. Suicide proved them anything but shameless and hence showed them to be people of honor. Reuters got their genre wrong. This is not comedy, but the stuff of epic and tragedy. Baosheng and Qu Junmei were people who still understood the style and spirit of the heroic.

Money and the Gift Shop

Money has peculiar traits, as economists have known for a few centuries and theologians have suspected for even longer. It works well in the world of commerce because none of its possessors' selves attaches to it once it is transferred. To the extent that any of our person attaches to money, the less useful the particular money substance is as money. We want money to move, to be current, to mean as much to one person as to another. It is a virtue for money to be promiscuous and perhaps that was why moralists of the Middle Ages had such a hard time with the idea of it, if not with the thing itself. What makes money particularly suitable as money, however, is what makes it generally unsuitable as a gift. It comes without any aspect of the giver's person attached to it.[36] No lines were waited in, no traffic jams endured, no particularizing of gift to receiver was undertaken. Nor, in most circumstances, are we willing to credit givers with the time it took them to earn the money they are giving, unless we suppose that the gift imposed a very real burden on them. Usually the clock starts running only when the donor consciously begins the process of giving.[37]

Although we feel that little if any of our inner being, our real selves, attaches to gifts of money, we also feel that money has an extraordinary capacity to bear the physical excrescences of those that have touched it before it gets to our hands and by those that will touch it after it has been in our hands. Money is magical, black-magical, in this respect. It carries the slough of others, which is always rubbing off it and dirtying those that touch it without ever becoming clean for all the filth that leaps from it. This idea is not inconsistent with our sense that money is current and promiscuous, that it is meant to stay with no one for very long. The main virtue of money is its ability to go out from us at a moment's notice, not unlike excrement in the broad sense of sweat, fingernail parings, hair, skinflakes, dandruff, saliva. Money is that which leaves us, try as we might to restrain it. We exude it, after a fashion. So money is doubly cursed as a gift. Not only does it convey none of our person, none of our spirit, but it also conveys too much of our person in the sense of dull matter and filth. Thus we make gifts of money with crisp new bills, sometimes in a special envelope. Such pristine money is not quite money because it is not yet filthy. This is why we are often reluctant to spend a new bill, especially one that has been given as a gift.[38]

Money is seldom an appropriate gift unless it moves down generational levels or down status gradients. The employer can give the employee a Christmas bonus, parents can give their children money as can aunts and uncles their nieces and nephews. If money moves up the status grades it is seldom by way of gift. It then takes on the trappings of tribute, taxes, or protection money. Medieval people understood this only too well. A real risk was incurred anytime a gift went from low to high. It raised the expectation that it would be made again on every anniversary of the first giving, because not to give under the same circumstances that had evoked the first gift would not be of neutral significance.[39] It is one thing not to give at all, it is another to give and then to cease giving. Discontinuation would suggest displeasure or disapproval of a superior, a desire to distance oneself, and as such would be a hostile gesture, a show of rebelliousness, which not giving would not have had if a gift had never been made earlier. Gifts thus had ways of rather quickly becoming mandatory exactions, of becoming customs, which still can bear the sense of exaction as in "paying customs." Gifts of the faithful to God, his saints, and his ministers here on earth are more complex, although in some respects they can be subsumed into any of the three categories listed above: tribute, taxes, and protection.[40] Some churchmen were able to complicate this picture, and not quite unconsciously, when they posed as humble and poor servants of the faithful, as lower-status beneficiaries of higher-status contributors. But they also played the lord when they extracted tithes from the poor, often rather indelicately.

If gifts moving up the status grades mimicked the behavior of taxation, gifts moving down the status grades mimicked the sociology and style of charity and alms. We can thus observe that our nervousness about gifts of money is more than just a function of such gifts being insufficiently individualized or inadequately time-consuming in the making. Because gifts of money almost always go from those who have to those who do not, from high status to low, from older established to younger unestablished, they can have the look and feel of charity. A gift of money suggests that the person to whom it is given needs everything, not just a particular thing, and as such it has the capacity to insult in a way different from the latent insult implicit in gifts in general. This is why the gift of money must be so carefully limited to the precise circumstances that normalize it and euphemize it. It is thus proper to give money at key life-cycle events that show passage from tutelage to emancipation, at times, that is, when all recognize that the recipient is young and unestablished, the very purpose of the gift helping him or her make the transition to establishment. Although practice varies enormously according to social class and ethnic identification, gifts of money thus tend to be made at confirmations, graduations, and weddings.° They can also be made at other times to people whose status legitimates the gift. The receiver of services in which the service involves bringing material things or taking them away can reward the server with cash; such are tips to waitpersons or Christmas gifts to letter carriers and garbage men. The custom changes when the servers are members of certain prestige professions, in which the services provided are more abstract and magical as with doctors, professors, lawyers. Gifts to these persons are never in the form of money.[41] We simply cannot give gifts of money to our equals or our superiors, only downward.[42]

Gifts of money, then, confirm relations of dominance and inferiority, whether the gift moves up as taxes and tribute or down as charity. They also prompt different kinds of expectations regarding recompense. If gifts of money had to be repaid in the same kind as in the case of gifts of durables with durables and gifts of consumables with consumables, it would be virtually impossible to maintain a fiction that the gift was a gift instead of a loan. Exchanges of consumables and durables are almost never identical exchanges: if I give you a book and you buy me a book sometime later, you will not buy me the same book. But money is money, a set of one member. It is thus that the requital of gifts of money explicitly takes on the form of admissions and confirmations of the status differences that legitimated the gift of money in the first place. Money gifts are not to be repaid in the same specie. Receivers are to give thanks and display gratitude; they are to feel constrained to use the money "wisely"—a euphemistic way of saying that they should use it in a way that accords

°The structural resemblance of gifts of money to charity helps legitimate for some the practice of actually giving money to a charity instead of to the person who is the subject of the occasion. For example, a common bar-mitzvah gift is to give to a charity in the name and to the honor of the boy getting bar-mitzvahed. How is a thirteen-year-old supposed to understand or reply? Most mothers insist on thank-you notes from their reluctant sons, and of one it is reported that he took vengeance by writing the exact same thank-you note that he sent to those who had given him conventional gifts: Dear Mr and Mrs G——: Thank you very much for the $20 contribution to the Torah fund in my name. I will put it to very good use. Sincerely yours, Bill M. Such gifts are clearly public gestures of the giver to an audience that includes the boy's parents but not the boy at all. He incurred no obligation to the donor, only the parents did, who conspired to make the boy act as if a gift had been made to him. If he had any obligation in the matter it was prior to the gift; it was the obligation to obey his parents or at least not to embarrass them before their friends.

with the values and expectations of the giver. Receivers often feel that such gifts oblige them to make similar gifts to others when they acquire the means to do so. Children repay their parents by being generous to their own children, the student abroad repays foreign generosity by giving to nationals of that country when they are here, and so on. In such a way, even if the original recipient understands vaguely that money is indeed moving to requite the initial obligation, it still does so in a way that reaffirms the original gift as a gift and not a loan and reconfirms the social differentiation it helped constitute.

Even where gifts of money might be desired by the recipient and rendered acceptable by the setting, donors are often unwilling to give it, preferring instead to buy a durable.* Some recipients even self-deceive into thinking that they prefer the durable rather than the money. I am hinting here at one small facet of the collection of practices which surround graduation and wedding gifts.[43] This is a rich area of practice with much local variation, and so I restrict my discussion to two points: the functions of the gift shop and the bridal registry. The taboo against gifts of money drives the custom of the self-signatured GIFT, those objects that proclaim their status as gift. These are what a gift shop sells, the myriad of items of minimal utility, usually slightly overdone even when bearing other signs of tasteful-ness, and generally priced higher than one suspects that they are worth. Items often are silvery, feathery, translucent, or transparent, as if giving them a certain liminal quality. If the object purports to be useful its use must be severely limited. Thus eating utensils and table settings bought for gifts are not earmarked for daily use. They are to be SPECIAL and as such are intended to stand in some kind of constantly messaged and obvious symbolic relation to the occasion that elicited them. They must bear the markings of a gift, that is, of something one would never buy for oneself.

It may be that a few people like to receive such things, but many

---

*Some people retreat to the gift certificate, a kind of money substitute, which serves to launder a gift of money. Givers get to show that they took time and endured hassles; they also get to spare the hard work of having to guess their recipients' more exact preferences, while enabling recipients to fulfill theirs. The gift certificate func-tions to allow those who could not properly give a gift of money the chance to do so in spirit, if not in form, and in these matters form means everything. The gift certificate plays some havoc with economic theory. It is often preferred by both giver and receiver even though it is less malleable to individual preferences than the money it is pretending not to be.

people prefer to give these things rather than objects marked by evident utility. The practice is not without its reason. The giver of a gift-shop gift is seldom a close relative. Close kin can give money or more personal gifts, such as clothing. Gift-shop patrons are people who feel gifts of money inappropriate and who are not intimate enough with the recipient to select truly personalized gifts. They are often people who are obliged to make a gift by virtue of a relation to other family members or friends of the recipients; their gifts are more to the occasion itself than to the person. These people do not want to enter into a cycle of exchange with the recipients at all. They seek a gift that signals that they have fulfilled the social demands the occasion arguably obliged them with, a gift that seeks no return beyond a thank-you note. Gift-shop gifts proclaim that they come with as few strings attached as any gift possibly can. They are ritual artifacts, given not to benefit the recipient so much as to indicate the proper ritual behavior of the giver. The joke (a joke at least to those familiar with the elaborate practices of cyclical gift exchanges of Melanesia and New Guinea[44]) is that these ritual objects end up as objects of one of the few cyclical exchanges we modern Americans engage in: the regiving of gifts from gift shops, in an eternally recurring cycle, to others on their weddings and for the births of their children. No cowrie necklaces for us, but an occasional silver ashtray may pass from hand to closet to hand to closet to hand to closet and never come to its final resting place.

To whom belongs the credit for the morally ambiguous but diabolically ingenious invention of the bridal registry—that list kept by the gift shop that shows not what the newlyweds need but what they expressly want? The registry seeks to resolve the coordination problem that arises when a multitude of prospective givers is about to have their gifts converge on one small receiving point. China and silverware patterns, the items already purchased, and sometimes even the identity of prior purchasers are indicated. The couple and the retailer are thus spared the labors of exchanging unwanted pieces, but these efficiencies are funded by greater constraints imposed on the giver. Givers, however, do not only lose thereby. They gain insurance against the risk that they will choose something inappropriate or not desired by the recipient. As I have already noted, the giver bears risks when giving: the risk of rejection. To this might now be added that the giver also bears the risk of giving the wrong thing even when it is accepted. Buying a gift means making choices, often hard choices, about what to give. The choices are hard because what you give indicates to the recipient not only what you think of them in the broad sense as someone that you are obliged to or that you like well enough to give a gift to, but in the narrower sense of thinking of them as someone with certain kinds of taste in clothing, furnishings, music, art, literature, or in other matters of style. Getting it wrong not only insults the recipient but types you the giver as socially or intellectually deficient or merely as someone who doesn't know the recipient as well as you think and hence not well enough to have given a gift in the first place. But if getting it wrong hurts or insults, getting it right is what makes a good gift good. Both the perfect gift and the bungled attempt depend on the existence of choice, because choice enables surprise, and a certain amount of surprise is a nearly indispensable feature of the perfect as well as the disastrous gift.

The registry saves the giver from the risk of his own ineptitude, but at the price of forgoing the chance to make a perfect gift. There are other costs too. Sometimes the cost is monetary. The registry might show that the only things left to buy cost more than you intended to spend. Sometimes the price is the risk of humiliation, as when the only remaining item is a gravy boat. But, more likely, the registry leads you to save face by spending more than you wished to in order to avoid getting stuck spending not enough. The registry creates a minimum and shows you clearly the amounts people before you were willing to spend. These minimums can be quite high, but minimums they are nonetheless. If you buy at the minimum it is not always easy to avoid paying a little extra in intimations of embarrassment or shame.[45] But the registry also, by its very existence, sets an upper limit too. It admits implicitly that no one is expected to buy a whole set of china or silver. Gifts can now be just parts of a larger wished-for whole.

The efficiency of the registry also is funded by subtle frayings of the veils of illusion we like to construct around the morality of giving. Although in premodern societies it was not unusual for people to ask for gifts without shocking their interlocutor, in our culture to ask for a gift denies our ideology of the free gift. If the registry maintains decorum, it does so just barely by allowing some choice of gifts. The giver is still allowed his several ounces of freedom, not enough to make a perfect gift but not enough to blunder too greatly either. Moreover, the registry has already been so well integrated into our expectations surrounding the gift-giving practices of weddings that the veils can remain intact. We mostly shrug off the request for a gift that the registry makes and treat it as if the request had been made by the occasion itself, not by the couple, no different, in other words, from the kind of importuning obligation that Christmas, birthdays, and the mere wedding invitation itself raise.

Concluding Observations

This account has been somewhat misanthropic. I do not mean to deny the pleasures of giving and receiving. Some of the pleasure is what we might call genuinely innocent; it is pleasure at no one's expense. Both giver and receiver play it right and both are happy. Some pleasures are not quite so innocent. These derive in part from the competitive aspects of giving gifts. We can thus feel pleasure at another's discomfiture and relief at our own having traversed the field of action without having suffered shame, embarrassment, and humiliation. On the other side of these darker pleasures are the pains: the vexatious burdens imposed, the humiliations and embarrassments suffered at our own or at others' ineptitudes, the guilt at withdrawing from the exchange, and so on. The suggestion implicit in this chapter is that our gift-exchange practices share features with the game of honor, albeit with stakes considerably smaller than they were when Egil and Einar played the game. Gift exchanges cannot avoid the adjustment of status and dominance between the parties to the exchange and occasionally among third parties as well.

Let me conclude with a brief final example that illustrates this point with painful clarity. I return to Valentine's Day, not to the one we previously examined, but to the one experienced by most American grade-school children. It is the custom for school children roughly between the ages of six and eleven to exchange cards with hearts on them or with little messages saying "I love you" or "Be my Valentine." Children bring the cards to school and time is set aside for exchanges. Some schools require that each pupil give a valentine to every classmate. Other schools let the children decide to whom they will give valentines. In schools of the first sort, a child indicates how he or she values relations with a particular person by the expense, beauty, size, "neatness" of the card, as well as by the written message it bears. Classmates the child cares about get nice cards; others get nondescript or damaged ones. In schools of the second sort, preferences are displayed less subtly. Cards are given only to those valued above a certain threshold, and then rankings among those who get cards are as those in schools of the first sort. Opening the cards is an occasion of some anxiety. Did the people I sent nice cards to send nice ones to me? Even the most popular find themselves having declared greater admiration for one or two children than those children have shown for them. And in schools of the second sort there are the poor souls who get absolutely none or only one or two. Theirs is the greatest, but not the only pain. No doubt even the popular children feel burdened by the nice cards they get from nerds, for they may have to be nice to them now too.

The hostility in the unilateral creation of obligation figures here also. This is what happens when the unpopular kid imposes on the popular kid by sending a special valentine. It is all the uneasinesses that arise any time an exchange between any two children is not roughly equal.[46] The particular structure of valentine exchange also reveals another fertile ground for hostility and discomfort in matters of gift exchange: the giver cannot avoid making invidious distinctions among recipients. Christmas puts us in this predicament, even birthdays, for the rankings that gifts accomplish need not depend on the simultaneity of the transfers. The fact is that giving gifts is one of the ways in which we display how we rank people. Giving forces us to make a visible sign of our preferences among the people we know and as such it has the capacity to insult, to create envy, to honor, and to dishonor. The valentine exchange reveals this forcefully. Even if the various donees are spared the knowledge of what you give others, you know that you gear the expense and the quality and the amount of your self that is in a gift to how you value the bond that links you to the recipient, or to how you value the recipient.

But gift exchange is not just a way of registering preferences. These children are not voting; they are giving gifts. When they want a popularity contest they know how to have one: they elect queens and kings and captains for all kinds of occasions. To characterize the exchange of valentines as nothing more than a popularity contest would be to get it all wrong. When people give gifts they think in the idiom of gifts and this means that the meaning of what they do when they give is not the meaning of what they do when they vote. They are working with the signs and practices of positive sociability, and they are being sociable even if doing so comes at a price to some. People can be conscious that they rank others when they give or that their act of giving will rank others, but ranking is never the sole reason they give. They give to connect with others in a way that brings with it the cultural signs of sociability and conviviality. They give because that is what friends, kin, and on this one occasion classmates do. And because gift exchange bears the signs of positive sociability, it can also do the work of admonishment, correction, and social control. Dealing with others convivially involves strategy, anxiety, and pain as well as spontaneity, disinterest, and joy.

The practices of gift giving are so rich that an essay treatment can hardly hope for comprehensiveness. But it should be evident that the vignettes presented here are not intended as examples of social deviance, or of cultural rarity, or of strange practice. There is no norm of the pure disinterested gift from which the practices I present deviate. Yet we so often convince ourselves that there is such a norm, feeling small and mean for feeling put upon by the gifts we receive and the dinners we are invited to, for keeping track of what we owe to whom and who owes us what, for noting who buys and who doesn't buy the beer, for seeing where we stack up in the gifts we receive from others and worrying about how others will take the gifts we give them. The norms, in short, that govern this complex arena of social interaction are many and varied and not always consistent. The practices I described are utterly "normal" and the glitches that occurred were glitches that are themselves predictable and have been experienced in one way or another by most of us. The remarkable thing about these practices is how complicated they are, how nuanced, how infinitely varied and textured, and yet even more remarkable is that we all know (more or less) how to negotiate this complexity, a complexity every bit as complicated as language itself. We all "know" the rules at some level of consciousness. But knowing the rules consciously does not seem to correlate with how well we actually do in the world of gifts and invitations.

There does appear to be, however, a foundational norm that generates much of the behavior in this arena. My account attributes a lot of power to a norm of reciprocity, to an undeniable obligation to return a gift with a gift, a norm quite opposed to the idea of the pure gift. This norm, along with the inevitable ranking of others inherent in giving, gives the gift its aggressive aspect, its capacity for annoying and offending. The Icelanders of saga times keenly understood the hostility of the gift, as I described earlier; among them the obligation to repay a gift and the obligation to take vengeance were not distinguished.

Wrongs that needed to be avenged were so many "gifts" that needed to be repayed. We thus can find an Icelandic woman telling her husband and sons that the shameful insults that had been bruited at their expense were gifts: "Gifts have been given to you, to father as well as sons, and your manhood will suffer unless you repay them" (*Njáls saga* chap. 44). In a world of feud where repaying what one owed was the very basis of honorable action, the gift, with its overpowering capacity to oblige, became a central metaphor for the honorable life. In our world, the norm of reciprocity still works to give gifts the power to honor and dishonor, to bind people to one another, and hence to impose on them. But we prefer to deny that; because we long ago delegitimized the homology of gift exchange and vengeance we have been able to construct for ourselves an ideology of the free gift, the gift that looks for no return, the gift that is utterly disinterested.[47] There appears to be an intimate connection between our official view of the sweet disinterest of the pure gift and the official view of evil and senseless vengeance, condemned both as immoral by moralists and irrational by economists. Lowering the morality of vengeance raised the morality of the gift. We, officially at least, prefer a culture in which debts both of positive and negative moral value do not make strong demands for repayment. So we criminalized vengeance and decriminalized debt: the law of the talion gave way to the law of bankruptcy. We are supposed to believe that when we give a gift we are making no demand for a return, and that when we are the victims of hostile actions we have not been obliged to pay back the wrongdoer. We tell ourselves that it would be childish, immoral, unchristian, irrational, barbaric, to do so. Yet despite this official ideology, the norm of reciprocity holds a remarkable grip on our beings. The law may outlaw revenge, but people hunger for movies, books, and tales of vengeful justice clearly invoking sympathy and admiration for the avengers; we thrill to their vengeance. On the other hand, if the recipients of our "free" gifts fail to make adequate requital we do not fail to subject them to social sanction.

By juxtaposing the Iceland of the sagas with our present, even though I took care to catalogue the differences between us and them in matters of exchange, I might be read to claim universality for a norm of reciprocity in matters of gift exchange. Is there such a thing? Does a gift always seek its return? Not surprisingly, some say yes[48] and some say no. As usual, it falls to anthropology to make the negative claim. There is always some group or some practice somewhere that undercuts universality. Just as the Roman Egyptians made mincemeat of the universality of the incest taboo with their simple preference for brother-sister marriage, so certain Hindu practices, it has been argued, do the same for the universal pretensions of a norm of reciprocity. In Jonathan Parry's analysis, the exception to the rule of reciprocity depends on treating gifts to God as gifts. The reciprocated gift is the gift in the profane world, the sacred world often requires unreciprocated ones. Yet it seems to me that, even in the Hindu practices Parry refers to, the gift demanding no return is marked as exceptional and strange precisely because it violates a norm of reciprocity. The free gift is thus parasitical on a "normal" gift requiring requital. Parry might say it is the other way around. Somewhere somehow, as an evolutionary matter, the first gift had to be made before the practice and norm of reciprocity were established. In light of that primordial case all reciprocity would be parasitical on an initial free gift.[49]

Questions of the universality of social and psychological phenomena have a way of pitting precommitted universalists arguing the generality of a very generally defined thing against precommitted localists focusing on variations in the meaning of what to an external observer look like similar activities. Very little gets resolved. Do gifts demand returns everywhere? I am inclined to believe that some gifts demand some kind of return in every culture.[50] Yet that is to make a very empty claim, because the circumstances that determine if there is to be a return, who is to make it, when it is to be made, what the substance or style of the return is to be, and what the whole exchange is to mean are so affected not only by different values across cultures but also by the spin individuals in each culture are willing to give it, that universals, if such there be, end up being too unspecified and unnuanced to be very interesting. What then is the latent claim in the comparison of Iceland and us? It is this: that despite the claims of the law, the state, and certain religions, within certain groupings we still live as if we were people of honor. True, not all or even most of the roles we play function in the way the honor game does, and it may be that even the roles we consider most important have very little to do with the mechanisms of honor. But it is hard to get through a life without having a feel for some of the things at stake in the world of honor, whether they be in the horrors of high school, in the pressures of career, or in the simple exchanges of gifts and meals with family, friends, and workmates. Amazingly, in spite of the reputed all-intrusive evil hegemony of modern institutions, we still manage to create spaces for ourselves within which we function rather preindustrially for all that.[51] And it is in these spaces that we often find our deepest being engaged.

Egil suggested that, for him at least, the imposition of a gift was justification for violence. In his world, gifts and violence ran in the same grooves. Gifts were the means of both challenge and apology. They could provoke, but they could also disarm and repair. But when we left Egil for settings more familiar we left violence behind too, suffering instead mere annoyance or chagrin over the gifts we give and receive. We repressed the violence that Egil could not or did not care to, but in the next chapter the repressed returns.

2

Getting a
Fix on Violence

The day before yesterday they broke on the wheel the fiddler who
had started the dance and the stealing of stamped paper; he was
quartered . . . and his limbs exposed at the four corners of the
town. . . . They have taken sixty townsmen and will start hanging
them tomorrow. This province is a good example to the others,
teaching them especially to respect the governors and their
wives . . . and never to throw stones into their gardens. . . . Mme.
de Tarente was here yesterday in the woods in delightful weather.
                                    —Madame de Sévigné, 1675

As I slooshied, my glazzies tight shut to shut in the bliss that was
better than any synthemesc Bog or God, I knew such lovely
pictures. There were vecks and ptitsas, both young and starry, lying
on the ground screaming for mercy, and I was smecking all over my
rot and grinding my boot in their litsos. And there were devotchkas
ripped and creeching against walls and I plunging like a shlaga into
them, and indeed when the music, which was one movement only,
rose to the top of its highest tower, then, lying there on my bed with
glazzies tight shut and rookers behind my gulliver, I broke and
spattered and cried aaaaaaah with the bliss of it. And so the lovely
music glided to its glowing close.
                        —Alex, in Anthony Burgess, *A Clockwork Orange*

There is an allure in violence. Homer seemed to have known this, as
indeed has every epic author and tragedian since. Hollywood knows
this, and even of late so do academics. History, at least political history, has always had violence as its substance, even though academic
historians did their best to try to relegate violence to the Other, or to
the happily Overcome, or to the justly Outmoded. To be sure, there
were those gun lovers, the military historians, but they came to be

marginalized in the academy; after all, their books were read by high-school history teachers and adopted by book clubs. The mainstream academic historian generated tales of the rise of rational government, of the pacification of the countryside by efficient administration. But then came the social and cultural historical turn, assisted by post-modernism and Geertzian interpretivism. Cultural history, which used to satisfy itself with morris dances, turned instead to cat massacres. Michel Foucault, as a prelude to what has become the most influential piece of social theory since Max Weber's work, quotes a very circumstantial account that gives us a front row seat to the gruesome execution in 1757 of Damiens, a failed regicide who was even harder to kill than Rasputin.[1] We are spared no horror, no brutality, no cries of agony. On the literary side, new historicists have taken their turn. Stephen Greenblatt, for instance, in an introduction to a collection of essays on a variety of topics that luxuriate in violence—for example, "Filthy Rites," "Murdering Peasants"—gives us an equally circumstantial account of the torture and murder of a Chinese goldsmith by English traders in Java in the first decade of the seventeenth century. This poor soul turned out to be as durable as Damiens and his tormentors even more debased. Foucault had a counterintuitive agenda. However revolting the torment of Damiens, it was an emblem of a regime less intrusive and thus preferable in some important ways to the regime of discipline and surveillance which replaced it. Greenblatt's agenda seems to be a simple fascination with the lurid over which he wrings his hands somewhat guiltily.[2]

I too am drawn to violence, or, at least, I have been unable to avoid it gracefully, having been immersed in the bloodfeuding culture of saga Iceland for a good portion of my scholarly life.[3] Most people consider the society of the Icelandic sagas a violent one, an excessively violent one for that matter. The sagas, after all, are stories of feud, vengeance, and honor. The style of violence of the sagas is some of what makes even jaded third-year law students love them and is no doubt exactly what leaves others thanking their lucky stars for the state, cash-nexus, and the suburbs. But let us leave the sagas aside for now; my aims here are much more general.

We are used to thinking of violence as a problem, yet we only rarely think of it as a problematic analytical category. We all think we know it when we see it. Our conversations assume that it is bad, that it would be better if there were less, that it always seems to be in Lebanon and the inner city and not in Japan, that it is about to break forth, that we have to apologize for why we find stories that involve it so entertaining, that sports involving it always seem more interesting on account of it, that it is gendered masculine in the dishing out but feminine on the receiving end, and so on. Our rough and ready sense, which serves us passably well when violence is not the substance of our inquiry, is really not all that useful when the task is to discern the relative successes or merits of various social orders or the relative costs of certain social and political changes. What I explore in this chapter is the content of our intuitions about violence, as a prelude to getting at certain moral issues that underlie inherently comparativist accounts in social science and historical writing: just how does a historian or anthropologist or literary critic for that matter decide that one time or place is more violent than another and then negotiate the value judgments that such a decision entails? What does it mean to say that the twentieth century is more or less violent than the eighteenth or that the United States is more violent than Japan or less violent than medieval England? Are questions like these simply means of expressing preferences or are they more complexly situated than that? Many of our judgments about quantities of violence, for example, might turn out really to be judgments about qualities of violence. A nation that breaks people at the wheel, we seem to think, must be more barbarous and hence more violent than one that injects its capital criminals privately and quietly. One caveat: the subject is hydra-like; almost anything in social and political theory is but one step away from arguable relevance. This is but a beginning.

Whose View?

Violence is perspectival, and not just at the level of scholarly discourse on it but at the site of the event itself. For often what is at issue in many kinds of interaction is the very definition of the activity as violent or not.[4] The basic structure of violence involves a play of three perspectives: those of victim, victimizer, and observer. Victimizers, according to our common notions, will tend to be male, and victims, if not female to the same extent as victimizers are male, will, in many settings, be gendered female nonetheless.[5] A male victim is a feminized male. The basic structure can accommodate nonhumans at two of the three positions. The victim, for instance, needn't always be human, nor for that matter the perpetrator either. We can imagine property and animals as victims, and animals and, in some cases, acts or vicissitudes of nature such as hurricanes as victimizers. The observer, however, must always be conscious and perhaps self-conscious and hence human.

The perspectives can also be shared by the same agent in the same act. In self-mutilation one person plays all three roles: he cuts, is cut, and watches the cutting. In certain types (indeed, perhaps all types) of violence there is complex melding of sympathetic imaginings which confuse the roles of violator and violated and observer.[6] Not just intellectuals complicate the difference between hitting, getting hit, and watching someone get hit, for whether one is victim, victimizer, or observer is often contested by the participants themselves. The battered wife who torches her husband identifies herself as victim while her husband's relatives may have a very different view. The ordinary German soldiers who watched, or cheered, or even turned their heads in disgust when SS troops machine-gunned unarmed Jewish women and children can claim themselves actors when writing home or observers and victims after the war.[7] But even if we can imagine, especially in clearly erotic violence, that the psychological component of each role has complex identifications and involvements with the other roles and that each role is also highly contingent culturally, at some strongly intuitive and visceral level we admit a real difference in these roles nonetheless. In spite of the permeability of the boundaries separating the categories of victim, victimizer, and observer we readily recognize easy cases, made easy by their relatively uncomplicated conformity to the paradigm of hitter, hittee, and uninvolved observer.*

---

*Some would deny the very possibility of the easy case. Such denials are often supported by a Freudianism of an especially sophisticated literary kind that delights in the paradoxes of character and finds much of the key to character in sado-masochism. For an able performance in this genre see Bersani and Dutoit, *The Forms of Violence* 31–39. Compare, however, Primo Levi, the least lurid and the least sentimental chronicler of life in an extermination camp: "We do not wish to abet confusions, small-change Freudianism, morbidities, or indulgences. The oppressor remains what he is, and so does the victim. They are not interchangeable. The former is to be punished and execrated . . . , the latter is to be pitied and helped" (*The Drowned and the Saved* 25). And "I do not know, and it does not much interest me to know, whether in my depths there lurks a murderer, but I do know that I was a guiltless victim and I was not a murderer. I know that the murderers existed, not only in Germany, and still exist, retired or on active duty, and that to confuse them with their victims is a moral disease or an aesthetic affectation or a sinister sign of complicity" (48–49).

Fairly consistent problems, however, complicate a variety of cases. As a social and political matter we have the problem of determining whose view is to be privileged when there is a dispute as to how to classify the activity and who played what role in it. And as a psychological matter we have the problem of discerning to what extent each point of view is influenced by sympathies, identifications, and meldings with the other roles. As a rough rule we might imagine victims to be more likely to perceive violence than victimizers; that is, people will tend to overvalue the harm done them and to undervalue the harm they do others. But this rough rule runs up against another that cuts in the opposite direction. Victims often do not perceive their own victimization, or when they do perceive it, they blame themselves and not the other for the harm suffered. It is thus, as a political matter, often the case that the victim's perspective is really the perspective of observers imagining themselves victims. The sociology of many radical and reform movements is a special example of this case, in which the elites are those who discern the victimization of the people they will lead by teaching them about their victimization. Whether victims are likely to overvalue harms or fail to recognize them at all varies greatly across cultures. Even within cultures there is great variation along gender, class, and ethnic lines. Among us, men are more likely to blame others, women more likely to blame themselves. In honor-based societies people are more likely to be extraordinarily sensitive to anything that might be deemed a harm or an insult, whereas one could argue that among us honor lies less in showing signs of acute sensitivity to wrongs done you, which might type you as a whiner or as unduly sensitive, than by showing how much you can take without complaining.

As a rough rule, victimizers will be less likely to see their own activity as violent than as, say, discipline or justice or simply doing one's job. Much victimizing is also what economists would categorize as "externalities," that is, a cost (or benefit) imposed on others which is not taken into account by the person imposing the cost (or benefit). Tort law thus makes sure that neither tobacco farmers, cigarette companies, nor cigarette vendors have to think of themselves as having injured the lung cancer victim. Even self-aware victimizers have little inducement to claim themselves as such publicly. It is easy to see why. Victimizers do not have the moral basis for continuing to victimize. It is having been a victim that justifies violence, and skillful victimizers know this full well.[8] But against these instances in which victimizers are ignorant or self-deceive or even innocently believe themselves not to be victimizers, there are settings in which being recognized as a victimizer is status-enhancing. This is the ethic of "in-your-face," toughest guy around, fastest gun in the West. This style is normalized in some (not all) honor systems and is often the stuff of a peculiarly male competitiveness. As a style of political discourse, though, it is marginalized. Some old imperialists may exult in simple domination, but even the aggressive nationalism of America Firsters mixes a delight in victimizing while posing as the victims of insidious and evil forces of blacks, Jews, and Japanese.[9] Nonetheless, self-identifying victimizers are not infallible on the question of violence either. They clearly have inducements to claim themselves more violent than they may have been.

The classification of an event as violent or not is not left just to the principal actors. It is socialized by the judgments either of actual observers or of any audience for whose partial benefit the activity was undertaken. Moreover, the principal actors themselves will usually have the social competence to hypothesize the judgments of observers whether the latter are there or not. In a sense the observer's position is embedded in the social norms that govern the situation. These norms can be understood to be constituted out of observer judgments, a congealing of them into rules of action and rules of interpretation of action. Some of them are even institutionalized legally where, even if notions of violence do not figure in the actual determination of liability, they are still reflected indirectly in the amount of damages or the length of sentence.

Not all actors, however, are equally competent in gauging what propriety demands. Consider, for example, the whiner. Whiners do not usually complain about nonexistent wrongs; rather, they complain more than is seemly or they complain in those situations when grandness of character or proper behavior would require ignoring the injury. But admirable action in these settings still depends on what observers would recognize as an injury or slight having been suffered and then ignored or forgiven. What, though, of the person who claims injury but no social paradigm exists that confirms his sense of injury? If this claimant is listened to and granted victim status, we also oblige ourselves, by that very move, to entertain a claim for justice,[10] unless we decide instead to lump him with the whiners. Different claims have different histories depending on their substance, who raises them, how many people are making the same claim at the same time, whether these claimants recognize affinities with one another, whether a substantial number of people positioned as observers become sympathetic to the claim—that is, in brief, whether the time is right for advancing such a claim. And if whiners, and some justified complainers too, are annoying, we surely need to worry even less about the person who sees himself as victimizer but is not confirmed in this view by anyone else. He may be a guilt-ridden neurotic, but the world is probably better off with more such souls than fewer.

It appears from just this brief bit that, as a matter of social theory, the observer's position is the arbitral one, generally empowered to define the nature of the event at stake. Victims often do not see themselves as victims and many who do obtain their realization only at the moment they are killed by the very violence they had up to then denied. Victimizers may not see themselves as victimizers, because they often do not see or know their victims. But the observer always imagines himself as one or the other or as both; it might even be claimed that victims must imagine themselves as observers in order to recognize themselves as victims. It is thus the observer's mental state, particularly his or her sympathetic or aversive imaginings about the event at issue, that is crucial as to whether the event will be perceived as violent as a social matter, and even as to how it will be perceived by the principals as a psychological matter. My stressing the importance of the observer does not mean that I am ignoring the reality of the victim's pain or the victimizer's exultation or guilt; both are part of what violence is about, but we can get at the violence of the matter, as distinguished from the pain and glory of it, only by socializing it via the observer's position. Nor do I want to be understood to be reducing the question of violence to mere subjective takes of various third parties. It's more than "my God, I hope that doesn't happen to me." The observer's view is richly situated culturally, historically, and normatively. It brings to bear the relevant social norms and cultural competence by which the action will or will not be comprehended as violent.

The observer is aided by the fact that violence tends to be perceived when the action follows certain expected scenarios or paradigms. Much violent action is thus conventional action, fitted into ready-made categories, such as hitter vs. hittee, criminal vs. victim, fist vs. face. Most violent interaction falls into the category of the easy case, about which no sane person would dispute the appropriateness of the interaction being labeled violent or disagree as to who was the victim and who the victimizer. The way we talk about violence organizes the category for us: violence is thus something that operates by being unleashed, by breaking out, by bursting forth, by exploding. It is nervously bounded but is always breaking boundaries, the boundaries that constrain it and the boundaries of others who are its victims. Victims are thus penetrated, invaded, violated, smashed, torn to shreds, pierced, pushed back. Violence is force,[11] but force characterized variously by suddenness, uncertain warrant, the capacity to induce terror. It is distinguished from more generalized force because it is always seen as breaking boundaries rather than making them.

Our root notions, the organizing metaphors of violence, support the role differentiation we started out with. There is that which breaks out of boundaries to break down other boundaries and that which gets its boundaries broken. Yet even in these paradigms ambiguity lurks: boundaries may seem clear in the abstract or on a map (this is probably one of the few places they are ever clear),[12] but when transferred to actual social action, boundaries, especially boundaries of personhood and self, are never so clearly demarcated that the possibility of dispute is obviated. The very notion of boundaries, it could be claimed, can never be divorced from disputes over their location or from competition between the entities they separate.

Mental States and the Violent Body

Our perceptions of the quantity and style of violence are in some nontrivial way connected to the array of emotional and mental states which might characterize each role.[13] The victim is usually apprehensive, maybe terrorized, or can be guiltily eager, anticipating pleasure (as with masochism), or simply numb. Hitters have an even richer array of appropriate emotions at their disposal: they can be motivated by anger, righteous indignation, hatred,[14] resentment, jealousy, vengefulness (notice that these emotions usually indicate the hitter was previously a victim), glee, pleasure, satisfaction (implying sadism or simply a sense of justice), or spite, malevolence (implying mean-spiritedness), or simply cold calculation and pure instrumentalism.

The observer can feel whatever the victim or victimizer does, but mostly as second-order emotions. That is, the observer's emotions depend to some extent on what he perceives or imagines to be the emotions of the first two parties, on, for instance, the presence or absence of apprehension or terror, shame or humiliation, in the victim, or on the presence or absence of glee or indignation in the victimizer and then also on his own sense of justice or commitment as between the parties, which in turn will depend on what he imagines their emotions to be. We thus have the strange history of the guillotine, which was intended to curtail the violent spectacle of public executions that involved torture and mutilation and to replace it with something predictable, efficient, surgical, and mercifully quick. But it was the very quickness that started people wondering. Could it be that the head lived after its severance from the body long enough for it to be conscious of its own detruncation? Did it actually get to witness, as an observer, its own decapitation?[15] And could anything be more terror-inducing if it did? Here the violence of the guillotine was purely a function of the musings of observers and third parties, for even if the decapitated heads were capable of such musings they were surely incapable of communicating them. The observer's position depends then on sympathetic imaginings and on the fellow-feeling or revulsions that those entail.[16] But it is not just that observers' emotions piggybacked on the emotions, real or imagined, of the principals, but that the principals, when playing out their roles, felt or tried to feel as they imagined they would feel when they were observers.

When the violator's state of mind eludes us we tend to use the terror of his victim or the anxiety he inspires in us as a way of defining the violator's mental state: that is, as one producing terror, as terrifying, as dangerous,[17] as violent. One effect of this imputation is that the more fearful the victim acts or that we imagine we would act were we him, the more he begs, the more he disgusts the violator and us, the more we are likely to find the violator violent. This violence will shock and appall us when we feel the violator is predatory—that is, when it is easier for us to imagine ourselves as his victim rather than as him—but will provide catharsis and pleasure, both aesthetic and erotic, when we feel the violator is justified, as when he acts with righteous indignation and vengefulness—that is, in precisely those situations in which the violator's state of mind does not elude us at all. In revenge, as the standard film genre would have it, we do not deny the presence of violence. We in fact hunger for it. What we do instead is redefine who is playing what role. The morally and emotionally satisfying feature of revenge is that it is the person typed victim in our model who is doing the violence and the person typed violator who finally is humiliated and victimized.

What is fear-instilling about victimizers is obviously more than just the mental states observers impute to them, but also how those mental states are physically embodied, what the prospective victimizers look like. Big people thus seem to have more violent possibility than little people, thick people than thin people. Self-consciously violent souls have an array of culturally coded ways of presenting themselves to indicate that they are violent souls. Bikers have one style, jocks another, street toughs others. They consciously cultivate certain styles of carriage, speech, facial expression, hair, body markings, and clothing. The recombinatory inventiveness of these codes can counteract the effects of most body types. The short and thick have no trouble intimating suggestions of violence; they have an easier time of it than the tall and skinny. Yet the tall and skinny are not utterly without strategies either; they can cultivate a certain look and posture that mark callousness and violence. And then it is remarkable what carrying an Uzi will do for the shortfalls of genetics.

Clearly, I have been talking about male codes. To the observer, the class of possible violent victimizers is made up of men. The ancient cultural stereotype of female victimizer is the sultry seductress—Eve and the Sirens, evil more than violent. The figure of the Amazon actually proves the point, because she genders herself as a warrior-aged male in order to fight. Not just any male will do. Little boys do not instill terror; yet inexorably their capacity to be cute recedes as their capacity to terrorize increases—by age thirteen few boys are cute any longer. But violent males cannot be old either. This fact is one of the pathetic paradoxes of bringing Nazi war criminals to justice when they are decrepit eighty-year-olds. The Israelis are only too aware of the dark comedy of meting out justice on the body of an old man for the unspeakable crimes of the young man. But if old age cannot excuse the visitation of justice (it cannot), old age can certainly deprive one of the pure satisfaction of just requital. It is more like hanging a man in absentia than hanging a man. One cannot help but feel a little foolish. Punishment should be visited on the body that violates, on the body that terrorizes because of the violence it wreaked and could be imagined still to wreak, rather than on a body that invokes pity (or disgust) because it reveals a certain common humanity with its victims in its mortality. It is almost as if the curse of bodily decay dedemonizes the devils who committed the crimes.[18]

Yet Hannah Arendt's point is that the most appalling crimes were committed by insipid little functionaries.[19] The age of technology allows victimizers to be puny and retiring. Evil becomes banal. One could feel little more satisfaction in killing Eichmann young than in killing him old. In either case he was too pathetic a correlative to the enormity of the acts he participated in. Eichmann did not fit the mold of the violent victimizer; his banality, in fact, is that he was not at all violent; he was just a person who affixed signatures to orders. Evil is banal when it does not require violent men to do its work. Violence is precisely what is needed to debanalize evil. Evil is much more grand when it comes embodied in Attila rather than in Himmler or Eichmann. Eichmann thus raises different issues than does John Demjanjuk, who may or may not have been Ivan the Terrible, a sadistic guard at the Treblinka death camp. He was evil in the old-fashioned way, not as a bureaucratic banality. Demjanjuk, once big and thick, now old and blind, makes us confront rather directly the issue of punishing old bodies for the actions of violent young ones.

If victimizers can self-create by adopting certain styles of self-presentation, they can also be created by observers. Observer perceptions of violence are a nice index of observer phobias and inner demons. The lower classes look violent to the upper classes, blacks to whites, men to women, and so on. There is not just a simple and necessary correlation, however, between instilling fear and being perceived as violent. Jews, for instance, have for centuries instilled fear in Christians and likewise women in men, but it is the fear of being tricked, outsmarted, poisoned, set up. Neither Jews nor women instill fear by being marked as violent. Both Jews and women (of course) are feminized. They are violated, they do not violate.[20]

Our discussion of emotional states and the central role of the observer's position suggests that much of violence involves the fear of violence, the universe of threat and danger. We feel that the fear of violence is restrictive. Perhaps a way of getting at the quantity of violence and the consequences of its varying styles would be to consider how the fear of violence works to restrict the freedom of the anxious person. The violent culture of my high school, for example, led me consciously to limit my range of social options: where I could walk or drink or with whom I could go out or even gaze wishfully and wistfully at. It led to restrictions on my body: how straight I stood, the gait with which I walked, the accent, timbre, and volume of my voice. An objective measure of the actual number of fights at that school could lead the sociologist or historian to describe the culture as "pacified," but that pacification was insufficient to prevent the psychic costs to people who organized their lives around the constant *prospect* of violence. Efficient totalitarian regimes and even some democratic ones know that they needn't be all that bloody to achieve stifling conformity to a desired standard. The terror of torture or assassination will lead people to restrict their behavior "voluntarily" through what some social scientists have pretentiously called adaptive preference formation. Perhaps sociologists could devise surveys to quantify this restriction, although I doubt it, and it would be virtually impossible for historians to get at the extent to which people in the past limited what they would otherwise have done for fear of reprisal.[21]

The obvious consequence of these observations is that we also seem to need a theory of coercion and a theory of consent, the kinds of things that political theorists worry about, to make sense of violence. But then again we do not want to so broaden the category that we call, for example, pre-1990 East Germany violent. One might want to say that whatever the initial violence that brought such a reality into being, it did not create a violent present, simply a very restricted one, maintained as much by people's views of the ranges of possible behaviors as it was by the occasional random violences of the police.

I do not want to press the point about fear too far. There are people—victimizers mainly, but not exclusively—for whom the prospect of violence generates little fear. Those people in my high school, for instance, who were the restrictors of my freedom knew that they were violent and recognized the violence of their world. They were just better at it than I was. But just what were they better at? Being violent or being able to absorb my violence and still do what they wanted to do? In the close world of face-to-face interaction the violent person is often, paradoxically, not the one who dishes it out, but the one who can take whatever is dished out and still have enough to get the original violator to back down. That is, at some level, we are still dealing with the ability to instill fear in others, with the suggestion of ominousness and threat. Yet we surely do not want to make the presence or absence of violence a function of the views of those brutalized so long as to have become inured to pain and violence. At some point we may want to say that coercion and restrictions of opportunity are so great as to be violent independent of the preferences of the people so constrained. But we have not yet begun to fathom our intuitions.

Aspects of Our Grammar of Violence

Our root notion of violence as boundary-breaking, the fist-meets-face view of violence, has a seductive essentiality to it. It makes us think that the category is timeless and relatively context-insensitive. Yet at the same time our views of violence depend on so many variables of sight, sound, pain, on categories of law and morality, on levels of technology, on rules of group formation, on legitimacy and status, among other things, that whatever essence violence might have it is unlikely to be found independent of the various social, cultural, and individualized settings in which it is situated. In this section we examine some of the variables that affect our perceptions of violence.

We tend to perceive violence when blood flows outside its normal channels. Ax murderers are thus more violent than poisoners. A fight that produces a lot of blood but no serious injury may well be perceived as more violent than one that causes internal injury but leaves no superficial manifestations. Violence is also felt to be noisy: the victims' screams and groans and the victimizers' shouting, the crowds' cheering (as in public executions), guns' reports, and bones cracking. Ax murderers are thus again more violent than poisoners. Part of the humanizing of capital punishment as it changed from public drawing and quartering to the lonely electrocution of a sedated victim or to permanent sedation by lethal injection was not only the reduction of pain but the reduction of noise and mess. Extraordinary efforts were made to achieve silence in executions. To make hangings quieter the English baffled the drop doors of the gallows platform with bales of cotton, and later, when the technology was available, rubber cushions and spring catches were used.[22] And if we don't quite see a gun with a silencer as all that less violent than a gun without one that is mostly because the silencer is sinister. A silenced gun undoes the illusion that the gun is intended to defend rather than offend.[23] The silencer allows one literally to get away with murder, whereas the noise, although disruptive of another's blissful ignorance, is literally a report. The unsilenced gun does not deny its dirty work. The point I am making is nicely captured by an early English law of King Ine of Wessex dating from the late seventh century:

If anyone burns a tree in the woods he shall pay the full fine: he owes 60 shillings because fire is a thief. If anyone chops down many trees in a woods and it is discovered he shall pay 30 shillings for each of three trees. He need not pay more no matter how many there are because the ax is an informer, not a thief.[24]

We tend also to associate noisiness and bloody messiness with pain, and in turn we have a sense that pain bears some relation to violence. We subscribe to a rough rule of thumb which says the more pain the instrument of death causes, the more violent it is. But pain is hard to get at. As Elaine Scarry reminds us, it is a private experience and incommunicable; it is language-destroying.[25] Messiness and noise are so closely connected with violence in part because pain needs a sign system to be identified. Screams and groans, blood and broken bodies, replace the words that pain cannot find. Without this cacophonic accompaniment, pain is not believed as pain, nor is it perceived as violent.[26] Silent suffering may be a consequence of violent activity, as when a parent grieves for a murdered child, but the parent's grief is not a part of violence in the same way that fear of violence is part of violence, unless the grieving is itself carried out in a violent manner, as, for example, in funerary customs in which self-mutilation or flagelation or immolation are the signs of grief.

Not all pain is violent. Violent pain must be focused, not just a cumulation of aches and pains. An act that causes three units of pain per day for a year will not be judged to be as violent as one that causes one hundred units of pain on only one day, even though the total quantity of pain inflicted is more than ten times greater.[27] Most medical procedures (if the patient consents to them) are not perceived as violent. Yet we would be inclined to think that a painful and intrusive procedure is more violent undertaken without anesthetics than with them. This intuition is yet another aspect of our beliefs in the barbarity of earlier times and other places. We think their medical practices violent and assume that the only reason they didn't (if they didn't) was because the levels of pain and violence in their times dulled their senses. Although it is likely that the immunity medicine has from being considered violent is mostly a function of its legitimacy, its cultural and legal privilege, it just might be that the modern unassailability of that privilege owes a lot to the availability of anesthetics. This basis for the privilege is more clearly revealed with regard to dentistry, whose cultural privilege has never been quite so

unassailable as medicine's. Until anesthetics became routine the association of dentistry and violent men was an easy one to make, as, for
instance, is exemplified in Frank Norris's *McTeague*.

Nor is all violence painful. Property destruction, corpse mutilation,
and the murder of a sleeping victim are a few of the many cases that
suggest themselves. A little more complex is the problem raised by
individual variations in thresholds of pain.[28] Is it that some people can
endure pain better than others, that is, that they are tougher, or does
the fact that they can endure it indicate that they simply do not feel it?
For courage to be a virtue, the first alternative would have to be the
correct one. We want heroism to involve some amount of self-
overcoming.[29] The person who fears nothing or feels nothing might
himself be an object of awe for those strange qualities, but we would
resist thinking that having no nervous system is a virtue. The Norse
called such people berserks and counted them useful only in battle
and as major liabilities at all other times.

Pain is recognizable in others only by surrogate senses. We see or
hear others in pain, but we do not feel their pain; we may feel certain
sympathetic twinges and kinesthetic dislocations, but not the pain
itself. Perhaps the fact that so much of violence from the observer's
point of view is independent of tactile sensation, that it is sight and
sound, does much to account for the prevailing view that representations or staged depictions of violence are themselves violent. A cover
story in *Newsweek* titled "Violence in Our Culture" turned out to deal
entirely with movies, television, and theater with a minor concession
to psychological studies that "prove" a correlation between watching
depictions of violence and a life of crime.[30] I do not want to repeat
here the various analyses about the relationships of representations to
the thing itself, if such a thing there be. The relationship of violence
and representation has been to some extent trivialized by some post-
structuralist literary criticism, which is especially liberal in what it is
willing to consider violence: thus reading and writing are violent, and
of course representation, to the extent it reproduces discourses of
domination, is violent; and it is even supposed that authors and literary critics lead lives of danger by reading critically.[31] But I don't mean
to suggest that there is not a serious issue here. We may want to test
our intuitions regarding whether we think the judge who signs the
death warrant to be as violent as the hangman who executes it. We
may want to test whether our emotional reactions to depictions of
violence that are marked by the conventions of film or novel differ

from our reactions to depictions of violence via media marked with conventions of reality, such as newscasts and newspapers. We may very well find that we are disgusted and terrified more by fiction than by fact, and in turn moved more by stylized representations of fact than by eyewitness involvement.

Violence is bound up with technology. Efficient means of killing are perceived as less violent than messy ones. Ax murderers are thus violent in a way that gunmen are not. Some of our perception of what is felt to be the excessiveness of Viking violence or the violence of other preindustrial raiders is partially dependent on the fact that they were relegated by their weapons technology to being ax killers. Clearly, it means something different for us to kill with an ax than to kill with a gun, but when the choice was not available, the meaning of killing with an ax was different. We all know this but we do not quite feel it, and hence we blame the earlier age for the vulgarity of its way of killing.[32]

Part of the substance of this vulgarity is not only the mess created but the particular type of mess. Axes and chainsaws dismember or decapitate. They destroy, more manifestly than a bullet, the external integrity of the body. They cannot kill without also mutilating. Broken bodies, partial bodies, are the stuff of horror and require great force. That force, sometimes exceeding the strength of four horses in drawing and quartering, suggests a violence greater than that which kills but allows the body to continue to look like one. Dismemberment and mutilation figure importantly in atrocity, a notion bearing an intimate connection to manifestly unprivileged violence. Atrocity often has more to do with what is done to corpses than what is done in making them corpses in the first place. A corpse, however, can be mutilated by those who venerate it as well as by those who are intent on humiliating it and its kin.[33] It was not unknown for the impatient faithful to assist death a little in order to obtain corporeal relics of dying holy men and women.[34] The very idea of body parts as relics seems to suggest that desecration and sacralization often must go hand-in-hand, yet the worshipful intent of these mutilators is often not sufficient to undercut our sense of the violence of their actions. Recall the morbid comedy of the Ayatollah Khoumeini's funeral procession during which grieving mourners tore his clothing and knocked him off the bier. It was comic in a way that the mutilation of an enemy's corpse could never be. The worshipful, after all, did not kill the object of their worship. The comedy (for us), however, requires that we perceive violence, whether in the frenzy of the worshipful or in the mutilation itself. We thus do not necessarily perceive violence to be exclusively the domain of the serious or of the tragic and epic. Violence does not undercut the possibility for comedy and in fact seems to be a necessary underpinning to much of the darker side of it.

Consider a variation on the theme of vulgar lethal technology. We are more likely to perceive violence when the victim meets the inflicter face to face than when the inflicter can effect his harm at a distance. This is one of the moral solaces of technology. Technology dispenses with actually having to lay hands on the victim. Thus, Miles, an inner-city youth, can claim that he was nonviolent when he killed his robbery victim with one shot. "Using a knife. . . would be violent. Stabbing and shooting is different," he said. "I never stabbed a person in my life. If you stab somebody, you got to feel the knife go in and you got to pull it out and stab 'em again and pull it out and stab 'em again. . . . I don't consider myself no killer."[35] Relative distance also accounts for our intuitions that Lieutenant Calley engaged in more violence when he gunned down women and children in My Lai than did the Phantom pilot who killed as many women and children with a single bomb. Our intuitions on these matters have survived rather insistent challenge since the Vietnam years: the face-to-face killer is more violent and more morally culpable.

We perceive the pilot as less violent than Lieutenant Calley because we believe that Calley, being on the scene, could carry out his mission with more particular attention to his choice of target than could the pilot whose distance from his target made for less precision in target choice and hence a greater likelihood that death would occur by causes that we might tend to perceive as "supervening." Because the pilot is far from his victims we even suppose that his primary purpose is to fly neat airplanes rather than to kill, whereas the technology of search and destroy missions lets us assume that Calley likes to kill more than the pilot does. We believe that if you can see your victim die before you then your own mental state is more intensely focused, more willing to visit focused pain, and hence more violent than the disposition of the person who is able to harm those he cannot see. Because the pilot cannot see his victim we attribute less malignity to him, and excuse him more for not having the fellow-feeling we expect a child's vulnerability should elicit from the face-to-face killer.[36] The commando is more violent, more immoral, either because he feels nothing or because we suspect that he may be feeling the wrong things. He is either an insensate brute or a pervert who derives aesthetic and erotic pleasure from the sights and sounds of carnage he effects. The pilot too may be insensate, or he too might thrill to the beauty of the fireworks display he causes, but his distance keeps him from the screaming, beseeching, and body parts of his victims and so we accord him the possibility of more refinement. After all, it is fireworks not begging that gives him pleasure; and if he is unmoved in spirit, well, that's just the consequence of his being removed in time and space. I think that it is important to observe that the fairly close fit here between claims about relative levels of violence and claims about moral culpability does not allow us to dismiss our views on violence as simply indirect ways of talking about morality. Our perceptions on violence are just as likely to be generating our moral judgments in this particular setting as our moral judgments our perceptions of violence.

Omissions are not violent, only commissions are. This view is consistent with our notion of violence as a type of force. If an adult watches the drowning of a four-year-old child to whom he is a stranger and whom he could have saved without risk to himself, he is not deemed violent (and furthermore the common law does not hold him liable, either criminally or civilly) for his inaction. If he were to rescue the child and spank her very soundly for putting herself in such danger he would be liable for the spanking unless the child were his own. The omission-commission distinction also helps explain why we might experience a coldly selfish culture of self-seeking individualists as less violent than a feuding culture with strong community solidarity, charitable to its weaker members, but aggressive to outsiders. Omissions can be cruel but not violent, and many violent acts may not be thought of as cruel.

The cruel and the violent no doubt share large points of congruence, but they differ in several ways. Violence can bear positive moral significations in certain settings; cruelty seldom can.[37] Cruelty always bears with it a sense of disproportionality.[38] It exceeds the precise demands of justice even in those instances in which it is claiming to do justice. We think of violence as sudden, noisy, boundary-breaking, claim-enforcing, having the capacity for innocence; we think of cruelty as insistent, cold, jaded, and decadent. Cruelty more often than violence is its own reward, for it usually means taking pleasure in another's pain.[39] Violence is always active; cruelty does not have to be.

Although a gaze may violate, it is not in itself violent; but we can think of someone as gazing cruelly without extending our sense of the cruel though not of someone gazing violently without extending and poeticizing our sense of violence.

If our focus has been rather local till now, at the level of event, let us shift for a moment to cultural styles. What is the basis for making judgments about the violence of whole cultures? Is a nation that has a low homicide rate at home but is a brutal aggressor abroad more or less violent than another that is rough and tumble at home but too unorganized to export its violence, for example, Japan in the 1920s and 1930s versus Lebanon today? Cross-cultural studies, if they are to be relied on, tend to reveal a correspondence between internal and external violence.[40] We have, however, a real problem in determining criteria for distinguishing internal from external. In these studies internalness is defined by the boundaries of nation-states (a very crude boundary at best), not by class, race, kin group, or the perceptions of killers and victims, and to that extent the experience of violence is misrepresented. Are the types of violence we direct toward our own the same as those we direct toward the Other? Anthropological and historical evidence shows that we use different weapons and different styles and intensities of fighting according to the relational distance, age, sex, and status of the people we are fighting against. A Viking raider may toss babies up in the air and spear them when raiding abroad, but when feuding at home he may well spare his enemies' children.[41] Among the Nuer, men of the same camp fight with clubs, but if the fight is between people of different villages it is with the spear.[42] In such situations the very style of violence is the recognition of group membership or otherness. Some might argue that all violence is inflicted on the Other,[43] that violence in fact makes the Other, defines the Other. In the view of the perpetrator, the victim might always be on the other side of the group boundary as he defines it in the heat of the moment. But if this is so, what do we make of masochism or suicide? A kind of *deus ex machina* can resolve this problem simply by populating personhood with more than one self. Instead of having a pleasure principle and a death instinct at war within a single self we might have instead a pleasure-seeking self at war with a death-seeking self occupying the same body.

Different times and different places have different styles of ostracism. Assume one society whose ultimate sanction against an unwanted member is to hang the offender and another in which all the members turn their backs on the unwanted member, who then reads these signals as an invitation to hang himself for shame in a tree, which he does. We have examples of both cultures.[44] The suicide culture is not perceived to be as violent as the homicide culture, other things (such as means of death) being equal. Why is this so? One could argue that in a society of suicides we would not experience the fear of others who might kill us and would have nothing to fear but ourselves. When we fear ourselves we entertain the notion that we are somehow in some control of the source of our fear, and to that extent fear is less fearsome. (In fact, when we say we are afraid of ourselves we usually use the expression metaphorically and not a little bit self-indulgently.) On the other hand, one could argue that a society of suicides has the same amount of fear as the hanging society, but the fear is directed generally toward all those others whose opinions would make us despair ourselves unto death. The superficial appeal of this latter proposition seems, however, to depend on a metaphorical extension of the core sense of fear. It is unlikely that general fears are different only as a matter of degree from focused fear; nor does it make much sense to think that a lot of small fears can be summed arithmetically to produce one big focused fear. The fear of one's self and general fears of others have more points of congruence with despair and anxiety than with focused fear. But it seems that our feeling that the violence of homicide is greater than that of suicide flows formally and easily from our perspectival model of violence. Simple paradigmatic violence involves, as a first-order matter, victim, victimizer, and observer, each separately embodied. Homicide, according to this model, is more fundamentally violent than suicide. Suicide requires second-order refinements to the basic model involving the role interpenetration and confusion discussed earlier. From the observer's perspective the violence of homicide requires little labor to discern; it is a public drama with a prelude that can be seen, while with suicide there is nothing to see until the corpse is created. Its drama is played out in the head of the suicide, leaving the observer only to clean up afterward and feel disgust or pity, but not to feel the terror or exultation that the violent drama of homicide produces.

Violence, Hierarchy, and Legitimacy

All historical work and most sociological work on societal violence focus on public violence of private citizens: crime, riots, strikes, rebellion, and war. What escapes view is intrahousehold violence on the one hand—men beating wives and parents beating children, masters abusing servants, various types of sexual exploitation—and on the other hand the violence the state uses to keep order and maintain its position—prisons, police, the impoverishment effected by exploitive taxation, and the violence of law itself.[45] It is clear that the perception of violence is intimately connected with social structure and one's position within it, and with the normative ordering(s) of the culture.

Inside the household most violent actions of the head of household were once privileged. Much violence went unperceived, categorized instead as instruction or correction. But sayings like "spare the rod, spoil the child" show that the privilege did not blind people entirely to the violence of instruction, correction, and discipline. Private violence was conscious, instrumental, and good policy, distressing few, if any, in the public realm. It took the labors of the feminist movement finally to expose the internal workings of the household to public view and show us the costs to women of the public/private distinction, the distinction that made the household door the boundary of a liberty (in the medieval sense) in which men were free to rain violence on women and adults on children.[46] One strand of feminist scholarship portrays women as victims of both direct male violence and the indirect social structural violence of patriarchally organized societies which kept them poor, disempowered, and dependent. Although it is impossible to deny the grim truth of most of the claims, the picture is partial. Not only does it exclude the achievements of women who triumphed in spite of legal and social disablement, but it also costs us a view of woman-on-woman violence. Middle-class scholars may not know that it is not all that unusual for lower-class adolescent females to settle disputes with each other by fighting just as their male classmates do. Tough high schools are tough for the girls because of the girls as well as because of the guys. And it is not clear that the girls are simply adopting male standards of behavior as their own. Yet because violence is gendered male, violent females are considered more deviant than violent males.[47]

Although until recently most historians have passed over intrahousehold violence as if it did not exist or, if it existed, as if it were not violent, those historians who have had their sensibilities affected by the present concern with such matters and who are eager to discover such violence are thwarted mostly by the inscrutable silence of the historical record.[48] The violence of law and order, however, has always been available to historians and sociologists, but until quite recently they generally ignored it.[49] Clothing violence in legitimacy makes it hard to recognize.[50] The presumption of legitimacy given to the state, for example, makes state violence almost invisible.[51] We accord state action a naturalness we do not accord to the identical act not legitimized by the law or state. Consider for a moment in this context what we mean by nonviolence as a strategy for social change. A strategy of nonviolence is invariably a strategy of lower-status claimants. A constituted authority that governs with restraint is not thought of as pursuing a strategy of nonviolence. Nonviolence is a term of art. Nonviolence clearly anticipates violence and, depending on the stakes, it anticipates corpses too, for the strategy of the lower-status claimants is to force higher-status authorities to overt acts of violence against them or, if the authorities refuse to engage on such terms, the lower-status claimants might simply do violence to themselves. "Nonviolence" (which by now may have earned its quotes) seeks to make the legitimate authorities act in such a way that others will indeed perceive them as violent and hence as illegitimate. The strategy makes its claim about the unendurability of the violence of the present order by engineering a situation in which those who benefit by the present order will be forced to use what everyone will recognize as violence to maintain it. And if that strategy fails because the authorities act in a way not perceived as violent, then the alternative strategy of self-immolation—by fire, by hunger-strike, by civil disobedience leading to imprisonment—seeks to reveal the invisible violence that the lower-status claimant believes is inherent in the social and political arrangements of the polity. In brief, nonviolence simply means that the corpses will be those only of lower-status claimants, not that there will be no corpses.

Of course, the state does not monopolize legitimacy, for it is intimately involved in all social hierarchy and is an issue in most all social action. Violence that works its way down the hierarchy is viewed as legitimate, order-effecting, and is often thus not even recognized as violence, or when recognized as violence is seen as less violent than the same amount of force opposing it. Violence is understood to be disordering and hence disruptive of established boundaries and established orders. This is perhaps the most consistent intuition we have about violence. We are thus less likely to perceive violence when we believe for whatever reason that it is merely the coercion necessary to make things the way they ought to be. If a parent disciplined an unruly teenage son by administering a sound beating and then the son, angered by this discipline, beat his parent, most of us, I wager, would view the son as more violent than the parent (even if this parent were father rather than mother), and some would go so far as to believe that the parent's actions do not even raise the issue of violence. But the son may be perceived as more violent because he is more likely to be more violent. A whole set of social and normative constraints govern the parent's violence, but there are few indeed left to govern the son's once he is embarked on being violent to his parent. The norms that govern the son have already been broken the instant he strikes back.°

Because violence is often associated with suddenness, regularized and predictable violence is often perceived as less violent by virtue of its regularity. The Viking raider is more violent by this account than the royal official collecting taxes. Regularity of expropriation has the look of state bureaucracy, of rational social organization, of the rudiments of the rule of law, whereas irregularity has the look of disorder, uncertainty, and randomness. Regularity is arguably less terrifying than randomness, if only because regularity of expropriation and application of force inures the victim to it and what was once perceived as violent by the victim comes to be perceived as the natural order of things. It also gives the victim the chance to prepare. Yet one of the more sinister achievements of certain police regimes is to have regularized violence while still preserving its suddenness. If the citizens are conscious of the regularity, then affliction comes when that consciousness is in abeyance. Hence the Gestapo preference for arresting people in the middle of the night.

Consider the issues raised in the following passage from Thucydides, in which a nameless but oratorically gifted Athenian addresses the Spartan assembly justifying Athens treatment of her allies. It is so rich that I quote it at some length:

> It has always been a rule that the weak should be subject to the strong; and besides, we consider that we are worthy of our power.

°We must be careful here. We do not want to let authority privilege its violence against indignant attack simply by virtue of its power to make the rules. It was, after all, not sons who made the rule that thou shalt not strike your parents. Here we would want to make some assessment as to the general acceptability of the regime making the rule and whether it provides a fair benefit in return for obeisance to it.

Up till the present moment you, too, used to think that we were;
but now, after calculating your own interest, you are beginning to
talk in terms of right and wrong. Considerations of this kind
have never yet turned people aside from the opportunities of
aggrandizement offered by superior strength. Those who really
deserve praise are the people who, while human enough to enjoy
power, nevertheless pay more attention to justice than they are
compelled to do by their situation. Certainly we think that if anyone
else was in our position it would soon be evident whether we
act with moderation or not. Yet, unreasonably enough, our very
consideration for others has brought us more blame than praise. For
example, in law-suits with our allies arising out of contracts we have
put ourselves at a disadvantage, and when we arrange to have such
cases tried by impartial courts in Athens, people merely say that we
are overfond of going to law. No one bothers to inquire why this
reproach is not made against other imperial Powers, who treat their
subjects much more harshly than we do: the fact being, of course,
that where force can be used there is no need to bring in the
law. Our subjects, on the other hand, are used to being treated as
equals; consequently, when they are disappointed in what they
think right and suffer even the smallest disadvantage because of a
judgment in our courts or because of the power that our empire
gives us, they cease to feel grateful to us for all the advantages
which we have left to them: indeed, they feel more bitterly over this
slight disparity than they would feel if we from the first, had set the
law aside and had openly enriched ourselves at their expense. Under
those conditions they would certainly not have disputed the fact that
the weak must give in to the strong. People, in fact, seem to feel
more strongly about their legal wrongs than about the wrongs
inflicted on them by violence. In the first case they think they are
being outdone by an equal, in the second case that they are being
compelled by a superior. (I.76–77)

This brilliantly self-serving speech is filled with the complacent
clichés of power which suppose that self-interest is the only serious
motivator of action, but several points touch directly on our discussion. One we mentioned earlier: the extent to which perceptions of
constraint, harm, and grievance are functions of a baseline of expectation and relative to it. With the expectation of the good comes greater
sensitivity to the bad, or, more precisely, the expectation of the good
expands the content of the category of the bad. The Athenian notes
the relativism of claims of harm and perniciously suggests the exis-

tence of an objective standard, the eternal standard of human misery, the standard of low expectation. If one is to compare, he argues, one should always look to compare one's standing with those who are worse off. It is one of the complacencies of Power to argue that the comparison must always be made to worse situations, never to better, precisely because one of the incidents of Power is to be able to compel others into that worse situation. This is a sick joke disguised as an argument.

A related point is that the perception of wrong and hence the perception of violence is sensitive to the relative status of victimizer and victim, for status determines expectations, and expectations, in turn, create sensitivity to the consequences of their denial. In a regime in which one is a juridical equal among other equals and does not expect to be oppressed by authority, one's antennae are finely attuned to insult, grievance, and injury from one's peers. Equality in this setting means the publicly recognized right of the wronged person to redress. Should redress be denied, more is at stake than the narrow legal matter of the denial of a cause of action; what is at stake is one's continued status as an equal. And in a society with institutionalized slavery such denial is a prelude to the forthcoming violence of slavery. No wonder the grievants the Athenian complains about feel legal wrongs done them by equals more strongly than violence inflicted on them by a superior, for in the former is the promise of the latter. In this regard note how the subtle Athenian claims gratitude as his due for the advantages conferred. He is aware that gratitude is an emotion that fares awkwardly in conditions of social equality, the experience of it often being an admission of inferiority and the constitution of hierarchy.

Violence may simply be what we accuse the Other of when we are contesting interests. It may be little more than a rhetorical play in the game of self-legitimation or the delegitimation of the Other. Or, at the very least, the word *violence* is a depository for a large number of utterly incommensurable activities, each with its own sociology and psychology. Both these concerns are plausible, but I do not think that they sufficiently dispose of our topic. There is indeed a strong normative component in the concept of violence which makes it suitable for use in the rhetoric of asserting and justifying claims. But that does not account for the special force of claims involving violence; it does not account for the fact that the concept of violence is called upon to do this kind of justificatory work and not any of the myriad others that might have been called on. Violence, we feel, is no less substantial than any of several concepts that are partially congruent with it, including justice, freedom, autonomy, coercion. It is true too that the concept is a catch-all category drawing together activities as disparate as war, spouse abuse, street life, barroom brawls, football, movies, and crime, activities that may be characterized more by differences than by similarities. But the very fact that we have organizing scenarios or paradigms that make the similarities salient (or for that matter call them into being) argues for not dismissing the conceptual power of the category. Violence means something to us, and like other complex concepts its particular applications may not always paint a coherent or consistent picture. But we do not ask for abstract consistency in such big concepts, only that they do their work of description or prescription in the local settings where it is plausible or possible to use them.

That violence is perspectival, that it may be intimately connected to notions of legitimacy and thus also to politics and rhetoric, does not mean that there have been no real changes through time in the way social control has been exercised or power relations constructed. Nineteenth-century discussions on the similarities of slavery and wage slavery notwithstanding, the market and industrial production controlled bodies in ways different from those the master used for the slave. The sanction of the whip was replaced largely by economic sanctions. The style of coercion was different, and these differences greatly affected the way in which the particular society was organized. The broad move from sanctions operating directly on the body or on one's property—beatings, raids, forced gifts—to sanctions operating economically and only indirectly on the body—firings, lockouts, wage reductions—might not have diminished misery or even cruelty,[52] but it surely meant something for what we like to think of as violence. In short, much of the style of dominance moved from a regime of irregular face-to-face encounter to regularized control effected from a distance.

Nature versus Culture

As a corollary to the invisibility of the violence of legitimate authority, violence, as we usually understand it, is anticulture, anticivilization. It is raw unmitigated nature and what culture has worked for years to cabin. Culture, in this view of things, represses violence, working desperately to keep it sublimated, repressed, bounded. Violence is the eruption of nature through culture's defenses. The nature/culture paradigm has a long and hallowed tradition in political and social theory. It informs the work of many historians as well as the Freud of *Civilization and Its Discontents*. But there is also a well-established countertradition that accepts the nature/culture dichotomy but valorizes its members differently. In this tradition nature is honest, and if not always serene it is never spiteful, decadent, or perverse. Violence, according to this tradition, is an aspect of the fall from the state of nature. It is this fallen state that brings us the unnaturalness of greed and acquisitiveness, pride, envy, lust, and the whole array of deadly sins. By this account violent *human* nature is unnatural; violence is man's very own creation, the product of the social and cultural universe he chose to create and chooses to recreate. Most of our intuitions about violence follow the first tradition—nature as violent—and are greatly assisted by our misunderstanding the significance of human nature in the second tradition as precultural or natural rather than as a creation of culture. In other words, the violent human "nature" of the second tradition ends up supporting the view of nature as violent in the first tradition by an accident of the multiple referents of the word *nature*. Thus we see violence as sudden, instinctual, primal, insistent, as erupting, tumultuous, disordering—as raw, visceral, and following the law of the jungle.

The Conservation of Violence

It would be interesting to know, if there were some magical way of knowing, whether the violence the state uses to impose its order is greater than the sum of anarchical violence which would be suffered if the same polity were broken down into smaller stateless communities. Or phrased less spatially and more temporally: is the amount of violence in a particular society relatively constant? Is orderliness in the streets bought at the price of greater abuse behind the doors of the citizenry, and if not by private violence, by the violence of the state itself in its prisons, schools, and law? I think most of us feel rather firmly, myself included, that violence is not subject to the second law of thermodynamics. There can be more or less at one time than another. A consistent claim of many legal, political, and social historians is that progress has been made in controlling the violence of humanity.[53] According to various versions of this account the development of the state, of conscience and good manners, of liberal democracy and bureaucratic and economic rationality, has made us less violent, more civilized, less childlike, more repressed, less superstitious, more rational than we once were.[54] Criminal law thus becomes mild-mannered: public execution gives way to the reformatory and prison. Mutilation and whipping are replaced by psychiatrist and social worker. Wars of succession give way to orderly elections. Cultic human sacrifice gives way to symbolic sacrifices of God/man in the Eucharist or simply to rational secularization.[55] Animals end up being the object of a certain solicitude.[56] Children are spanked less and lectured more in school and at home. Circumcision is redefined as a wise hygienic practice. And cultures that practice clitorectomy or infibulation allow us to congratulate ourselves on the cultural evolutionary ground we have covered. Of course there is a dark side to the tale and not all people are quite sure the price was worth paying. Foucault, following Nietzsche, thought that we lost more than we gained. He clearly preferred the outrageous but intermittently intrusive violence of torture and public execution to the omnipresent subtlety of the disciplinary style of social control which replaced it. Some see only a change in the styles of violence, not a diminishment—from an early barbaric ferociousness to bureaucratic callousness.[57] The dispute has hardly been settled: some think things have gotten better, some think they have stayed the same, and some think they have gotten worse.[58]

But we can also ask other questions or tell other stories that, if they do not quite make the thermodynamic model respectably plausible, might make it less implausible than the civilizing and rationalizing models and some of our own intuitions would have us believe. In any event, they will reveal some of the complacencies of the civilizing model. We have already noted that strategies of nonviolence mean only that the lower-status claimants will not resort to violence against the constituted authorities, not that they will not invite violence directed toward themselves or not even that they will not be violent to themselves. Consider next the civilizing paradigm's view that the advance of the state brought about greater bodily security and less violence. The state's claim to a monopoly on the means of violence has an uneven application in fact and even in some ways in theory. The state never claimed a monopoly on all violence. It left some very substantial areas free of the claim. It always, as already noted, turned its eye from the brutality of the family. As a rough rule, which I set forth more by way of provoking than by way of real commitment to the notion, the state was much more concerned with prohibiting the return blow of a wronged citizen against the wrongdoer than in prohibiting the initial act of aggression which prompted the return blow.[59] Surely this is the present perception of those who believe that the state has let them down in these crime-ridden times. The state went after feud and vigilantism and it populated the category of crime with the acts that earlier had constituted the feud, but to the extent it was successful in eliminating rough justice it also lost the deterrent to the aggressive acts which this rough justice had provided. Something may have been lost when actions of vindication and vengefulness— that is, when some of the rougher forms of social control—were assimilated to crimes of pure aggressive and invasive predation.

There are at least two reasons why the state would concentrate its energies on eliminating the return blow. One is a matter of efficiency: avengers are more predictable than initial attackers. The class of people who owe return shots are more easily identifiable, and hence more sanctionable, than the class of prospective aggressors. The former is made up of people who have been done identifiable wrongs, the latter is made up of everyone. For this latter class, the effectiveness of the state's sanctions had to be substantially discounted by the likelihood of being caught. For the class of wronged people the discount rate was much lower. Against the initiator of violence, the original predator, the state opposed, in effect, the moral force of the rule prohibiting the conduct, but there is no reason to believe that the moral force engendered by the rule was any more effective in restraining the initial act of aggression than it was the return blow. True, the state had a rule against the first wrong but the rule was more likely to be enforced when it was the victim who violated it by taking revenge.[60]

The other reason is a matter of practicality and self-interest: who were the wrongdoers who benefited from the state's style of pacification? During the early stages of state formation, at least, they appear to have been primarily the state and its agents. The tithe and tax collectors often did not look very different to the peasant than did a local ornery knight or a Viking raider.[61] Both beat him up, violated his women, and took his horses. One was no less bribable than the other and no more controllable. I do not mean to say that there is no difference now in the amount of threat and violence needed to support the state apparatus than there was then, or that the violence and threat are of the same types. Regularity of application, the rule of law, the acquiescence and even active support of populations for the state apparatus eventually made for real differences in the amount of violence needed to mulct a peasant in the thirteenth century and a professor in the twentieth, but when later historians describe the early period of state formation as rationalizing and pacifying, ordering and succeeding in suppressing violence, we are surely entitled to distrust the complacency of the account. The advantages that certain elements of the population gained with pacification were not achieved without substantial violence. And though these advantages might be maintained with less violence than was needed to secure them in the first place, it is too often the case that the violence of order and order creation is ignored.

Consider too this rather bizarre ethnographic example: the Gebusi, a small society of some 450 people living in a lowland rain forest in south-central New Guinea, are a society characterized by very low aggression.[62] They are almost too good to be true. They are indulgent to their children. They are egalitarian; male social life is without any evidence of status rivalry. The emotional tenor tends to be relaxed and unpretentious. There do not appear to be any signs of competitiveness at all. The few quarrels that do arise are quickly quelled by third parties and the ill feeling dissipated by joking and other diversion. Here's the catch. These people have the highest measured homicide rate in the world, some 419 per 100,000 from 1963 to 1982 and an astounding 683.0 from 1940 to 1962. Let me make a long story short. The high death rate is a function of their belief system. Any time someone dies of illness, someone gets blamed for causing the death by witchcraft and is killed. The witch is identified by seance and killed immediately upon the ascertainment of his or her identity. The kin of the witch, while not altogether pleased, do not avenge the killing, and in general the community's feeling is one of relief that a lethal-sickness-sender has been eliminated. The rather strange Gebusi evidence can be read to suggest that the connection, if any there be, between gentle socialization and homicide is fraught with complications.[63] The Gebusi also call into question certain easy assumptions about the connection between homicide and certain varieties of emotional economy. Here killing is not a function of rage, anger, hatred; it is undertaken almost fatalistically, with a sense of regret.[64] One of the strangest suggestions of the Gebusi evidence is that the highest homicide rate in the world coincides with an absence of any perception of violence.[65]

Thus stoning, spearing, and strangling, in short what we would think of as rather violent killing, may not be wholly included in a category of violence. A belief in nonaggression can coexist with a high homicide rate without appearing contradictory to those on the inside and can even be explained to be consistent by outside observers. It appears that the cost of constant amiability is the fearsome witchcraft apparatus that discourages the emotions and thoughts that lead to quarrels and competition, such as envy, hatred, pride. If that is indeed the case, the Gebusi material gives life to the hydraulic theories of human aggressiveness. Repress it here, it will pop up there. But we are jumping to too hasty inferences. One can surely imagine a system of beliefs which could support cultural amiability and nonaggressiveness shy of lethal witchcraft accusation.[66] The Gebusi system has in effect doubled the population's mortality rate, and the society, not surprisingly, cannot reproduce itself.

But if these examples call into question some of the more complacent assumptions of the progressive and civilizing paradigm of Western civilization, we know that life can be better or worse and that some of the variables for making it better rather than worse are less pain, less suffering, more freedom, more bodily security, and less violence. Though the civilizing model might have its share of complacency, and though life in the suburbs might lead to its share of complacency, no amount of complacency can undo our sense and the fact that the suburb is a lot less violent and a lot more enabling of good things than is the inner city.

Violence and Statelessness: Honor, Insult, and Threat

Our root notion that violence involves physical impingement, where fist meets face, leads many to believe that verbal abuse, that mere words, can never be violent except by metaphorical extension. But surely this is a very culturally specific view. The sagas, in contrast, reveal that medieval Icelanders, living in an honor-based culture, perceived little difference in the amount of wrong done by a blow or by a verbal insult, even a homicide or an insult. Verbal affronts and physical affronts were collapsed into a single general category of impingements on one's self and one's honor.[67] Surely, even among us less heroic souls, any scale of the violence of acts would not simply run from physical brutality at the high end down through all types of physical violence before it passed into verbal violence. Honor is not quite dead among us: we can all imagine blows we would rather endure than verbal insults.[68]

A look at the world of the sagas will let us get a quick glimpse of a culture of honor and threat in which insult made the world go round. Anyone who has taken an undergraduate introduction to medieval culture knows that something happened when the world of epic became the world of romance.[69] But what happened is less clear. Was it merely that literary styles changed, or was the style reflective of an underlying change in people's affective lives? Or did the change only reflect a relocation of the centers of literary production from the halls of warriors to the courts of kings and clerics who were now claiming to form something we would later identify as states? One could claim that epic is the literature of statelessness and that romance is part of an incipient ideology of state building. It cannot be an accident that the heroic has only the thinnest notion of the state.[70] With the heroic we are in the world of honor conferred by a community of equals or near equals, by players in the game of honor;[71] with the romantic, although honor still figures importantly, we enter a world of honors conferred by a superior. It is in the honor of the epic, the honor of heroic society, that we find an insistent logic to violence sustained by its own particular emotional economy.

One way of defining honor is as a susceptibility for having a certain set of dispositions and the likelihood that certain emotive states will be evoked in certain settings. Honor is above all the keen sensitivity to the experience of humiliation and shame, a sensitivity manifested by the desire to be envied by others and the propensity to envy the successes of others. To simplify greatly, honor is that disposition which makes one act to shame others who have shamed oneself, to humiliate others who have humiliated oneself. The honorable person is one whose self-esteem and social standing is intimately dependent on the esteem or the envy he or she actually elicits in others. At root honor means "don't tread on me." But to show someone you were not to be trod upon often meant that you had to hold yourself out as one who was willing to tread on others. The style of honor did not mean you were reluctant to give offense because you knew the other would retaliate, it meant that you had to look not at all fearful about giving offense. Hence we observe the ubiquitous feature of virtually all saga conversation: it hovered on the edge of insult.

In the culture of honor, the prospect of violence inhered in virtually every social interaction between free men, and free women too. The violence that free men rained on their children, servants, slaves, wives, and mistresses is not what the sagas are interested in, and as I indicated above was not all that likely to be perceived as violence, but simply as the natural way authority cashed in on the prerogatives of its position. But among free men, nervousness and anxiety, threat and anticipation of shame and humiliation, lurked even (or rather *especially*) in the most convivial of gatherings. Take the case of seating arrangements at feasts: the shame and envy felt by people who were not seated in the place they felt entitled to led to some of the best-known saga feuds.[72] For shame and envy are quickly reprocessed as anger, and anger often is a prelude to aggression. Let me treat you to a well-known saga example in which two men, one a powerful chieftain named Gudmund and one a substantial farmer named Ofeig, contend for precedence in seating arrangements at a feast given by a follower of Gudmund. Gudmund was appointed the seat of honor and Ofeig was given the seat next to him.

> And when the tables were set, Ofeig put his fist on the table and said, "How big does that fist seem to you, Gudmund?"
> "Big enough," he said.
> "Do you suppose there is any strength in it?" asked Ofeig.
> "I certainly do," said Gudmund.
> "Do you think it would deliver much of a blow?" asked Ofeig.
> "Quite a blow," Gudmund replied.
> "Do you think it might do any damage?" continued Ofeig.
> "Broken bones or a deathblow," Gudmund answered.
> "How would such an end appeal to you?" asked Ofeig.
> "Not much at all, and I wouldn't choose it," said Gudmund.
> Ofeig said, "Then don't sit in my place."
> "As you wish," said Gudmund—and he sat to one side. People had the impression that Ofeig wanted the greater portion of honor, since he had occupied the highseat up to that time.[73]

It is not hard to discern why festive meals are charged with such energized significance. This was a culture without formal titles and in which the law made no distinctions in value among free men. Seating arrangements at feasts thus provided one of the few occasions when relative ranking was clearly visible. Of course, clarity could be suffused with irony, as when magnanimous men made grand gestures in the interests of festive concord by agreeing to sit in places less honorable than everyone knew they were entitled to, but irony was only a possible strategy in such situations because they were so dense with meaning and danger.

But there is no violence here. Ofeig does not hit Gudmund. There is only danger and threat. Threat bears an intimate connection to violence, but is hardly coterminous with it, covering a wider conceptual terrain.[74] Nevertheless, it helps us understand just why violence can inhere in words or in any sign capable of threatening, and not just in physical impingement. Threats are words, postures, or actions intended to coerce or influence someone else's behavior by emphasizing the costs to the other of not conceding the threatener's position *and* by suggesting that the threatener will somehow be involved in bringing those to bear.[75] (For the rather bloodless "emphasizing the costs to the other" we should understand "scaring the other.") A substantial segment of the universe of threats does not involve violence at all, but the shadow of violence colors, to some extent, even the most benign of threats. It seems we understand the archetypal threat to be a threat of violence (I'll knock your head off), which then fades off by degrees into its paler cousins (I'll take my ball and go home, I'll take my business elsewhere). And even though not all threats involve violence, it seems that most all violence involves threat, and this very state of affairs tends to give threat its ominous tinge.

There does not always seem to be a satisfactory way to distinguish a threat of violence from violence itself. We can demonstrate the lack of discreteness between the category of violence and the category of threats of violence in another way. Suppose I threaten to hit you if you disagree with me. No one, you would say, would have a hard time distinguishing the threat of violence here from the violent action threatened. But now suppose I hit you for disagreeing with me. That blow does not function just as the completion of my earlier threat. The punch is also a new threat, a threat not to stop with one blow, a threat not to pull the next punch, a threat to aim it differently, a threat, in short, to escalate. The truth is that a new threat inheres in every action taken as a consequence of an original threat of violence. The logic of violence in this scene is not the logic of blows, pain, and death, but the logic of threat, nervousness, apprehension, and shame. This—threat, danger, shame, and competition—was the necessary logical precondition for violence pure and simple: killing, beating, maiming. The scene suggests that in this culture the violence of words and insult preceded the violence of sheer physical mass invading physical mass.

I think that we run a risk of censuring honor-based cultures as excessively violent because we see so much threat lurking in the air, because the violence is so personalized, because we imagine ourselves back then as having to suffer the depredations of aggressive men and, perhaps even more unnerving, as having to fulfill the awesome responsibility of righting our wrongs, of taking vengeance. The logic of heroic violence is that violence is never separated from individual or small group responsibility. The people who benefited from violence against their neighbors also had to bear the costs for that violence. There was as yet no state to assume the burden of violence.

The Style of Violent Stories

Violence is the stuff of good stories, as I said at the outset. I use "good" advisedly. It has been felt to be the proper stuff of narrative since the first written records. Epic is nothing if not violent, for whatever else characterizes the genre, killing or the susceptibility to being killed must be there. Yet it takes something more than violent subject matter to make us sensible of violence, to make us feel that the story is itself violent. Even to begin to account for this phenomenon would require a long detour into aesthetic philosophy, theories of narrative, theories of representation, the psychology of reading and cinema, in other words, too far afield from our present immediate concerns. Some of the issues have already been touched on above, so I will content myself with a few quick supplementary observations intended only to be suggestive.

We seem to prefer our violence mediated in certain styles. Given the same subject, a verse rendition is not as likely to be perceived as violent as a prose one. For us, violence tends to get lost in florid styles but is manifestly discernible in terse styles. This effect is partly an aspect of fashion and taste and partly a facet of the gendering of violence. We now think of high style and florid styles as feminine, terse styles as tough and masculine. And in any set of contrasting pairs such as received standard or dialect, stylized or "realistic," we expect that our violence should come packaged in the one valorized as masculine. Yet when these expectations are thwarted, violence does not necessarily become less noticeable; it may become even more peculiarly unsettling. We have come to understand that certain kinds of stylizations go hand-in-hand with a peculiar type of overtly eroti-cized violence, made especially unsettling because we perceive it as perverse, as kinky, as against the usual masculinization of violence. The violence of ambivalently gendered males has its cold wit. In this it is not unlike the terse hypermasculine Clint Eastwood style, but its cold wit bears the markings of decadence, dandyism, and effeteness, and this gender-bending helps make dandyish violence particularly unsettling and more violent in its way than just plain old rock 'em sock 'em. This reaction should hardly be all that surprising. If vio-lence is more easily perceived when it is a force running counter to the usual forces of order, when it is force contrary and uncertain of its warrant, we are more likely to see it as violent. In this view, rock 'em sock 'em because conventional must appear less unsettling, even less violent, than feminized dandyish violence. Hannibal Lector of *The Silence of the Lambs* and Alex of the movie version of *A Clockwork Orange* are thus more terrifyingly violent than the average thug. Further, the violence of dandified decadence not only thwarts the usual gender typing of violence, it also bears the markings of the cruel. This kind of violence seldom pretends to moral justification; it is unaccompanied by excusing anger or justifying indignation. It is simply for the beauty of it, the fun of it, the pleasure of it.

Everything else being equal, is violence more likely to be per-ceived in epic, tragedy, or comedy? Violence is essential to epic, usual in tragedy, and hardly at all strange to comedy, but where it is consid-ered ho-hum, where amusing, and where extremely unsettling, I would suspect, will not vary randomly. Here I am not sure which way things cut. The violence of epic is generalized; its topic is war and feud. In tragedy, violence is particularized, although here too war and feud often provide the setting for the action. Tragedy is consciously designed to elicit greater empathic response—pity, fear, and catharsis—but Aristotle also indicated that it should be presented in the most embellished language. With one hand our violence is granted, with the other it is taken away. But violence is not essential to tragedy in the way it is to epic, and even in some ways to comedy. Tragedy needs death, but does not require violence. Comedy, in fact, needs violence more than tragedy does, but it has a hard time with death that is not clearly connected to rebirth. Thus the convention in animated cartoons of universal resurrection for every "lethal" blow endured. Those few cartoon characters who don't literally bounce back to life have the good fortune to sprout wings and take up harps as they float heavenward.[76]

The presence of suspense and surprise bears some connection to perceptions of violence. This connection too is tricky. We would expect that less formulaic and less conventional violence should appear to us as more violent than the routine and predictable. If it does, does ritualized violence appear less violent than less-structured violence? Or must it be that if violence is the conscious object of the ritual, the ritual is not doing its work unless its violence strikes home as violent, unless it has the power to terrorize and hence to provide catharsis. The violence of charivari, of rough music, must really feel rough or the ritual will fail of some of its purpose. Cat massacres and religious riots, to the extent they can be subsumed to ritual, must showcase violence, not repress and metamorphose it into attenuated forms not felt as violent.[77] Ritual may well be able to do without surprise, but what it cannot do without, if it means to be felt as violent, is the aura of threat.

Just as our perceptions of violence are intimately connected with our notions of legitimacy and justice so too we are less likely to perceive violence in narratives when it is the good guy dishing it out, when it is evil that gets punished rather than evil that punishes. The underlying values assumed in the narration thus affect our perceptions of violence. The unironic view that war is glorious rather than hell might well mean that *The Song of Roland* will be seen to be less violent than *Catch 22*, even if allowances are made for the differences between verse and prose and nearness in time versus farness in time, or just for the fact that when bodies are broken in epic there is no discoursing on pain. Not a few of these observations raise again the problem of how the observer mediates violence and suggest that from the observer's viewpoint all violence comes packaged as a kind of narrative. Some narratives present violence more to our liking than others do, and it is clear that fashions in narrating violence change. It has always intrigued me that students in a class on epic can read the *Iliad, The Book of Samuel, Roland,* and *Njáls saga* and recognize violence only in the saga, in which there are significantly fewer corpses and mayhem than in the others. Their reaction is partly due to the fact that the sagas are saturated with the *prospect* of violence, with threat, in a way the other epics are not. The other epics seem to regulate threat better, making it more periodic and confining it to arenas clearly devoted to violence, such as battles and trials. The sagas (and especially their translations) are terse and ironic in the tough-guy style in which we like our violence served up. The styles of the other texts type them in the students' minds as classics of literature and thus not dandyish or decadent, as high style, as poetic, as disembodied, and hence not very violent no matter how many corpses pile up.

Concluding Observations

What would it be like to have lived back then? Which time (place) was the best of times, which was the worst of times? These are the kinds of questions which drive the production of written history. Even the most dry-as-dust professionalized historian is driven by them. The questions are moral ones. They require us to make judgments about the good life, about justice, about bodily security, about wealth and its distribution. They invite us also to personalize and romanticize, to wonder whether we would have been better or worse off then, feared more or less, been safer, more secure, more fulfilled, less harried. The professional historian is required by the conventions of academic discourse to deny the motivating force of such questions. But they are asked and answered nonetheless by indirection and suggestion, often unconsciously. And how we ask and answer them types us politically and dispositionally: as Whigs, romantics, conservatives, communitarians, libertarians, feminists, pessimists, optimists, reformists, or revolutionaries.

It seems that to answer these kinds of questions we need to get a fix on violence and that need has motivated this essay. But it should be clear by now that cross-cultural or transtemporal comparisons about levels of violence are fraught with difficulty, most of them insurmountable. Even our own intuitions are made up of inconsistent notions operating at different conceptual levels. Other people's fears and anxieties, the actual lived experience of domination, pain, threat, and violence, the nuances of meaning in richly varied practices, are largely unrecoverable except in very impressionistic ways. We can do better recovering certain structural coercions, the violence of the state and law, but the paucity of the record costs us the actual experiences of women, children, servants, and slaves. How do we account for the fact that the concepts embodied in our word *violence* may not have lexical counterparts in the other culture? In other times the "violence problem" was not an easy conceptual dumping ground for everything ranging from sport to child abuse. Old Norse had no word that ran the semantic range of our *violence*. Nor for that matter does French *violence*. Many core French uses of the term would seem metaphorical, tendentious, or vastly extended in English. French might use *violence* where we would think *domination* or even *constraint* more apt.[78] Thus Bourdieu talks of the open violence of asymmetrical economic relations, as of employer-employee, landlord-tenant.[79] Some of Foucault's claims in English translation have a greater tinge of melodrama and exaggeration than they do in French in those locations where the claim is about the violences of certain discourses. Because French *violence* is often indistinguishable from domination, coercion, or power, we can find Foucault appearing to support a thermodynamic view of violence when what he is really claiming is simply the ubiquity of constraints imposed by discourses:

> Humanity does not gradually progress from combat to combat until it arrives at universal reciprocity, where the rule of law finally replaces warfare; humanity installs each of its violences in a system of rules and thus proceeds from domination to domination.[80]

Historians and sociologists who have tried to get a fix on these things have had to develop quantifiable or easily observable surrogates for violence.[81] Charles Tilly, following in the tradition of Georges Sorel, focuses on civil strife or collective violence, rather than homicide.[82] One can count the number of strikes and riots much more easily than the nonquantifiable features of what we perceive as violence. Criminologists who have done cross-cultural studies of violence have retreated to using homicide rates as the indicator of relative levels of violence. It is not hard to see why. Homicide has two virtues. It is fairly uniformly defined across cultures, unlike assault or rape. And nearly all societies consider it a serious matter, so that it tends not to suffer from underreporting.[83] In contemporary cultures some of the problem of underreporting can be compensated for by victimization surveys, but even these misrepresent the levels of stigmatizing crimes such as rape. The crudeness of homicide rates as an indicator of violence should be readily apparent. The Gebusi have already shown that.[84] We can also imagine that if two cultures have exactly the same cultural predispositions toward violence, the one in which guns are readily available will have a greater number of homicides without necessarily for that reason being more violent, unless, as in the case of the United States, advances in lethal technology are paralleled by advances in medical technology which can make what once would have been homicides into mere attempts.[85]

If measurements of the quantity of violence will forever elude us, interpretations of the styles of violence should not. Foucault's *Discipline and Punish* is one grand example showing us that interpretive approaches to issues of punishment and social control can tell us much about modes, if not quantities, of violence. We should even be able to discover the changes in the emotional concomitants of various styles of violence. If these approaches won't quite answer our moral questions, we still will have some feel for the way it was. We certainly should have enough basis for recognizing that a violent society may not for that reason be an unfree or unjust society. And that is probably the best we can do.

The next chapter combines and foregrounds two themes that have figured in the background of these first two chapters: emotions and honor. It deals with two particular issues: how to talk about the emotions of another time and place and what emotional configurations support and maintain a moral economy of honor. The raw material from which the exposition is constructed is drawn mostly from the sagas of medieval Iceland. Those put off by medieval things will find the sagas very unmedieval, more like our westerns and Mafia movies than like Arthurian romance or pious devotional literature. They are smart, unsentimental texts that display a remarkable critical insightfulness into the culture they describe. They offer as good a view as there is of the moral, social, and cultural mechanisms of honor.

3

Emotions, Honor, and the Affective Life of the Heroic

The striving for distinction keeps a constant eye on the next man and wants to know what his feelings are: but the empathy which this drive requires for its gratification is far from being harmless or sympathetic or kind. We want, rather, to perceive or divine how the next man outwardly or inwardly *suffers* from us, how he loses control over himself and surrenders to the impressions our hand or even merely the sight of us makes upon him.
—Friedrich Nietzsche, *Daybreak*

We are ambivalent in our views of the emotional universe of medieval people. We think of them as puerile, as quick to fly into rage and then just as quick to swing to almost equally violent and public displays of remorse for the consequences of that rage.[1] Yet we also think of them (at least most nonmedievalists do) as benighted, insentient, too brutalized or primitive to have a subtle emotional life. The same ambivalence often characterizes upper-class views of the lower classes: they are vulgarly too emotional in their displays of anger and raucous joy (the image of professional wrestling seems to bear some connection to upper-class contempt and fear of the lower classes). Then there is the upper-class sense that the richness of one's emotional life varies directly with one's education, refinement, and wealth.[2] The poor and the medieval, by this account, do not feel as much as do the sociologist and historian who study them; and although the poor and medieval may experience lust, rage, anger, hate, and joy, they are unlikely to experience angst, ennui, pity, embarrassment, and those aesthetic emotions that are elicited by the reading of good books.

Part of this ambivalence is a function of the difference between our sense of what an emotion is on the one hand and our sense of what it means to be emotional on the other. People are "emotional" if they are quick to anger or quick to shed tears for joy, sadness, or fear, especially if they do these things when we would not. But we do not tend to think of people as emotional if their emotional life is characterized by feelings of guilt, interest, envy, depression, a sense of duty, even if we would not have reacted in the same way. Yet these too are emotions by most anyone's categorization. We understand certain emotions to be more emotional than others. These are the emotions that tend to be accompanied by acts of violence or obvious somatic disturbance. That is, rather strangely, we most easily see emotions in others when their display engenders in us either fear or embarrassment.

Ultimately, however, our sense of the quality of the emotional life of another depends, to a large extent, on how much we can identify with the other. Sympathy and empathy (or disgust and revulsion) are thus the necessary emotional underpinnings to understanding the emotions of others. We rely on various keys and clues to generate our sympathetic (or aversive) understanding of the richness or poverty of another's emotional life; we do likewise when we try to determine the emotional styles of another culture. We look at how or to what extent emotions are talked about; we look at socialization practices, at basic patterns of behavior, at somatic displays, at how children or animals are treated, at the style of certain types of key rituals, such as mourning, marrying, and even (and not just for the sake of alliteration) murdering. It seems that our sense of another culture's emotional regime is often formed by our view about how violent it is, by our attraction to or disgust with its styles and levels of violence. I do not wish to push this idea too far. Understanding emotions does not always lead to the topic of violence in the same way that discussing violence, as observed in the preceding chapter, leads to a consideration of emotions. But there is some kind of nontrivial connection nonetheless, which will lead us eventually to reconsider in greater detail the emotional style of honor, an issue touched on briefly in Chapter 2.

This brings me, by a very personal association of ideas, to the sagas, which will provide us our Other, an Other in which issues of violence and emotion are closely intermeshed. Readers' initial impression of sagas is that the saga world is coldly unemotional—not only the sensibilities of its characters, but the sensibilities of the narrative style as well. Readers are amused, or repelled, by the laconic way in which rather gruesome events and grievous losses are experienced or described. Consider, for example, these cases. In *Njáls saga* a certain Kol, on seeing his leg hacked off by Kolskegg, comments casually, "That's what I get for not having a shield," and the saga continues thus:

> and he stood a few seconds on one leg looking at the stump.
> Kolskegg said, "There's no need to look; it's just what you think—you're without a leg." (*Njáls saga* chap. 63)

In the same saga Hallgerd questions the man standing before her who has just killed her beloved husband. He is holding a bloody ax:

> "What's up? Why is your ax all bloody?"
> "I don't know what you'll think of this," he responded, "but I announce the death of [your husband]."
> "Then you must have done it," she said.
> "Right," he answered.
> She laughed and said, "You sure don't play around." (chap. 17)

Or Gudrun, in *Laxdæla saga*, who smiles and converses casually with the man who wipes his bloody spear on her sash right after he has killed her husband, a husband, however, for whom her feelings were somewhat ambivalent (chap. 55).

None of these incidents is really unemotional or even described in that way, but the emotions that are indicated, either by words or by gesture, are ones we feel evince a lack of concern for life, a kind of nonchalance which borders on insensibility or cruelty. Kol, after all, expresses quite clearly the emotion of regret. What amuses or shocks us is that he chooses to express his regret as regret for not having had a shield rather than regret, shock, and horror for having lost his leg. Hallgerd's laughter is clearly a marker of emotion, but we are unsure of the propriety of its motivation. The laugh could represent shock, upset, and horror, a kind of nervous laughter, in which case it is hardly an indication of lack of emotion. Or it might be a strategic and coldly rational move on Hallgerd's part to disarm her husband's killer. Or she might combine both emotion and reason: she laughs in shock and then quickly recovers to make strategic use of the representational ambiguities of laughing in such a setting. In fact, Hallgerd does immediately give her husband's killer some "friendly" counsel that she knows will send him to his death.

If Hallgerd's laugh, as is likely, is largely involuntary, Gudrun's smile is more voluntary and appears to be motivated somewhat by reason and strategy. Here we do not need to rely on our own hunches but can make use of the view offered by a character who was present. Several members of the killing group offer the opinion that Gudrun could not have felt the loss of her husband very deeply, considering the easy way she conversed with them. But Halldor, one of the killers, corrects their impression: "It's not my view that Gudrun doesn't care about Bolli's death; I think that she chatted with us because she wanted to know absolutely for sure the identity of the men who made up this expedition. It's not exaggerating to say that Gudrun is the most fearless and determined of women. And it is to be expected that she would be upset at Bolli's death" (*Laxdæla saga* chap. 56).

This scene reveals that the modern reader is not alone in being taken in by the ways certain saga characters express emotions. The men who read Gudrun's smile as evidence of a lack of great feeling for her husband are revealing that smiles were not quite appropriate in this particular setting. They expected signs of grief, tears and wailing, not signs of casual cordiality, smiles and conversation. This is a nice bit of information, for without it we might be led to believe that in saga Iceland smiles only rarely indicated easy cordiality. Halldor's views happen to be entirely in accord with the usual meaning of smiles in the saga world of feud and vengeance, where they are markers more often of hostility than of amiability.[3] But if Hallgerd's laugh or Gudrun's smile are in any way rationally motivated facial expressions, coldly designed to mislead, their calculation, if calculation it be, depends on a culture in which smiles and laughs are by and large disarming rather than threatening. For if everyone knew that smiles forebode only evil they would hardly be a practical strategy for misleading others. And although Halldor sees the method in Gudrun's smile he does not go so far as to say the smile indicates lack of emotion. He claims only that it represents a set of emotions and dispositions different from what less perceptive people might conventionally assume. Basing his assessment on her character, he suspects that she is sufficiently motivated to commit herself to a course of vengeance. Halldor suggests intimate connections among grief, anger, vengeance, strategy, reason, and the display of emotion. Here too we note the same ambivalence presented at the outset: some suggest that Gudrun feels nothing, one person that she feels indeed, but feels things that will lead to vengeance and death, things we officially like to think are not proper justifications for action.

But these preliminary examples aside, first impressions are often our best impressions.[4] Just because the three brief incidents I presented here might often be mistaken by readers as representing the sagas at their most coldly unemotional does not mean that there are not many good reasons for finding saga narrative rather unemotional. One might well wonder whether the cultivated nonchalance and understatement in the face of death that is the hallmark of the heroic style does not reveal a socialization very successful in killing some of the softer types of sentiment rather than simply in covering genuinely felt feelings with cool wit and taciturnity. Imagine, for instance, what the emotional state of Ketil of Mork might have been after hearing that his wife's brother had just killed his (Ketil's) brother. Ketil is everywhere in the saga presented as a decent and honorable man, very close to both his wife's kin and his own. We can imagine that he would feel an array of emotions, including anger, grief, uncertainty, anguish, anxiety, a sense of betrayal, frustration, outrage, despair, depression. Yet the saga treats of his predicament as follows: "Ketil of Mork was married to Thorgerd, the daughter of Njal, but he was also the brother of Thrain [the victim]. He thought himself to be in a difficult situation and so he rode to Njal and asked whether he would compensate for Thrain's death" (*Njáls saga* chap. 93). That is all the saga cares to tell us about how awful Ketil must have felt. True, there is the offhand reference to his feelings of uncertainty ("he thought himself to be in a difficult situation"), but by far more narrative effort is devoted to the genealogical setting that explains why Ketil is in a difficult position: he is married to the sister of his brother's killer. Perhaps the genealogical information was a sufficient cue for the medieval audience to fill in what the expected emotional state of someone so trapped in the tangled web of kinship and affinity would feel. But we can hardly be sure of that. It is after all not so easy to reconstruct the emotional style of another culture, across eight centuries, through imperfect sources.

My prior work with some exception has tended to emphasize the strategic aspects of social behavior, particularly feuding behavior in saga Iceland. I have perhaps tended to portray people as more manipulative, more in rational control of their choices than they in fact were or could have been.[5] Here I make a start at getting a fuller picture of motive and motivation and this means getting at the emotional setting of social action. The task is fraught with difficulties, but we are not without good clues. First: the presence of emotion words. Are people described as angry, envious, grieving? Do the characters describe their own mental states or the psychological motivation of others? Second: descriptions of somatic responses. People swell up, they turn red, they blanch pale, they shed tears, they laugh, smile, and move their brows. Third: dialogue and the action itself, that is, the whole range of behaviors, which simply wouldn't make sense unless we make certain inferences about the possible range and styles of emotions that motivate the action. Fourth: the whole system of beliefs. Because so much of emotional life is intimately connected to beliefs, a comprehensive study of emotions would also involve a comprehensive social and cultural history, and that is too large a task. Instead, I touch on some of the salient issues raised by the historical consideration of emotions in a bloodfeuding society and go on, in the second part of this chapter, to a discussion of some of the emotional underpinnings of that key cultural system, honor.

In Search of Emotion

Language and Emotion: Some Problems

There is an enormous literature on emotions in at least three disciplines: psychology, of course, but also anthropology[6] and philosophy. None of these disciplines goes at emotions in the same way and none has addressed the particular problems raised by the attempt to recover the emotional life of people long dead. One of the obvious problems the historian and the anthropologist must confront, and the psychologist and philosopher often ignore, is the extent to which the emotional categories of English can be trusted to represent human universals rather than local cultural particulars.[7] To what extent, for example, do Old Norse emotion terms track English categories? Would Icelandic carve up anger the way English does, as in rage, fury, wrath, indignation, annoyance? Would it distinguish at the level of the word among envy, emulation, spite, jealousy, grudgingness, malice, and resentment? Mapping the linguistic terrain of saga emotions requires the kind of lexical work that is only now becoming possible thanks to the soon-to-appear saga corpus in machine-readable form.

From cursory impressions, however, one can safely say that neither saga diction nor saga style will give us the richness or distinctions that Proust does.

What is the connection between the richness or poverty of a vocabulary of emotions and the richness or poverty of emotional experience? If we want to think that speakers of languages with poor emotional vocabularies experience a similar level of feeling as those with rich vocabularies (i.e., that a grizzly bear chasing me will elicit a feeling we call fear in me whether or not I have a distinct lexical equivalent for that concept), we cannot be so sure that there won't be some difference at the level of consciousness regarding that feeling. Consciousness about a feeling may well affect the substance of that feeling. The sadness I feel when I know I am sad may be different from the emotion called sadness I feel when I don't know I am sad.[8] Some emotions, such as anger and fear, are more visceral than others, and presumably language and social and cultural norms would not affect them as much as the more obviously thought-dependent emotions such as regret, guilt, embarrassment, shame, self-respect. Yet even relatively visceral emotions are thoroughly mediated by culture. Can we ever experience precultural fear? It is culture that sorts out among the fearful who will scream and who will sit silently. Among us, women are allowed to scream, men are not. A man who screams is feminized. Fear might make some run and some stand paralyzed and some prepare to fight to the death, but which people will do what is not randomly distributed across cultures or within cultures across class, gender, or age. Culture also determines the secondary emotional accompaniment of fear: whether one who is fearful is also likely to be embarrassed, or angry, or despairing, or accepting. Universalists on this issue might argue that the internal feeling of fear is uniform across cultures, and that culture affects only how we will act and think when we are fearful. But how can we get at this feeling ridded of its cultural and cognitive baggage to know? Anger reveals similar cultural impingements. Who will blow up and scream and who will eat themselves up in frustration or drink themselves into a stupor are not randomly distributed.

If consciousness of a feeling changes that feeling, then cross-cultural variations in how emotions are conceptualized, or in whether certain emotions are conceptualized at all in language, should affect the way people feel.[9] Certain Australian aborigines use the same word to describe both fear and shame.[10] Surely this fact must affect how they think about how they feel and possibly, by various feedback mechanisms, affect how they feel too. Does it make a difference in the actual substance of the feeling to have a single word describe a particular emotional state rather than a variety of more paraphrastic or circumlocutional descriptions? Consider, for example, what might be your emotion if you had to live with the killers of your kin. There is no simple word for it in Old Norse, or in modern English for that matter. But whatever the emotion is, it appears to motivate Olvir to ask to leave King Harald's court: "[My brothers and I] are not in a mood to drink and sit with those men who bore weapons against our kinsman, Thorolf" (*Egils saga* chap. 22). Is it a feeling that prompts Olvir's request? Or is it the structural setting he finds himself in? And does it make all that much difference? There is an intimate connection between the breach of strongly held social norms and certain emotions. If people are not supposed to be convivial with the killers of their kin, then properly socialized persons will feel that they should not do so and will feel the array of whatever feelings (shame, guilt, frustration, embarrassment) properly socialized persons will feel when they violate a norm whose validity they accept. And if they do not feel the appropriate emotions but still act in the accepted manner, others will assume that they have the feelings appropriate to the situation anyway. The effect may well be that the expectations of others has a lot to do with triggering the emotions appropriate to the setting. I have digressed a bit from my immediate concern with vocabulary. Even though Olvir has no simple word for what he feels, he has means of expressing it by referring to the norm that legitimates his request to leave the company of his kin's killers. The problem then appears to be not one concerning the number of precise words devoted to emotions but one concerning more general habits and styles of talking and thinking about emotions.

Those who prefer to think that there is a meaningful reality of emotion independent of language might imagine a universe with as many different emotions as there are situations that elicit them. In this view the anger you feel when stubbing your toe might not be the same emotion as the anger you feel when someone vandalizes your car or when a person cuts in front of you in line. The emotions may be rather closely related, but there would still be, according to this view, qualitative differences (not just differences of intensity) among them. We can imagine an emotional taxonomy in which each of these "angers" would have its own word.[11] Some psychological studies have conceptualized the world of emotions to be a plane or a space with an infinite number of points measured along various axes, axes that indicate the relation of the emotions to pleasantness, attention, certainty, perceived obstacle, anticipated effort, responsibility, control, and so forth.[12]

But surely having a word or a ready-made concept must affect our emotional life.[13] Convenient easy simplex emotion terms or phrases, it seems, tend to act as *evaluative magnets*. The existence of the concept and term, say, of anger might cause us to ignore the differences between closely related hostile feelings and lump them together. Such terms also save us the work of having to think all that precisely about how we feel. They tend to make us subsume our emotional states, or at least our understanding of our emotional states, into the ready-made category the word provides. Emotion terms, like all words, generalize and in the process fuzz over a lot of individual variation.

One important caveat. Emotion terms in some settings might be terms of art which are not intended to indicate the emotions, but which serve instead as surrogates or shorthands for describing ritualized behavior or for making normative claims. Thus the shame and humiliation of having a certain event befall you might be more a normative assessment about how you should feel than a descriptive statement about what you in fact do feel. And love, anger, shame, and grief, among others, can define social as well as psychological states, with no necessary claim being made about the feelings of the person in the social state.

The Body and the Appropriateness of Emotions

At times the sagas give us descriptions of somatic changes in heightened emotional situations. Some of these are among the best-remembered scenes in the sagas. Flosi's extreme agitation after being charged to take vengeance by Hildigunn in a most grisly fashion (she dumped the flakes of the victim's clotted blood all over him) is marked on his face, which "one second was as red as blood, another as pale as grass, and another as black as death" (*Njáls saga* chap. 116). Reddening is probably the most frequently referenced somatic indication of emotion in the sagas, although tears and swelling are not infrequent. Even though it might not have been the saga way for

people to talk about emotions, their bodies were not always so obliging. When Thorhall Asgrimsson hears that his foster-father had been
burned to death, his body swells up, blood flows from his ears, and he
faints. He feels himself humiliated by what he felt to be the unseemli-
ness of his body's reaction, and he swears to avenge it on those who
burned his foster-father. Kin and friends try to humor him and keep
him calm by insisting to him that "no one would consider [his bleed-
ing and fainting] shameful" (*Njáls saga* chap. 132). But because of the
general nervousness about shame in this society, Thorhall is not ap-
peased by the judgment of his friends. He is only too aware of the
style of competition which would use any ambiguous unconventional
act to the detriment of someone's reputation if it could be so used:
"and he said nothing could stop what people would say."

Other incidents in the sagà reveal that Thorhall has a most expres-
sive body whose actions are beyond his conscious control. On another
occasion, his face turns red as blood and tears like hail burst from his
eyes (chap. 142); on yet another, his leg swells up from an infected
boil, which if not an indication of emotion, soon becomes one when
both Thorhall and the author make it a symbol of pent-up frustration
and vengeful fury (chaps. 135, 145). (After the blunders of the man
he is advising in a complicated lawsuit ruin their case, Thorhall lances
the boil in frustration and rage with a spear and then, with it still
dripping with pus, impales the first opponent he meets). Everyone
knows that Thorhall is an emotional fellow and they know because his
body tells them so, even if he doesn't readily verbalize his interior
states. No one thinks Thorhall a lesser man for being emotional,
although a fair inference in the bystanders' expressed view that his
fainting is not shameful is that his reactions are involuntary. Thorhall's
friends and kin would not have suspended their reproach if his emotions had presented themselves in the touchy-feely style of talking
them out. His remarking that he feels humiliated is made not in a
pseudo-intimate, confessional, and revelatory style but in a matter-of-
fact way of justifying and explaining a resolute commitment to vengeance.[14]

There are other views, largely those of psychologists, which make
universal and objectivist claims about emotional life. Some experi-
mental work has been interpreted as supporting the claim that happi-
ness, surprise, anger, fear, disgust, contempt, and sadness, and perhaps shame and interest are universal as are the facial expressions
associated with them.[15] The readily observable variation in the emo-

tionality of people of different cultures, this work claims, has been misunderstood by those who argue the social and cultural contingency of emotional life: that variation is not in emotion, which is a given of human neuro-psychic organization, but in the events that elicit the emotions and in the culturally acquired traits for suppressing or disguising these emotions once elicited. The suppressed emotion, they claim, is still there, for before culture can suppress it, the emotion reveals itself in fleeting contractions of the facial muscles called microexpressions. These expressions, like the emotions they represent (or, according to this view, like the emotions they are),[16] are also universal aspects of human behavior. But the universalism gained for this set of emotions comes at the cost of the general impoverishment of the emotional universe, for to these researchers the emotions, by definition, are to be restricted to those affects that occur before thought gets involved to complicate things. Such theories have little place for emotions like embarrassment, relief, remorse, or envy. Yet we needn't accept such a narrowly physicalist position to suppose that certain roughly articulated core emotions may be present in most adult affective life. It is not as if the emotional experience of a person from culture A has no points of congruence with the emotional life of a person from culture B; or even if it is conceded that there may be no precise points of congruence, there are nevertheless rough ranges of emotional experience which can be fairly well understood and imagined if not precisely felt across cultures, just as on an individual level we manage to communicate and understand each other's emotional states even if we cannot be certain of the precise feeling of the other.[17]

If some emotions produce predictable somatic displays, those displays are often susceptible of more than one emotional meaning.[18] Silence can indicate sadness, grief, or rage. Redness can indicate embarrassment, jealousy, anger, indignation, humiliation, or shame. Laughter can indicate vengeful fury as in the crazed laugh of the "killing mood" (*Víga-Glúms saga* chap. 18), or the relief of the prospective vengeance target who finds he has been let off the hook (*Ljósvetninga saga* chap. 17). And if a person is not sufficiently berserk-like to have the crazed killing-laugh come over him, propriety may demand that he forgo all laughter until he has avenged himself (*Droplaugarsona saga* chaps. 12, 13; *Njáls saga* chap. 136). That is, mirthful or polite laughter is inconsistent with the social obligation to take vengeance, but crazed malicious laughter is proper, as are ominous grins and equally ominous failures to laugh politely when polite laughter is appropriate. Although the body, then, is not a perfect signifier of emotion, it helps make up for some saga reticence in talking about emotions; at least it can save us from denying that emotions are being felt and observed, even if we cannot be certain precisely what they might be.

Consider this case, in which a face reddens: Bergthora, the mother of Skarphedinn, has just heard that her husband and sons have been viciously insulted. She tells the men about it as they are seated at the table, and Skarphedinn responds as follows:

"We don't have women's dispositions, getting enraged over everything."

"But Gunnar got enraged on your behalf," said Bergthora, "and he is considered even-tempered. If you don't avenge this, you'll never avenge any shame done you."

"Our mother, the old gal, is having a lot of fun," said Skarphedinn—and he grinned, but, nevertheless, sweat showed on his forehead and red spots appeared on his cheeks, and this was very unusual. (*Njáls saga* chap. 44)

Here the characters actually have a discussion of feeling anger, not by admitting it, but by denying it, or by projecting it on to second and third parties, Bergthora and Gunnar. It is women who get angry, suggests Skarphedinn, not men, who are to keep their cool. By so saying he reveals what the content of Bergthora's speech says already: that she for one is displaying anger. He also reveals what his body will confirm in spite of his effort to suppress it with a grin: that he too is seething with rage. The game of indirect emotion talk is played beautifully by both son and mother. Son takes out on his mother the fury he can barely restrain by treating her with a bit of contempt. She is thus subjected to the trivializing banter of "our mother, the old gal" and a round of culturally available antifeminist clichés, which gender easily aroused anger as feminine, slow anger as masculine. His expression of irritation to the woman egging him on is a conventional move in the ritual of goading. Women are expected to goad their menfolk to vengeful action, and men use their goading as an opportunity to discourse disapprovingly about female vengefulness and irrationality.[19] But mother is more than son's match in this give and take. With brutal economy she gives a rational riposte to Skarphedinn's views on the propriety of quick anger and couples that with a needling insinuation about her son's lack of manliness. After all, she says, Gunnar, well known to be the greatest of warriors and thus not especially effeminate, who is even-tempered and thus a model of the emotional style you, my son, consider manly, has already blown up on your behalf. The "on your behalf" is especially cutting, reminding her son that not only is he slow but that he appears sufficiently pathetic to third parties that they feel obliged to express the feelings of rage for him.

The real sting in Bergthora's argument, however, depends on a theory of the appropriateness of emotions to their settings or eliciting conditions and to precisely who is justified in displaying them. Just as it would not be appropriate for a distant cousin to cry and mourn more ostentatiously than the children or spouse of a deceased, so it is not proper for Gunnar, who is not the object of the insult, to be more enraged than the insult victim. Bergthora's point is that the even-tempered Gunnar is unlikely to make inappropriate emotional displays, so the sole source of impropriety here would be her son if he should not be even more angry than Gunnar. Gunnar is no mere third party. He is the husband and cousin of the insulters and the head of the household in which the insult was composed. He is liable. Still, his anger and outrage should by Bergthora's argumentative strategy have somewhat less intensity than that of the targets of the insult. Real men, in situations like this, get enraged, and in case the point has been too subtly made she abandons indirection completely: "If you don't avenge this, you'll never avenge any shame done you."

Such can be the indirection of actually talking about emotions in the sagas. Body language is somewhat more direct, but not without ambiguities. Take Skarphedinn's unnerving grin, which suggests sadistic urgings and hostile sensation at the same time that it manifests desperate efforts at self-control. The grin is multiply determined. At some level it means to cover up and control, at another it means to reveal, and at yet another it cannot be meant at all because it appears involuntarily. But in this scene much of the ambiguities and ambivalences of the grin are resolved by the other somatic indicia of emotion: sweating and flushing.[20] These clearly indicate some kind of emotional tumult even if the somatic indicia alone do not reveal just what that emotion might be. Whatever it is, the sweat and the flushing confirm a desperation in the grin. Clearly Skarphedinn is furious, consumed with indignation, but he also is shamed and humiliated, hence, in fact, his fury.[21]

The bodily indicators of emotion vary in their degrees of voluntariness, moving along an axis with sweating, blinking, blushing, and flushing at the involuntary end, sliding by degrees toward physical illness, nervous grins, shrugs, spontaneous or hysterical laughter, hand gestures, tears (all of which admit of some degree of conscious control), to more controlled smiles and laughter, to being quiet, to highly staged symbolic postures, such as breast-beating or simply going to bed. Let us examine a few of these at the more voluntary end of the spectrum. Older men, old enough to be at the end of their vengeance-taking vigor, often take to bed in grief for the violent loss of a kinsman and in despair and frustration over their inability to succeed in exacting revenge. Havard lies in bed three years before his wife goads him to action to avenge their son (*Hávarðar saga* chap. 9); when Kveld-Ulf hears of the fall of his son Thorolf he takes to bed, says the saga, "on account of grief and old age" (*Egils saga* chap. 24).[22]

Some of the cultural senses of taking to bed can be teased out by following that consummate of cynical ironists, Sturla of Hvamm, to his bed. When Sturla heard that his old enemy, a woman named Thorbjorg who had once tried to gouge out his eye, had died, he took to his bed

> as was his usual practice when he was depressed. People asked him why he was doing so and he answered, "I have just heard some news which I consider quite distressing."
>
> "We hardly believe that you would grieve Thorbjorg's passing," they responded.
>
> "There's another reason why I am suffering. I figured that there would always be grounds against her and her sons while she lived, but now it wouldn't look good if I continued hounding them once she's dead." (*Sturlu saga* chap. 36)

Sturla is not the type from whom one would expect great fellow-feeling for his enemies, and we are not disappointed. He stages a clever little black-humored comedy, manipulating the cultural meanings of emotion display to make a witty and mean-spirited point. Like other old men, Sturla takes to bed out of grief for someone's death and in despair at his inability to take revenge. But Sturla is inverting all the moral and emotional valences involved. He is indeed grieving Thorbjorg's death, but his grief is motivated not by love but by hate; Thorbjorg's corpse does not make an unfillable demand for revenge, it undoes the basis for vengeance. Sturla is astutely aware that we often need the people we hate as much as the people we love in order to maintain our sense of personhood and purpose. Thorbjorg's mere existence always provided him with the justification for continuing his feud against her sons. As in the cultural motif of taking to bed for grief he is parodying, he is depressed because he will now be unable to take vengeance, not because he lacks the will or means but because it is no longer politically feasible.

Sturla cleverly orchestrates the cultural expectations surrounding the conventionality and decorousness of certain emotions and their somatic and ritualized accompaniment. He is truly depressed, but his depression does not prevent him from also feeling no small amount of *Schadenfreude*. The depression is a consequence of regretting the loss of pretext; the *Schadenfreude* is evidenced by the fact that Thorbjorg's death is the excuse to stage a joke; it is a cause for laughter and pleasure in another's misery. That Sturla can joke in the midst of depression shows his kinship to other great wits, but it also reveals again just how reluctant these people were to talk seriously about their own inner states.

Going to bed might have been an appropriate behavior for old men, but it was not so for young men. If it was proper for old men to have their grief mixed with frustration and despair, the grief of younger men was supposed to produce anger and, depending on the precise source of the grief, shame, spite, vengefulness, a most punctilious sense of duty, and violent action.[23] When old Kveld-Ulf went to bed after the death of his son, his other son kept urging him to get up instead of lying around uselessly: "It is rather my view, that we should seek vengeance for Thorolf and it just might be that we will have the chance to get at some of them who were actually present, but if we can't, there are still those whom we can get at whose deaths will displease the king" (*Egils saga* chap. 24).

If the appropriateness of certain feelings and their display is a function of age it is also a function of status.[24] Thus kings and not their stableboys are the subject of tragedy. When players in the game of honor—that is, men and women of feuding status—express pleasure in another's misery, it may be a sign of wit, as in the case of Sturla, or simply a realistic admission that *Schadenfreude* is a necessary emotional companion to feud. But when someone takes pleasure in the misfortunes of his social superiors, those superiors do not always react kindly. Rather than warn Kjartan of a pending ambush, Thorkel, a poor farmer of mean spirit, prefers to watch the encounter from afar for his own amusement. His amusement costs him his life once Kjartan's kin find out about it (*Laxdæla saga* chaps. 49, 52).

Much of the expression of emotion is mediated by the knowledge that it is presented to a public. Emotions (or at least their display) form an important part of the work of legitimizing and justifying our actions. The more obviously public the performance, the more the performance tends to take on a quasi-formalized style, to have a ritualized aspect. Mourning customs are an obvious example, but there are other instances. Egil buries his head in his cloak for lovesickness (*Egils saga* chap. 55), and few readers of the sagas are likely to forget the alternate raising and lowering of his brows as he sits glowering opposite King Athelstan, feeling whatever feelings a halfberserk, intensely violent man might feel after he has lost his brother in the king's service and has not yet heard whether and to what extent he will be compensated. A twelve-year-old boy on an expedition to avenge his father is described as "swollen with grief" (*Laxdæla saga* chap. 63), but we can guess that the "grief" and the swelling are somewhat ritualized by the fact that his father was killed when the boy was *in utero*. Such grief thus appears to be less an emotion than a state or condition, in this case the state of having an unavenged father for whom one is now taking action leading to vengeance. Or better, this kind of grief is best described as a justificatory argument. Grief gives an acceptable reason for the revenge. It is what a twelve-year-old deprived of his father should properly feel before undertaking this mission, and so, because the author is also arguing for the rightness of the action, he describes him as swollen with grief.

Making Sense of the Action

Even if—despite the gist of most of the examples discussed so far—it were true that certain facial expressions indicate one certain universal emotion and even if all the problems of mapping emotion words and resolving differences in their referential domains across cultures and linguistic boundaries could be solved, we would still have to confront the unignorable problem that the saga authors and saga characters do not especially like to indulge themselves in emotion talk and that somatic description is also rather rare. Dialogue is introduced with "he said," "she said," and the verb is not varied to indicate the tone; when a rare adverb gives us the emotion behind the utterance it is inevitably "angrily." On the somatic side, pain is seldom mentioned, nor are most facial features except in moments of great agitation. The saga writers much preferred to type characters by general character dispositions and then let that disposition account for the type of emotional life the person might be likely to live. Thus characters are introduced as spiteful, hard-spirited, self-possessed, generous, cunning, wise, moderate, toughminded, brave, warriorlike; and generally their behavior is consistent with, if not always predictable by, the disposition attributed to them.

A preference for disposition talk rather than emotion talk has several consequences. In dispositional style, character or personality tends to be fixed once a person reaches adulthood. Personality approaches allegory. There are, of course, exceptions: some people change their dispositions,[25] others at least change their behavior, if not their dispositions. After all, aggressive and quarrelsome people may have peacefulness rammed down their throats. And eventually dispositions may start to accord with behavior. Some scholars, desperate to find people changing their characters in the best moral and Christian mode, have to resort to emending the text to get stubborn people to fall into line. Such is the case of a notorious passage in *Hrafnkels saga* (chap. 7) in which a mildly troublesome occurrence of the manuscript's *land* (land) is turned to *lund* (disposition, mind, temper), so that a change of farms becomes a change of dispositions. Despite the few exceptions, however, the general saga view sees character as fixed. This fact gives some indication of how little the penitential style of Christianity, which supposes that character can be trained and molded, had penetrated the native folk theories of psychology. Character change itself is rarely held out as a life-course paradigm, as a positive value in itself, as it has been held out in certain devotional and romantic narratives.

A brief digression: our own cultural views on the fixity of character are rather ambivalent. There are perhaps two roughly contrary positions. One view, shared by Californians, some sophisticates, and certain strains of Christianity, supposes that character can change or that with changes in the body come change in character. Whole industries are supported by this belief (the self-help pop-psychology industry, many other therapeutic styles, fat farms, health spas, cosmetic surgeons). The other position, however, is extraordinarily durable and similar to the dominant saga theory. We might call it the folk view, but that would be to imply that the first view isn't also a folk view, just a view of different folk. The wisdom of this position tells us that the leopard doesn't change its spots, the apple doesn't fall too far from the tree, or once an *X* always an *X*. Yet if such a view tends to push personality toward allegory, it is no less true to life.[26] We are, after all, a bit allegorical ourselves inasmuch as we are constrained greatly by social and cultural factors to play out the limited number of socially and culturally prescribed roles available to us. Some of us are tortured enough by this realization to feel a kind of vertigo when we find that the lines we are uttering, the postures we are adopting, sound and look strangely like the commercials and movies we have distaste for, strangely like our teachers and parents and colleagues whom we congratulate ourselves on having transcended. For saga characters, living in a simple, undifferentiated society with what divisions of labor there were largely molded on gender lines, there were even fewer roles, and so the range of possible characters one could become was even narrower.

One of the consequences of preferring disposition talk to emotion talk is a quasi-legal and moral one: dispositions are ways of talking about reputations, and reputations have a lot to do with one's legal and moral standing and the value of one's word, one's corpse, one's son's or daughter's marriage prospects, and so forth. Emotions are more particular, less durable, not ever-present, and hence less likely to imply a permanent juridical or moral status. Many attributions of disposition clearly involve a moral judgment. In honor-based culture the morality of an action was never separated from who did it. The deeds of honorable people were prima facie honorable, the deeds of dishonorable people dishonorable, independent of the particular emotions that may have motivated the particular action. Gudrun in *Laxdæla saga* can steal, commit adultery, be instrumental in the death of her husband and lover, yet never have her honor diminished, while Hallgerd in *Njáls saga* is given no such benefit when she commits the same actions. Snorri the Chieftain, like his descendant Sturla, can be hard of counsel, cunning, and ruthless and still maintain an honorable reputation. They are dispositionally and socially honorable men and thus they get the benefit of many a doubt.

Disposition talk does not, it would seem, indicate a weaker sense of individuation than does emotion talk, even though it may say something about views of the depth of the self. Dispositional traits mark people off from other people no less sharply than if these people are described in terms of a more specific and local motivation. Yet, if the way one talks about personhood actually constitutes the notion of the person, the saga notion clearly is not ours, but it is not its polar opposite either. If we were to take the Western concept of the bounded autonomous individual at one end of an axis and a role-based socially contextualized sense of person as the other,[27] the saga person would lie somewhere in the middle.[28] The demands of kin and household pushed that person toward a role-based sense of self, a self of weaker individuation; the demands of a punctilious sense of honor pushed more toward autonomy of self. To be sure, the honor of one's kin inured to one's benefit, but ultimately—for males especially and considerably less for females—honor meant the testing of a rather discrete and lonely individual who had to measure up against all the other discrete individuals in the game of honor (of which more shortly). I am not claiming that the saga sense of honor was the Western notion of the autonomous individual struggling to maintain itself against the claims of society. The honorable person was never understood to stand outside of the society in which honor was gained and lost. But neither were saga people the selfless unindividuated romanticized non-Westerns of certain styles of anthropology and political theory.

Emotion in the sagas, as I have noted, must be inferred. Inferring motivation and the emotional underpinning of human action is something we do all the time. In our own social interactions the problem is one not so much of gaining sure knowledge of the other's motives as of gaining enough to guide our responses and future activities in light of what we presume the other's motives and intentions to be. When we are dealing with living interlocutors we can crosscheck our first impressions against reputation and subsequent behavior; we can ask others to clarify their intentions; we build a mental file of how well we feel they know their own motives, how willing they are to tell the truth about them when asked, and how willing they are to act in accordance with the intentions they give others a reason to believe they have. With most others with whom we deal we also share language, culture, and a whole normative and social order that nicely constrains the realm of the possible. But we still have to interpret the other's actions, words, and very being, and that process is not much different from the one we undertake to get at characters long dead whom we know only through texts.

My point is not to secure the position of what we can know about the past by undermining the determinacy of the present. We muddle along quite well in the present. Yet the difficulty of getting at emotions across time, language, and geographic, moral, and cultural space, though not all that different in kind from the problems of negotiating intersubjectivity in general, surely makes our job tougher and our confidence weaker. The risk of misidentifying the emotions we assume are required to motivate action is greater when the actor is not our cultural and social contemporary and when the text in which the actor resides is reticent about talking about motivation explicitly.

Literary studies commonly avoid this risk by universalizing psychology; we are thus inclined to think *Hamlet* and *Lear* are great literature because we believe Hamlet's and Lear's psychological, if not social, predicaments universal and because we imagine that we feel the same way we believe they felt. Many of the standard justifications offered to students, legislators, and parents for teaching good literature or learning history depend on an assumed timelessness and transparency of emotional and moral life across time and space. It is fashionable now to condemn such essentialist complacency, and, fashion aside, the condemnation is richly merited. But still, just what makes *Hamlet* and *Lear*, or the Icelandic sagas, travel so well? Why do we feel that we understand the motivation of the characters, that the action is not random, that the sense of action is recoverable? Are our feelings of understanding simply an illusion created by universalizing tendencies in our own culture? Clearly some texts fare better than others, perhaps less because we are able to comprehend the motivation of action in them than because we are comfortable with the subject matter and their stylistic conventions.

This discussion raises difficult questions about the ability of words and discourses to be translated, the ability of interpretation, imagination, sympathy, empathy (and even philology) to get at the "truth" of their subject matter. Part of the reason *Lear* and *Hamlet* travel so well is that we tell ourselves repeatedly that they do; they are part of a consciously maintained tradition that makes them part of us and not exemplars of the Other. To deny that they are is to type oneself a philistine, unimaginative, or simply too lazy to check the bottom of the page for the gloss of archaic words or too dull to parse the complicated tropes and figures of early seventeenth-century verse. But whatever self-deception we engage in regarding our connectedness to great books is assisted by the genuine capacity of the text, in the context of other contemporaneous texts, to give us enough mate-

rial to understand it on its own terms. These works must bear sufficient normative, structural, and spiritual traces of the society and
culture that produced them to have them parse across so much time
and so much space.

Stories have the capacity to engender in the reader all kinds of
emotions. Some of these emotions piggyback on the emotions the
reader perceives the characters to have.[29] Others are elicited by larger moral issues raised by the account and by tactics and manipula-
tions of the author, who exercises a lot of control over who will be the
objects of our sympathy or aversion. But can we trust our emotional
reactions? If we can never actually know whether we have reex-
perienced the feeling a seventeenth-century Hamlet would have had
(or the feelings of a contemporary reader or viewer of the play) we
surely have no basis for denying that we can come pretty close.
Interpretive and philological techniques can do much better than
random in telling us how the text meant us to judge the morality of
certain actions, what the words mean, and what the values are that
make the story have sense. We can feel confident that when the text
says that a character loved, it does not mean she hated or was angry or
envious. Love might not have been the same as it is now, but it wasn't
something unrecognizably different either. Although we may never
have felt precisely as Hamlet did, we may never feel precisely as our
spouse or any of our contemporaries do either. We get at their emotions in life much as we get at them in books. We process both as
narratives or as a series of interlaced narratives in which rules of
appropriateness govern what others should feel if they are to talk and
act in the manner we see them.

These texts are accessible for other reasons. As I claimed in the
chapter on gifts, the values of honor, of paying back both good and
bad, are not quite strange to us and are perpetuated in some of our
most popular narrative traditions: westerns, gangster movies, even
our foreign policy justifications. And part of our social being is still
intimately involved in the honor game in which requiting wrongs or
insults is mandatory. We are still deeply committed to a norm of
reciprocity in spite of our official hostility to vengeance taking. These
values are not always respectable, but they survive nonetheless and
are sufficiently widespread because we live much of our lives in the
face-to-face settings of neighborhood, schools, and workplace; it just
does not take much for us to plug right into stories of honor and
revenge. These are what the sagas are and these are what so many of

our narratives still are. The motivations that sustain honor and that supply reason to vengeance—the very substance of *Hamlet* and the sagas—are not unfamiliar.

We are not without light then in recovering the emotional life of the sagas, even with some precision. There are many sagas, and after reading them with care one discerns that certain actions tend to elicit similar responses. The social and legal arrangements of the sagas have their own sense, a good portion of which is recoverable. A person familiar with the sagas begins to recognize a world in which people can make reasonable predictions about other people's behavior: they can plan ahead, they can be prudent. Events do not appear to happen randomly; they have a logic that the characters seem to rely on and understand and that the reader can recover for a significant range of experiences. Needless to say, many experiences cannot be recovered, especially those we would most like to recover. We will never know much about how women felt about their men or how servants felt about their masters. The experiences of childhood and sex are almost completely lost, for there are only brief anecdotes in these areas. But if we want to construct the experience of shame, courage, cowardice, and vengeance, or the whole panoply of feelings which honor demands or condemns, we are in a better position. A person who lives with the sagas knows that they are tense with emotions barely repressed, all the more moving to the reader because they are not obsessed on or talked about. And English emotional vocabulary can get at these emotions even though the natives clearly would have thought it bad form to be talking so much about them.

A Concluding Example

Let us try to make sense of a brief speech. It illustrates the difficulty of repressing the blood urge and the uneasy tension that arose when heroic honor faced the practices and demands of Christianity. Two brothers, Snorri and Thorstein, have been hunted down by the avengers of some people they had helped kill. They prepare themselves for execution by confessing to a priest, washing their hands and combing their hair "as if they were to go on a social visit."

> Then Snorri said [to his executioners], "I would appreciate it if I were killed before Thorstein, because I trust him better to be able to forgive you, even though he should see me executed."
> (*Guðmundar saga dýra* chap. 18)

In another place dealing with a different topic I wrote this about Snorri's words:[30]

> Besides showing remarkable courage, [the speech] reveals the cool rage of Snorri, who knows that he would be incapable of forgiving his brother's executioners and hence would risk undoing his final absolution with new sin. The milder mannered Thorstein, he supposes, will better be able to keep his soul safe. The ambivalences of the sentiment are striking. There is Snorri's refusal to give up his wish for revenge balanced against his fear of damnation; there is brother love and some small brother contempt. He cannot forgo the competitive urge to die more heroically than his brother, and his heroism comes at the expense of devaluing Christian values against the old heroic ones. . . . Even his fear of undoing his absolution is not so great that he forgoes completely a refusal of forgiveness. His concession to maintaining the purity of his absolution is simply to express his present refusal to forgive as a hypothetical future failure to forgive, a nicely casuistic resolution.

To make adequate sense of the passage, my explication provided as motivations the emotions of rage, vengefulness, love, contempt, fear, fear of shame (by implication), and I would also include courage or resolution, forgiveness, and competitive urges. Although I can hardly claim that this is the only way to interpret the passage, it seems to do rather well by most measures of plausibility given what we know about the heroic ethic as culled from other sagas, about Christian practice, and about the art of dying in saga Iceland.[31] It would be a thin interpretation indeed that avoided Snorri's motivations. This was a death speech, good enough to be recorded and recalled for a long time. Its motivation was clearly caught up in the emotional styles and commitments that supported the norms of honor. And we sense that we can understand these things. The emotional terms I use seem to do more than just interpret Snorri's words for us, they also seem to be getting reasonably close to what was motivating them.

The Emotional Economy of Honor

Our emotions are intimately connected to our beliefs and to the normative world of which we are a part. A culture in which honor is a dominant organizing principle is very likely to make certain emotional dispositions more salient than they would be in an American upper-middle-class suburb. We might expect emotions that depend on relative standing in a community, such as shame or envy, to be more prevalent than those that depend on self-evaluation independent of the views of others, such as guilt or remorse, or those that accompany alienation, such as angst and ennui. The well-known distinction between shame and guilt cultures, though rightly and roundly criticized, still captures a fundamental difference between the world of the sagas and ours, between a culture in which reputation is all and one in which conscience, confession, and forgiveness play a central role.[32]

Honor

Honor was more than just a set of rules for governing behavior. Honor permeated every aspect of consciousness: how you thought about yourself and others, how you held your body, the expectations you could reasonably have and the demands you could make on others; it determined the quality of your marriage and the marriage partners of your children. It was your very being. For in an honor-based culture there was no self-respect independent of the respect of others, no private sense of "hey, I'm quite something" unless it was confirmed publicly.[33] Honor was then not just a matter of the individual; it necessarily involved a group, and the group included all those people worthy of competing with you for honor. Your status in this group was the measure of your honor, and your status was achieved at the expense of the other group members who were not only your competitors for scarce honor but also the arbiters of whether you had it or not. In other words, your good standing depended on the judgments of your enemies. Your good standing was also aided by friends, not so much because of their judgment of you, but because you had them. Having friends was a sign to others of your honor and only the honorable had friends. Of course friends constituted the possible class of future enemies and in that sense their judgments mattered. I am overstating the case, but, for Iceland, not by much.

Although the honorable man might be emulated, the mathematics of honor usually meant you could never be just like someone else without taking what he had, appropriating his status to yourself. For the most part, people acted as if the mechanics of honor had the structure of a zero-sum or less-than-zero-sum game.[34] The shortest road to honor was thus to take someone else's, and this meant that honorable people had to be ever-vigilant against affronts or challenges to their honor, because challenged they would be. The man or woman beyond challenge was no longer in the game of honor, but in the world of lords and kings who conferred *honors* on retainers and courtiers who competed with one another for honor as measured by the *honors* conferred on them by a superior. And if some people got too big to play the game, others became too small. The person who could or would not respond to challenges eventually lost all honor and thus all his moral being by being condemned to the invisibility of the pariah or servant.

Yet the sagas show that some people were remarkably skillful in maintaining honor without having to settle every account, even some pretty big accounts. Snorri the Chieftain never avenged his father and was subjected to insults for not busying himself with revenge, but he was able enough at having his will in other dealings that he succeeded in leading a successful and honorable life nevertheless.[35] In the practical world of the sagas, the honorable person got a lot of benefits of the doubt, a presumption that his doings were honorable. As long as he could still elicit in others the expectation and fear that he would indeed avenge the *next* shame he suffered, he would still be counted a person of honor.

It should be clear that I am rejecting the thin notion of honor frequently encountered in moralizing accounts that caricature honor as only foolhardy aggressiveness. Honor was always sensitive to context and circumstance.[36] Bloodtaking was not the only course of honor. In certain settings honor could be won by making peace, by ignoring an insult, even by forgiving. Honor could be acquired by commercial success abroad (but not at home), by integrity and a sense of equity, as well as by success as an intrepid warrior. The antithesis was not honor/peace, but honor/shame, and shame inhered in much more than cowardice. It could also inhere in foolhardiness, stupidity, and imprudence. The thin notion of honor, however, bears some truth: as I noted in Chapter 2, honor, at root, still meant "Don't tread on me." For though the ability to make peace and be prudent could be honorable, it could be so only if the person making peace was honorable.

Shame

Honor goes hand in hand with shame. In a culture of honor one can be shamed only if one has honor, if one is a member of the group competing for honor. Shame is, in one sense, nothing more than the loss of honor. Shame depends on the failure to measure up to the external standard imposed by the honor group. Like honor, it depends on the judgment of others, although it can be felt without the actual presence of the judging group. One can feel shame even when no one is looking, for the judgment of others is already congealed within the social norms internalized by the person feeling shame.[37] The honorable person is socialized to entertain the sentiment and sensibility of honor; one judges oneself as harshly as one would judge others, even perhaps more harshly. A player in the game of honor suffers shame for shameful deeds. Not to feel shame for such acts would type one as shameless, as a person of no honor.[38] To the extent that a person's very social being is dependent on one's being honorable, one must palpably feel the loss of honor, that is, shame. The person who does not subscribe to the norms of honor will not feel shame for having violated them even if real third parties try to make him or her feel so.[39] This invulnerability is simply an aspect of the social quality of shame. Shame requires membership in a society, a community of people sharing norms of right action and caring deeply about what others in their community think of them.

It should be noted, as an aside, that honor and shame in the saga world are not like the honor and shame of the Mediterranean region in some important respects.[40] In Mediterranean cultures, according to the traditional ethnographic account, shame was the female condition and the moral condition of a man's female relatives.[41] More narrowly, shame was female sexuality itself, literally her sexual organs. As a consequence, a man's honor consisted in making sure his women remained inviolate. Honor also inhered in the whole system of challenge and riposte, but so much of the challenging was centered on the moral condition of one's women that even if the ostensible challenge concerned a man's ability to fight, an unfavorable outcome of that challenge would mean that his women could not be defended. Honor was thus never more than one remove from women's shame. Both honor and shame were obviously and clearly eroticized. The world of the sagas was different. Little premium was placed on a woman's virginity or on a child's legitimacy, for that matter, and women's lot was considerably better for that fact. Honor and shame were gendered to be sure, but they were not obsessively focused on the condition of the female genitalia and did not lead to an ideal or a reality of female sequestration.[42] In the Norse world the language of

challenge at its most vulgar and most provocative made sure to suggest the effeminacy of the insultee. The coward was the man who was
penetrated by other men, no different from a woman. But the actions
that were shameful and the shames that could be done the honorable
man involved the reputation of his women only occasionally.[43]

Shame has its obvious role in the socialization of honorable people
and in maintaining social control. In the sagas, the norms of honor,
the norms of proper behavior, in fact, are as often expressed nega-
tively in terms of shame avoidance as they are positively in terms of
honor acquisition. And shame—as skömm's synonyms óvirðing (literally un-honor), svívirðing (dis-honor), and ósæmð (un-honor)
indicate—is conceptualized as the negation of honor.[44] Shame is
seldom, if ever, described as a feeling. As a linguistic matter people
are not said to be shamed or to feel ashamed or shame. Shame,
rather, is something done to people, or people endure it or suffer it,
or it will come to them, or they simply have it. Skömm is also often
used to label the moral negativity of certain types of action. It is thus a
shame to take back what you have given (Njáls saga chap. 123), to fail
to show up for a duel (Finnboga saga chap. 34; Gísla saga chap. 2;
Vatnsdæla saga chap. 34), for three men to attack one (Hávarðar saga
chap. 4), for a man to be struck by a woman, to have an outlaw escape
your clutches (Gísla saga chaps. 32, 27), and so on. Conceptually
shame had the capacity to get at omissions as well as commissions.
Not only can omissions be shameful, they are cast in the image of the
archetypal shame behavior: cowardice, the refusal to act when right
action demands courage. Omissions are events for moral purposes
and, above all, they are events for the purpose of regulating relative
standing, even if, as I noted in Chapter 2, they might not always be
events for legal purposes.[45]

The connection between right action, duty, and shame, however, is
more complex than this easy sort of moralizing talk would lead one to
believe. The shameful could not be reduced to a litany of rules. The
particulars of context were crucial in the determination of how much
and whether shame was done or suffered. The identity of the parties,
their past history of dealings, their relative popularity, the particular
failing at issue, all figured in the moral calculation. Different people
held themselves and were in turn held to different standards. The
modest man of honor, maintaining a simple but dignified existence,
could more easily justify prudent action than could the man of honor
who held himself to the highest standards of heroic fearlessness.

Children were not capable of giving insult, and when they said things that if said by an adult would cause shame and be avengeable, they were merely disciplined—beaten and given other instruction (see *Njáls saga* chap. 8). Such, however, was the anxiousness of maintaining status that even the remarks of children, although not avengeable on them, could make adults laugh at one's expense and so still be a shame. Recourse was against the adults for laughing, for one usually stood to lose by contending with people who were not in the game. If a master was insulted by a servant his strategies were either to ignore the affront with studied contempt, to discipline the servant in a way that reaffirmed the permanence of the status differences, or to delegate the task of vengeance to someone closer to the rank of the servant.[46]

By nominalizing shame, as the Icelanders did, by making it independent of the self, they could readily subsume it conceptually into the structures and logic of the key systems of reciprocity: the feud and gift exchange.[47] A shame is, above all, something that is given or paid over and that needs to be given or paid back and avenged. Thus it is that shame is frequently coupled with verbs for taking vengeance and for paying and requiting.[48] But not anything designated a shame or a dishonor justified lethal vengeance. Designating various actions as shames, as noted above, was a way of doing a lot of the low level work of social control and moral educating. To encourage people to alter their behavior, one called what they were doing or what they were not doing a shame. But if all shames did not give rise to justifiable vengeance, all acts that required vengeance were shames, for shame and dishonor inhered in the very structure and rhythm of feud.[49] To have a shame of this sort done you was the same as being one down in the feud. It meant the ball was in your court; it was your turn to move against your shamer. In this way, shame provided the very opportunity for doing those things that made one a person of honor. Nothing is more honorable than reclaiming one's honor, than paying back affronts, humiliations, and shames. One of the many little paradoxes of honor is that the honorable person must not only be shamable, he must also occasionally suffer shame or remain forever untested. We can imagine, however, a regime in which a person is so dominant that no one would risk shaming him, where he could, in the proverb of the Kabyle, "sleep and leave the door open."[50] Yet in a world of honor the time would come, maybe in the next generation, when a challenge would be made. For where no challenge was forthcoming and where there was no prospect or fear that it would come, there was no game of honor, only the dominance of lordship or the bonds of patronage and clientage. In those situations, what was once the fear of affront became, if fear there was, the fear of revolt and insubordination.

The honorable person did not become dishonorable the moment he suffered a shame. He was dishonored but not dishonorable; he suffered shame but he was not shameless. We should distinguish between the experience of shame of the person shamed as a part of an expected continuing exchange of somewhat hostile social reciprocities and the experience of the person shamed as a result of a judgment by others and confirmed by himself that he simply cannot meet the standards of a fully moral and respectable being. The first shame is the shame of the honorable man suffering a dishonor in the game of challenge and riposte; the second shame is the shame of the person finally adjudged to be an inappropriate player in the game. This latter is the person who feels shame as self-loathing and despair, although to those who judged him so utterly shamed he is seen to have lost the capacity to feel shame. This is another paradox of honor and shame. The most deeply felt shame is that of the person who is finally adjudged incapable of experiencing honorable self-doubt. He is shameless. The honorable person feels shame too, but with a different admixture of accompanying emotions. In place of self-loathing sits anger, indignation, apprehension, and no small amount of anxiety.[51] For this person, the pain of self-loathing is held mostly in abeyance and remains ready to descend with full weight only when he has shown himself incapable of riposte. A clock started running the moment the shame occurred. It was now his turn to move, to show himself a person of honor. Honor was not to be reclaimed with indecorous haste. Vengeance was to be savored. Too quick a vengeance was only slightly more honorable, it was said, than never taking it at all. As the Old Norse proverb would have it: "Only a slave avenges himself immediately, but a coward never does" (*Grettis saga* chap. 15). If, however, requital never came and no honorable reconciliation had occurred in the meantime, the clock ran out. This was a serious matter, and it could, if it led others reasonably to assume a general incapacity to avenge the next offense, bring about a kind of social death as one passed from the ranks of the shamable to the oblivion of the shameless. Even those who had built up a lot of social credit and for whom the presumption of honor worked to great effect could not risk too many discomfitures of this sort.

Even though shame is conceptualized as a thing rather than as a feeling, the sagas do on occasion describe what people felt when they had been done a shame. *Skömm* at times finds itself bound by substantive and alliterative attraction with the noun *skapraun*,[52] which literally meant a trial of the mind, that is, vexation, frustration, feeling aggrieved, the sick feeling of shame and humiliation. These were the feelings that filled the period during which one was waiting for the chance to take vengeance and hence the chance to repair one's honor. Imagine the anxieties experienced during the time period when you have not been as hasty as the slave but were still not deemed a coward. You would be anxious and concerned lest the opportunity for getting at a worthy target not present itself in a reasonable time; nervous and perhaps fearful about the dangers involved; wary and ill at ease wondering whether people doubted your mettle; angry, indignant, aggrieved, sick at the *Schadenfreude* you suspected others might be feeling at your expense; shamed and humiliated at having been caught up short, and, as a corollary, full of self-doubt as to how you could have failed to prevent the shame from having been done to you in the first place. At some point people might start to insult you with the slowness of your hand. In fact, your wife, your old father, your sister, your mother were almost certain to. They had a repertoire of insults and ritualized goadings at their disposal to suggest that you were indeed shameless: "If you don't avenge this, you'll never avenge any shame done you"; "You'd have just about the right amount of spirit if you were the daughters of any old farmer."[53] But your kin, who shared your interests, were not about to wait until you were truly a person of no honor to suggest that you were. Their goads only made sense if they were made when you could still reclaim your honor, that is, when you were still shamable, when you could still feel the anguish of shame. Yet they were also revealing that they were nervous that time was running short, that soon others, less concerned about your regaining your honor, would be speaking about you as an object of contempt.

These shaming rituals were performed by those who had an interest that you feel your shame and who were concerned that you might not be feeling it enough. Even though the ritualized aspect of these performances made them expected and thus took some of the edge off them, they still provoked great feeling. Skarphedinn, as we saw earlier, was shamed in this way by his mother: "he grinned, but, nevertheless, sweat showed on his forehead and red spots appeared on his cheeks, and this was very unusual." Clearly he acutely felt the shame his mother was trying to make him feel.[54]

Another shaming ritual was employed to force assistance to those in distress. An Icelandic version of "sitting dharna" can be found in a couple of cases in which men in dire straits threaten to sit down and die right before the eyes of the man from whom they are beseeching aid if their request should not be granted (*Ljósvetninga saga* chap. 18; *Njáls saga* chap. 88). These ceremonies make a lot of sense in shame cultures. They induce by threatening to shame, by making open judgments about the loss of reputation to be suffered, and by appealing to other emotional states such as pity, guilt, grief, embarrassment, anger, or the sense of duty.[55]

Saga reticence aside, we can guess that shame was meant to be deeply felt because of the occasional assertion that it was better to die than to live with it[56] and because of the willingness of saga characters to act on that assertion. This is a world of shame and envy, the emotions of status, not of guilt and remorse, the emotions of conscience. The fact that saga people talked about shame more than they talked about guilt no doubt assists the perception of saga reserve and emotionlessness. Scholars who think that they see remorse and guilt usually attribute them to the effects of the Christian emotional style.[57] Even in clearly Christian situations we see shame more than guilt. Consider this case, one of the very few in the entire saga corpus in which we have the verb *skammask*, meaning "to feel shame."[58]

A priest named Stein doubted the holiness of Bishop Jon's bones. He was the only one of the clerical company unable to smell their miraculous fragrance. "Then Stein the priest felt shame at his lack of faith" (*Prests saga* chap. 22). Notice that it must be shame that is the emotion at issue. Here the group norm is a belief that saintly bones smell good, a belief our poor shamed priest accepts also. The fact that all the other clerics profess to smelling the good smell means there is communal agreement as to the dead Jon's status. If Stein did not believe in the ability of saintly bones to exude miraculous fragrance, he would not be shamed. But because he does, his inability to smell the good smell can only indicate his not being up to snuff in the community; it is a loss of face, a shame. Stein was not just shamed; he *felt* shame. The word *skammaðist* together with sufficient circumstance in the telling confirm this point rather nicely.

The passage goes on to show Stein repenting his lack of faith. He prayed tearfully to the holy bishop Jon for forgiveness. The tears were tears of contrition and remorse, tears indicating the emotional style of penance. He felt shame for his loss of status, and remorse for angering God and his saint, the occasion for his shame. Stein was thus forced to manifest signs of guilt as well as shame. But the guilt was elicited by his failings toward God and his saint, the shame was elicited by his failings to live up to the expectations of his clerical brethren.

Envy

I have already hinted that shame was not the only status-dependent emotion that informed the world of honor. Envy occupied just as important a place, but less obviously so because it occupied a distinctly lesser role in people's speech. Talk about shame, like talk about honor, was the way people talked about reputation; it was how they kept score of who was ahead of whom; it was how relative standing and status were determined and publicized; it was how people understood the results of the game of honor. Yet people talked about envy enough to provide sufficient textual justification for the claims I am about to make.[59] But they didn't have to talk about it, for it was largely assumed to be the motive and motivator of most action in the game of honor. To talk about it would have been bad form. Unlike shame talk, which clearly was within the game of honor, envy talk was more about the game as game. It was a kind of "meta" talk, a way of judging the game itself and not the play within it. One could gain little advantage in accusing someone of envious motivation when envy was virtually the way of the world of honor. It could hardly have been otherwise.

Honor was a system for judging relative merit. It was how prestige was allocated and a ranking was obtained among those people in the game. The very nature of the game meant that you paid very chary attention to how you stood relative to others, which in turn necessitated constant attention not only to the quality of your honor but to the quality of other people's too. The world of honor was obsessed with the act of comparing. The Icelanders even had a special name for this kind of comparing—*mannjafnaðar*, or literally "man-evening," "people-comparing or balancing"—and they also had a formal game of the same name in which man-comparing went on.[60] Such keen attention to the standing of others might be undertaken dispassionately and rationally, but not by honorable men or women.

The comparison of one's self with others of necessity meant invidious comparisons, meant jealousy and anxiety about one's status; it meant shame and humiliation at the loss of status or joy or even ecstasy at its recovery. It meant begrudging the advancement of others who were gaining on you, envying their position when they were ahead of you, and delighting in any discomfitures that befell them. Envy—the misery occasioned by another's successes[61]—and *Schadenfreude*—the pleasure occasioned by another's failures—were the consequences of comparing, and they in turn motivated the comparing in the first place. Although such comparisons might simply provide motive for competing for honor, the competition was not always innocent. Envy prompted strategies that might prefer hurting your opponent to benefiting yourself. Envy, in other words, often went hand in hand with spite, which might be defined (following Robert Nozick) as the preference that neither you nor the other have the thing rather than that both have it.[62]

Envy fueled the leveling mechanisms that kept people from getting too powerful to play in the game of honor. The sagas refer not infrequently to the envy that motivated people to develop enmities with big men and local leaders. Gunnar and Arnkel were thus brought down, ultimately, by the envy they elicited in others (see *Njáls saga* and *Eyrbyggja saga*). The acquisition and possession of honor had its costs. Acquiring honor meant having to step on a few toes and thus assuredly gave rise to specific enmities, but the simple fact of having honor meant incurring envy and hence eventually enmity from people with whom you may not have had any prior hostile dealings. Yet these costs were the very joys of honor. What, after all, was honor if not the ability to elicit envy in others, the ability to extract from them a judgment of your superiority? In this regard, La Rochefoucauld's "The mark of a special achievement is to see that those who most envy it are compelled to praise it" is almost tautological, for it is the envy itself that is the initial judgment of the praiseworthiness of the other.[63] The joy in the knowledge that you made others envious was the joy of knowing you were a person of honor, a joy that had its inevitable aspects of *Schadenfreude* because the honor it was based on was conferred by the estimation of a community of people who envied you.[64] But this joy had to be leavened by anxiety and vigilance, for the knowledge that you made others envious was also the knowledge that you might well become the target of envious people whose own sense of honor could most quickly be reestablished at your expense. The fear of being a magnet of attack might just keep your designs within the limit the community was willing to tolerate and lead you to sacrifice some of the desire to be envied in order to live to be capable of being envious.

Some might see in these leveling mechanisms an analogy with how envy works in witchcraft systems, where its leveling force is well known and nicely captured by the oft-cited Bemba proverb Max Gluckman (I believe) put into circulation: "To find one beehive in the woods is luck, to find two is very good luck, to find three is witch-craft."[65] But envy elicitation is not condemned in an honor-based system as it is in witchcraft systems. The moral regime is very differ-ent. Honor says you should not fear eliciting envy and in fact rewards it by making it honorable. The honorable person, above all, could not appear fearful. And although honor and prudence could coexist, the ability to behave prudently often had to be earned at the price of having a reputation for occasionally behaving grandly and impru-dently. People of honor knew the difference between foolhardiness and courage, but failures of courage were very seldom excused. It was one thing to avoid flaunting your position by obnoxious behavior toward others and quite another to avoid excelling out of fear for the consequences of excellence. Honor could have no truck with such pusillanimous people. If in the sagas people do not consciously limit their designs because they wish to avoid the envy of others, they are still treated to counsel warning them of the problems the envy of others will bring them (*Njáls saga* chap. 32). People were thus not unaware of the costs of provoking envy, but their tragedy was that they could not avoid provoking it if they succeeded in the game of honor.

The field in which envy operates, much of this discussion assumes, is bounded like the field of the honor game. If disparities among the players are too great there could be no honor game. As other anato-mists of envy have noted, envy is something that exists among near equals or among people in proximate social standings. David Hume sums it up:

A common soldier bears no such envy to his general as to his sergeant or corporal; nor does an eminent writer meet with so great jealousy in common hackney scriblers, as in authors, that more nearly approach him. . . . The great disproportion cuts off the relation, and either keeps us from comparing ourselves with what is remote from us, or diminishes the effects of the comparison.[66]

Jonathan Swift is more succinct:

> We all behold with envious eyes
> Our equal raised above our size.[67]

Honor, envy, and shame—all intimately connected to self-esteem—are also intimately connected to one another in a variety of ways.[68] In shame we feel the effects of the comparison that others make of our behavior, or that we imagine others could make of our behavior, with the demands of the norms of honor; in envy we feel the effects of the comparison we make of our own performance with those we judge to be doing better than we are. The comparison that produces envy could, under some circumstances, produce shame. Both emotions require us to make judgments about ourselves, and in both we judge ourselves inferior. In shame we fail against a standard or norms whose validity we accept; in envy we fail as against another person who possesses something or some quality we wish we had. We might imagine a sort of confusing of these two emotions as when the contemplation of someone else's good fortune not only produces envy of him or her for it, but shames us for our not having attained the social, cultural, and personal competences that yield those kinds of goods. And as envy might produce shame so too shame might produce envy. The very mechanism of shame, in fact, puts us in the position to be envious. For shame is our admission that we are lower, and now that we are lower what could be more natural than to envy those that are higher? Thus it is that envy strangely confirms the judgment of shame. The confusion is even more likely given the intimate connection of each emotion to hostile and violent action within the game of honor. We might suggest that as a rough rule of thumb opening moves in the saga game of challenge and riposte were more likely to be motivated by envy rather than shame and that subsequent redressive moves were more likely to be motivated by shame than by envy. But because it is never clear and always a matter for interpretation and negotiation whether any move is an opening move or a responsive one, it is nearly impossible to sort out the mixture of motivation which drove any particular action.

If the belief system makes envy, *Schadenfreude*, shame, and humiliation salient emotions, why is so much saga action perceived as grand action? Most of us, I think, would prefer less mean-spirited motivations; we think of these people as caring greatly about their reputations (which they did) without questioning too closely the emotional environment of self-esteem in an honor-based culture. We focus on their courage (which they had) without realizing that the socialization of courage means heavy recourse to the pains of shame and humiliation, spite and vengefulness. Our views of envy, pride, and *Schadenfreude*, the emotions of honor, are indelibly affected by the inversion of heroic values wrought by Christianity, whose moralists helped turn the emotions of heroic society into the deadly sins. The envy that helped sustain the egalitarian ethos of heroic society was metamorphosed into the sinful envy that questioned God's and man's uneven distribution of wealth and status; the pride of the warrior, of the man and woman who took pleasure in his or her honorableness, became pridefulness; vindictiveness slowly took on the negative meaning it has today, rather than indicating that set of feelings which obliged one to maintain face among equals. Competitive gift exchange became gluttony and avarice, and so on. Even without accepting the details of Nietzsche's tale of the history of morals, we would do well, as he did, to distinguish the envy of heroic, feuding, honor-based cultures and the *ressentiment* and envy of nonheroic culture.[69] Perhaps the greatest risk we incur in using English emotion words to discuss a stateless feuding society is not that we impose our theory of emotions and cognition with these words but that we thereby impose our moral values too. For to us emotions are not without their moral rankings. Some are good; some are bad; some evidence a grand spirit, some a mean one, and perhaps nothing fares worse than envy, an emotion we do not especially value, because with us it only leads to bitterness and chagrin over unequal distributions in a world with only unorganized notions of honor.

Envy has not fared well in the hands of moral and political philosophy. Aristotle lumps it with malice and shamelessness, as feelings that are evil in themselves and hence incapable of admitting a mean.[70] Medieval theologians and preachers uniformly condemned it;[71] monkish chroniclers had the habit of attributing it as the prime motivation of their enemies. Even Hume, who did much to reclaim pride as a virtue from the condemnation it suffered in the Christian tradition, did not feel the urge to make the same kind of case for envy.[72] In more recent times envy has been the whipping boy of certain right-wing idealogues who attribute the evils of redistributive legislation to the envy of the losers in the race for riches.[73] Only Nietzsche and John Rawls try to make limited positive cases for envy. The former, in an early essay, sees it the driving force of competitive contest;[74] the latter finds it, although normally a vice, excusable when it is prompted by differences in the distribution of primary goods so great as to lead to the loss of self-respect.[75]

The nice side of envy has a way of being siphoned off into other emotions. Thus admiring envy is understood as emulation,[76] and envy prompted by justifiable annoyance at another's situation becomes indignation or resentment. Even Rawls's case for envy becomes one of nomenclature. When envy begins to look as if it has a moral component, it becomes resentment. Rawls's defense of envy then means only that he recognizes a context or two in which envy can rightly be renamed resentment.[77] Rawls raises a few other points that are important to our business. He suggests that the emotion that motivates honor acquisition in an honor-based culture should be called resentment if social wealth is regarded as an "unchangeable zero-sum game." Of the envy "held to be pervasive in poor peasant societies" in which the quantity of social wealth is constant he writes: "In this case it would be correct to think that justice requires equal shares. Social wealth is not viewed as the outcome of mutually advantageous cooperation and so there is no fair basis for an unequal division of advantages. What is said to be envy may in fact be resentment which might or might not prove to be justified."[78] Rawls does not limit social wealth to concrete goods. In his view self-esteem (and thus apparently honor too) is a primary good. But Rawls ignores that the whole point of honor is to distinguish oneself from others at the same time that one accepts the basic rule upholding the *roughly* egalitarian assumptions of the honor game. No distinction, no honor. And no rough egalitarianism, no game. I do not think that Rawls means to suggest that an honor-based society could never be a just one. Peasants and Viking farmers are hardly his chief concern, nor was a view of justice as fairness theirs. Given the zero-sum nature of much of the honor game, envy can never be separated neatly from resentment or from plain old competition. But honor-based cultures were not only cursed by pervasive scarcity: scarcity also enabled grand action, without which life would have been pretty dull.

Dull. The very word suggests another emotion that figures centrally in heroic society: boredom. I conclude this chapter by briefly sketching how it figures, leaving the large question of how this emotion behaves to another time. Boredom is an unpleasant emotion that people try to avoid. And in materially impoverished cultures—which the classic honor-based cultures tend to be—there do not exist the variety of distractions we have come to rely on to alleviate us from its throes. In conditions of general material deprivation, people tend to find in other people and themselves, rather than things, the means to banish boredom, for people are not as rare as things.[79] But people as a general matter are not interesting either unless they can be provided with qualities that will make them so. What is needed is a means of giving people a general capacity for being interesting independent of the randomly distributed and rare talent some people have of being able to captivate others with their personalities. Competition, contention, conviviality generate this general capacity. These three things, as we have seen, promote concern about relative ranking, and such concern quickens interest in others and in where one stands relative to them; it prompts the desire to do the all-consuming work of acquiring and preserving honor.

The next chapter brings us back to present times again, but the issues remain quite similar to the ones I have just discussed. The focus will be on humiliation, an emotion that I postulate is central to our negotiation of face-to-face interaction, to social control, and to the complex psychology of self-presentation. In heroic society, honor, the positive side of shame, worked to create moral and social hierarchy within a group without formal hierarchical rankings. Hierarchy within the honor group was fluid, for people held their places only as long as they maintained their honor, while those below them were envious and only too willing to take it away from them and assume their positions We too create moral and social hierarchies, but given the vagaries of social differentiation, class, rank, and other forms of quasi-formal hierarchy, the emotional underpinnings of our self-esteem and self-respect are more varied. Shame still plays its role in our enclaves of honor: the schoolyard, the workplace. But in wider settings it is humiliation that undergirds the creation and maintenance of moral and social distinction and rank. It is humiliation that disciplines those who pretend to positions they are unworthy of filling. It is the fear of it that helps constitute the self-knowledge that makes one know one's limits. So much still hinges on our desire to look good and competent and, more important, on our fear of looking bad and incompetent. In both this desire and this fear lies the prospect of humiliation. This is what we turn to now.

4

Humiliation—
Part I: Its Domain
and Strategies of Avoiding It

Although humiliation figures in the life of almost all scholars, it has
itself had virtually no scholarly life. As an object of intellectual inquiry, humiliation has had a hard time extricating itself from its two close
cousins, shame and embarrassment, both of which from time to time
receive their share of scholarly attention. This fact means that I must
start inauspiciously with a digression on shame and embarrassment.
Shame, which was voguish among anthropologists thirty to forty years
ago, went into retirement until the various disciplines that hover
around the edges of the self-help industry and other more respectable psychotherapies brought about its resurgence, even meriting
cover stories in *The Atlantic* and *The New Republic* in 1992.[1] In the
view of this literature, shame, lost in guilt's shadow, has been unjustly
ignored as the underlying cause of most modern and postmodern
psychic misery and malaise—poor shame, unfairly forgotten, unsexy,
and dowdy, and utterly in need of a makeover. The makeover in many
cases makes shame look not at all unlike guilt, and, although I could
spend the better part of this chapter reviewing the various attempts
that have been made to distinguish these two competitors for the title
of "the emotion that ails you most," most of them, once poked a little,

end up giving us very little that looks like *that* much of a difference, in any event surely not a difference that justifies the claim that a major paradigm shift has occurred in how we view our inability to make ourselves or others very happy.[2] But for an explanation of what ails your soul to effect a cure, it must be fresh enough to surprise you into a state of self-knowledge. Guilt lost its freshness and became cheapened by its omnipresence as an explanation. Rather than provide a new substantive explanation, people perceived a need to revive the explanatory power of the old one. So guilt got rechristened. Remember, most of this literature takes place in the context of the problems real therapists face with real patients, and in that setting telling patients that their problems are ones of unacknowledged shame might lead to the self-knowledge that constitutes the cure; such epiphanies are harder to achieve now in guilt therapies than they were in 1910 when guilt freshly displaced a ho-hum and hypermoralized shame. It is not just in the world of psychotherapy that shame is being resurrected. Judges, frustrated with the manifest shortcomings and costs of prison and parole, have recently been reverting to formal shaming as a mode of punishment: if not quite brands, stocks, and pillories, at least scarlet letters in the form of bumper stickers and newspaper ads proclaiming one a drunk driver or a child molester are becoming more and more frequent.[3]

On the other hand, since the 1960s there has been a fairly steady stream of work on embarrassment, starting with Goffman's and followed upon variously by that of a few philosophers and a multitude of social psychologists.[4] But embarrassment has been only a little better at extricating itself from shame than humiliation has. Even Goffman did not consistently separate them, choosing instead to subsume shame implicitly into embarrassment rather than the other way around, a move largely reproduced by Christopher Ricks in his admirable *Keats and Embarrassment*.[5] As for humiliation, if it is treated as distinguishable from shame or embarrassment, it is dealt with mostly in the extreme situations of concentration camps[6] and torture chambers, so that humiliation is assimilated to pornographies of sex and violence.

The first chapter of this two-chapter essay attempts to map out a domain for humiliation differentiable from the domains of shame and embarrassment. This task will be all the harder because I avoid death camps, torture, and what were once referred to as perversions, and stay in the center of the familiar and the public. I advert to the extremes, Humiliation with a big **H,** only by way of contrast in order better to describe the middling and usual. I will come back to this point near the end of this chapter, for I can give it more flesh after working through humiliation with a small **h:** the humiliations of day-to-day interaction, the little falls and the barely perceptible attacks on our self-esteem and self-respect we all face, and the complex, but mostly self-defeating, strategies we use to avoid such humiliations. This is the humiliation that has more in common with embarrassments and even amusement than with torture, rape, and masochism. It still bears significant points of contact with shame on its dark side and with embarrassment and even amusement on its lighter side.

In many situations humiliation is linguistically coupled with shame simply as a reduplicative intensifier: they suffered shame and humiliation. On just as many occasions, humiliation could, with only a slight difference in intensity, be substituted for embarrassment: I embarrassed (humiliated) myself by being so totally overdressed. Nevertheless, some points of humiliation's domain do not overlap with shame or embarrassment without considerable alteration in nuance, sense, feel, seriousness, and quality. There may be times when we feel both humiliation *and* embarrassment or humiliation *and* shame, times, in other words, when the *and* is adding refinement to our description rather than merely indicating intensity by multiplying synonyms. The self, in fact, seems quite capable of entertaining more than one emotion at a time. None of the emotions excludes the possibility of feeling many others concurrently, even their opposites. The oxymorons of poetic discourse are thus more than figures of speech, O hateful love, O dull surprise, O attentive reader! It may also be the case that simultaneously experienced emotions compound in such a way that, say, joy and regret produce something that is neither quite joyful regret nor regretful joy but a vectored product of each.[7] In any event, one of our tasks will be to get at the contours of a separate and maybe unique realm of humiliation. But be forewarned. We will not be able to get at humiliation without also devoting considerable space to shame and embarrassment. What I am after is not hard and testable in the narrow empirical ways of a certain style of social science. I credit feels, hunches, and my method is largely the interpretation of what I consider to be recognizable situations involving the discomforts of norm violation and norm adherence, the awkwardnesses of self-presentation in simple social interaction, and the pains of social and minor moral failure. Parts of this chapter are not easy going, but they do the hard work that makes Chapter 5 accessibly direct.

The Domain of Humiliation

The Contraction of Shame

In a culture of honor, as in saga Iceland, shame was talked about as if it were a social state or a concrete thing and only rarely as a feeling. A shame was done to a person by the hostile challenges of another, or one was shamed by one's own failures to maintain standing in the honor group. If feelings were admitted they usually referred to the emotions or physical illnesses that being done a shame would tend to bring about. The shamed person would thus feel rage or outrage, or simply go to bed in despair. Shame was above all a status with an almost juridical aspect. The shamed person lost honor, and that loss was palpably observable by others because these others were in fact responsible for the loss of honor by their very way of seeing the shamed person. Being shamed, it was noted, did not necessarily require an observing audience. One needed only to be committed in a serious way to the values and standards of the community in which one claimed membership to feel shame (and to be shamed) for not measuring up to those standards or adhering to those values.[8] The community, however, was crucial in two ways. It was the source of standards and values and it ultimately would be what validated the appropriateness of any person's sentiments of shame. A person might, for instance, feel shame and not be treated as a shamed person. He might think himself not up to snuff, but that view might not be confirmed by others. And if not confirmed by others, this most social of emotions would lack the necessary eliciting forces to maintain the feeling associated with it—at least such would be the economy of shame in face-to-face cultures of honor.

That was then. Today, for some, shame has somewhat different contours. Anthropologists still accept the account I have just given, as do some philosophers.[9] In these literatures shame is described so as to distinguish it from and indeed to oppose it to guilt. Shame is the emotion of a universe that privileges ideas of honor, reputation, and respect, a world in which the public self dwarfs the private self. Its chief sanctions are ridicule and abandonment in its various forms:

exile and outlawry. In contrast, guilt is the emotion of a world of instituted authority, secular and religious, which can punish transgression and sin. Strategies of forgiveness, rather than vindication and revenge, become more permissible in this setting, and are correlated to confession and apology brought about by the workings of an active conscience. Both shame and guilt in this view are more than emotions; they designate social statuses, legitimated by the community and imposed on those whose fear of shame and guilt (the feelings) were insufficient to do the necessary work of social control.

In the psychological literature shame takes on different trappings and emphases. While Piers and Singer define it in such a way as to incorporate the anthropological view into the diction of depth psychology,[10] depth psychology talks about shame in terms of defenses against exhibitionism and voyeurism,[11] condemning it thereby to the marches of the uninteresting and marginalized.[12] The new shame psychologists privatize and trivialize it by making it less an emotion whose paradigmatic context is one of losing or maintaining face against challenges to reputation than the emotion of simply not feeling good about oneself, the feeling of low self-esteem. The social has a very small role in this kind of shame, if it has any at all.[13] The new shame might even be seen as the linchpin of a new politics of the antisocial, in which it is nearly supposed that a person should maintain high self-esteem no matter how inept or offensive he or she might be.°

Despite the new devotion to shame in the psychiatric and self-help trades, in our daily discourse shame does not figure as much as do humiliation and embarrassment, at least insofar as we are likely to use these words in actual speech. Shame is just a little passé except when used in the common collocation "What a shame," where it does not indicate an emotion at all but only certain misfortunes for which "it's too bad that . . ." is equally applicable. If someone were to describe

---

°The public schools of Ann Arbor are committed to virtues of self-esteem in this style. A first grader when asked by her mother how she was doing in school said, "The teacher says I'm doing great, Mom, but to tell you the truth, that's what she always says and I don't know if I am *really* doing well at all." This style of cultivating self-esteem patronizes children, yielding cynicism in the smart ones and deceiving the others, ultimately producing an ignorance not as easily corrigible as more innocent ignorances. Because this ignorance is eventually maintained by self-deception it often produces an effrontery that insists (often rather aggressively) on the excellence of its own mediocrity.

herself as feeling great shame or shamed, the speaker, if a literary type, would in many cases be considered slightly mannered and self-indulgent, or if a religious type, as influenced by an archaic language of penance and sin. There is shame's indelible association with the style of sanctimonious children who point the index finger of one hand scraping it with the index finger of the other at those children they considered rule breakers. The sentiment and style of that shaming gesture finds a close analogue in the parental and schoolmarmish "Shame on you," which is itself just unfashionable enough, kind of proto-archaic, so as to give the modern parent a mild twinge of embarrassment even as she scolds her three-year-old by saying it. The common discourse of shame comes less with "shame" than with "ashamed," where it also takes on itself the tones of parents and teachers, as when it operates as a slightly more acceptable surrogate for "Shame on you" as in "You ought to be ashamed of yourself." In both these cases *shame,* one notes, is not used to indicate a feeling but a status, although the latter instance is somewhat ambiguous on this score. It is in the construction "I am (felt) ashamed that . . ." that we seem to indicate most clearly a feeling, but even here the feeling is not always one that indicates the totalizing emotion of shame as much as regret or embarrassment. Then there is the work that *ashamed* does as an unfelt gesture of stylized conversation, as when one says he is ashamed for not having gotten around to reading Professor X's important contribution to the literature.

Humiliation: The State, the Feeling, and the Fear of It

It is, however, in the way we talk about humiliation that the distinction between an internal feeling and the social fact of an existential state is most clearly made. We have all witnessed what we would refer to as people humiliating themselves without themselves feeling humiliated: the fatuous academic who is too dense to discern that he knows less about the subject on which he is confidently lecturing than the audience he is addressing; Burns's woman with the louse in her hair is another example, but her situation is distinguishable from that of the fatuous lecturer. She would *feel* greatly humiliated if she knew what the observer knows. That after all is clearly indicated:

> O wad some Pow'r the giftie gie us
> To see oursels as others see us!

It wad frae mony a blunder free us,
And foolish notion:
What airs in dress an' gait wad lea'e us,
And ev'n devotion![14]

It is not clear that our pompous lecturer would feel the same mortification if he could learn how others saw him. Such souls have enormous capacities for self-deception, and the views of others, rather
than mortifying him, would simply provide the basis for justifying his
having contempt for them. No mortification is likely to make Burns's
lady give up her fine clothing and other indicia of wealth, but the next
time she goes to church she will undoubtedly take great pains to
comb herself ever so carefully and arrange that the pew behind her
remain unoccupied. Let me expand on these examples just a little
more.

Do we judge the lecturer and the churchgoing woman differently
because she is the victim of the fortuitous actions of a louse and he is
actively humiliating himself as a consequence of purely personal failures of judgment, of talent, and of preparation? I am not sure we do.
It is more than the chance lightings of a louse which led to the
woman's humiliation. She is cursed by being the object of the moralizing envy of poorer people among whom we can count the narrator, and she chose to dress in an inappropriately ostentatious style for
church. If she is not entirely responsible for the envy her wealth
elicits, she is surely completely accountable for the vanity that leads
her to display it in an inappropriate setting. Both she and the academic are vain and guilty of putting on airs. Both of their humiliations
depend on their being complacent, blind to their own inadequacies,
and generally inattentive to the meaning of the particulars of their
self-presentation. They seek deference from others, they mean to cut
figures before others, and in so doing they presume on others; those
others will get even. It is the presumption that enables the humiliation and justifies it. Vanity begs for humiliation.

One of the most salient distinctions between shame and humiliation is that, at root, humiliation depends on the deflation of pretension. Although both shame and humiliation work by lowering, in
contemplating shame the observer is more likely to be moved to pity
than glee.[15] In a rough, but very crucial sense, shame involves tragic
justice, humiliation comic justice.[16] Shame is the stuff of high seriousness, while humiliation often partakes of farce and fabliaux; such is

the case at least from the perspective of third parties. The pathetically vain and vulgarly fastidious Absolon in Chaucer's *Miller's Tale* is humiliated by having to kiss Alisoun's naked arse, but when Antony fled battle because Cleopatra had already fled, his was "an action of such shame" that "experience, manhood, honour, ne'er before did violate so itself" (3.10.22–24). I will return to this theme in much greater detail, for it is, I think, the key insight into what makes the categories of shame and humiliation distinct.

But then there is the *feeling* of humiliation, which can be quite private because it is often only on reflection that we realize that we were or could have been seen as contemptible fools. I venture to say that the feeling of humiliation is most often felt by those who most fear ridicule, fear being seen as fools, in short, fear being humiliated. The feeling and the state then may be related in a perverse if not quite inverse fashion. I don't wish to overstate the case. The fear of ridicule can at times make one look more ridiculous than if one negotiated social life with a little less self-awareness. Julien Sorel provides one example, and the myriad obsessive Dostoyevskian characters other examples. Some people are so in the grip of this fear that they are willing to die rather than risk looking ridiculous. This fear is something qualitatively different from the fear of shame which induces heroic action in feud or in battle; there, courage is at issue, but here it is not in the least bit involved. The fear of humiliation is the fear that causes people to feel greater mortification for being discovered violating norms of body control and decorousness (e.g., passing gas) than for offending against more serious moral and legal norms (cheating on income tax, stealing from the workplace, adultery, betrayal).* Shame occupies itself with the big, the moral, the religious; humiliation tends to be grounded more trivially, engaging the conventional and the decorous (much as embarrassment does), but that triviality seems to bear no relation to the magnitude of averseness it

---

*From what position am I making the judgment of seriousness of the norm if in fact the less serious ones are the ones that produce more emotional discomfort? One of the extraordinary powers of official moral, religious, and legal discourse is to have won for itself the category of the serious. Our viscera, however, seem more willing to accord seriousness to what moral discourse considers the trivial. The trivial world of appearance motivates us more, is inescapably present, and hence takes more commitments of time and energy than the serious world of essences. We will elect people to office who steal, lie, commit adultery, betray friends and values they have professed allegiance to, but not people who stumble out of airplanes.

engenders, or to the magnitude of the vindictiveness used to remedy it. I can think of no better example of the power of the fear of looking foolish, the fear of humiliation (or embarrassment in this case) than this: I know more than one person who has sat quietly choking to near death in a restaurant rather than risk looking silly by frantically gesturing or in any way interrupting the requisite decorum to beg for a Heimlich maneuver. Risking death can be more easily embarked upon than risking being seen as an incompetent fool for violating norms of bodily presentation and public decorum.

The fear of being humiliated can also often lead one to take up postures that are themselves pretensions, thereby making oneself ripe for the deflation that produces the state of humiliation (but in these sensitive souls, also the feeling of humiliation). Being cool or looking cool is asking for humiliation, as much as it is a defense against what it is asking for. A middle-aged academic man who greatly fears humiliation and as such is reserved and proper in the presence of female students, making sure to give no sense that he thinks them sexual beings, nevertheless might suffer humiliation if they do not consider him a sexual being. To this end he carries himself in a fashion that shows himself still physically proud and confident. Now imagine this same soul walking (I might almost say strutting, but that would misrepresent the skill with which the man makes himself look as if he is just walking and nothing more) and having to cross the path of two undergraduate women walking toward him. He does not look at the women, for to do so would be to run the risk of being seen doing so or even of incurring the self-generated hostility of engaging in such pointless folly. But he is keenly aware of their approach nevertheless, because it is the occasion of intense feelings of self-awareness and fear. Fear is perhaps somewhat of an exaggeration. Small trepidation, anxiety, is better. What if they were to laugh just at the moment their path crossed his? How would he be able to explain that laugh and still maintain his self-esteem? Up to now our man has not been humiliated but he fears that he will be, and if they laugh he will *feel* humiliated, if not be so (the latter depends on whether they are indeed laughing at him or not). But if the women do laugh, and they do so because of him, then he will have been humiliated *before* he felt it. That is, his pretension of self-presenting as a sexual being at age fifty in a public occupied by people less than half his age justifies his degradation. Even if they don't laugh he will have to explain to himself his trepidation; the very trepidation reveals him in his own eyes as somewhat obsessively self-referential with a self-conception that is built out of no small amount of pretension. This trepidation itself may subject him to mild feelings of humiliation.

Our man presumably should rethink his strategy. Surely the truly adept fearer of humiliation can avoid a good deal of it and especially that portion of it which comes his way as a consequence of that very strategy. Otherwise he would give his strategy up in despair, or at least such would be the suggestion of the rational choice theorist. Almost. That style of theorist would not give it up in despair but give it up crisply and with confidence in the wisdom of his choice. He would also be a bit better than I am about determining the precise conditions that would dictate giving up on the earlier strategy. He would give it up not simply because the strategy brought with it some unfortunate costs, but only if those costs exceeded the costs of the humiliations that would not have been otherwise avoided. But few outside of social science departments and a few law schools think in such a hyperrational way, and virtually no one lives this way even among those who must think that way as a matter of professional commitment. The commitment to strategies of humiliation avoidance is more than a rational choice. In one view, how we go about avoiding humiliation is us, is our very character. The person who fears humiliation would not be that person if he or she did not fear it. A constant concern to avoid ridicule is not a loose accident or casual adornment lightly adhering to some essential character that underlies it. A person who greatly fears ridicule and humiliation is so significantly defined by that trait as to be likely to have little quantity of self existing outside the trait which would be able to make the decision to jettison it.

Suppose, however, that there are steps the fearer of ridicule could take. His only ameliorative strategy would be to be relentless and brutal in all matters of self-assessment and to avoid studiously any manner of self-presentation which involved pretension or carried with it a more than modest risk of being perceived as pretentious by normal, decent people. But that strategy too is impossible, for pretension is not some essential thing that is insensitive to context. What may pass for normal among a bunch of academics would look pretty silly in a neighborhood working-class bar. Merely the style of clothing could be perceived as pretension. Pretension, in other words, is not only a vice of the pretentious; it is also, to our great chagrin, something that comes with certain territories by the very fact that we live in a hierarchical social world. That is, pretentiousness as a social fact need not require the will to fatuity; it can arise by simple incongruities not always within our control.

"Structural Pretension" and the Relation of Social Status to Humiliation

Here we need to differentiate two phenomena: the first, which was just mentioned, is the pretension of accident, a function of ranked difference, rather than of the active putting on of airs; it is what I call "structural pretension." The second is the somewhat paradoxical possibility of a sort of inverted pretentiousness that may arise from the failure to make certain small adjustments in one's own mode of self-presentation in order to accommodate the sensibilities of others. Academics or patricians who talk with excessively latinate diction to the barber or hair stylist may congratulate themselves on just being themselves, but the setting makes that less a virtue of integrity and truth to one's self than a vice of pomposity and social ineptitude.

The refusal to make changes in our normal diction, in the quality of our vowels and consonants, are strategies of distancing. When made, such adjustments are hardly the stuff of pretension or of being someone you are not; they are, rather, the stock in trade of skillful practitioners of face-to-face encounter, the very stuff of what we might call the style of democratic politeness and amiability. These are the signs and substance of the recognition of another as someone worthy of respect, in which respect takes the form of concession and compromise from one's own default position in consideration that one supposes that the other is making the same kind of small compromises in one's own direction. The compromises must, however, be small. If they are exaggerated they run the risk of mocking the other or of making the compromiser look foolish and pretentious as a hypercorrector if compromising in an upward direction, or a hypocorrector if going the other way. There are many types of linguistic hypercorrection. It applies not only to word choice but also to vowel quality and to grammatical structure. It is saying "It is I" or more vulgarly "between him and I." It is the pronunciation of *new* with a palatal glide (*nee-you*). Hypocorrection is a coinage to describe the practice of an educated person who adds too many goddamns, fucks, and son of a bitches, as rhythmic filler.[17] It is the affectation of rap jive by whites or drawled vowels by northerners. Certain usages are in a state of flux, like the status of contractions in academic prose. These are considered hypocorrection by those who avoid them, while those who use them consider not doing so a sign of a fussy hypercorrection.

This set of issues, however, is different from those raised by structural pretension, the pretentiousness that is an inherent consequence of ranked social difference. Some may object that structural pretension is not pretension at all, but simply class or ethnic suspicion imposed by people's uncharitable misinterpretations of the intentions of group outsiders. It is not just that, however, for the misinterpretations are not quite symmetrical. What I mean to capture is the difference in the figure a tweedy academic cuts in a working-class bar compared to the figure a working-class person cuts in a bar frequented almost entirely by academics.[18] Structural pretension is not merely a matter of a fowl among fish. It depends on the fowl occupying, by the usual social conventions of status demarcation, the higher position. The setting must be one in which the fowl has no moral or social right to assert the higher status, but also is likely to be seen as making such a claim because the context calls special attention to the status differential. In another view, structural pretension involves the (mis)interpretation by the lower-ranked person of the upper-ranked person's presumed intentions regarding his self-presentation. The only evidence of pretension, after all, is the accident of being out of place. Yet being out of place (and not knowing you are) is one way of understanding what pretension is. Still, it is not hard to distinguish the innocent assumption that you can unobtrusively occupy space in which others find you intrusive from the arrogation of a rank that you are not up to filling.

Both structural pretension and the usual conception of pretension as vanity depend on the judgments of observers, but they differ in the modes of intentionality imputed to the first party. In the pretension of vanity the pretentious one is completely responsible for the view observers are taking of him, whereas structural pretension is more a matter of accident. With the pretension of vanity we feel that the observer is correctly interpreting a consciously intended style of self-presentation which indicates some kind of moral failing, taking *moral* here to comprehend the claim we make on others not to be the object of their contempt. The vain pretender is not only claiming a role he is not entitled to but he is botching the job of filling the role he claims. It is for the community to determine the social position to which you justifiably belong. Your job is to know where they are likely to put you, based on both your knowledge of the relevant standards of judgment and how you stack up in relation to them.* And you will be punished if you are unable to do so. It is the temerity, stupidity, or whatever not to know where you stand and then to claim a higher place for yourself than you deserve which makes others see you as humiliating yourself. You make yourself the justifiable object of their ridicule and scorn. As an aside, it should be noted that the grounds of justification of the humiliator's role varies widely across cultures. By one account the humiliator can claim the moral high ground if he goes after either knaves or fools, but only for those things that such humiliation may work to improve or prevent in the future. In other words, it is only corrigible pretense and presumption that justifies satiric acid. Thus Swift in his own obituary:

> His Satyr points at no Defect,
> But what all Mortals may correct;
> For he abhorr'd that senseless Tribe,
> Who call it Humour when they jibe:
> He spared a Hump or crooked Nose,
> Whose Owners set not up for Beaux.
> True genuine Dulness mov'd his Pity,
> Unless it offer'd to be witty.
> Those, who to their Ignorance confess'd,
> He ne'er offended with a Jest;
> But laugh'd to hear an Idiot quote,
> A Verse from Horace learn'd by Rote.
> ("Verses on the Death of Dr. Swift," vv. 467–78)

Swift raises an issue that will be partially addressed below: the place of bodily defect in this whole moral and emotional economy. Physical defects can evoke shame, humiliation, and embarrassment in their possessor, and awkwardness, embarrassment, pity, and laughter in others. It took a long time for Christianity and civilized manners to delegitimate the delight the gods took in Hephaestus's deformities so that Swift could take pride in not stooping to laugh at such things.[19]
    I have painted a picture here that makes pretension a matter of

---

*The community's view, however, is not necessarily just, and sometimes should be resisted. But even in those settings it still behooves the seeker of social justice to know his enemy and to know how his enemy sees him, even if he disputes the right of the enemy to define him morally and socially. But clearly I am dealing with micro issues here, not the big questions of social justice.

one's being more a fool than a knave. The way we talk about humiliation as making a fool of oneself suggests the same. But we also give
the pretentious very little quarter. We hold them to an account that
suggests that we think of them as knaves too. It is not just that they
botch the job of seeing themselves as others see them, it is that they
seem to be botching rather slyly in their own favor.[20] The person who
pretends to less than he deserves is not scorned and ridiculed in the
same way. Such people may be the objects of pity, but are unlikely to
feel humiliated for being so pitied. In the Christian scheme of things
they should be admired unless their lack of recognition of their own
merit is also a form of despair.

That so much of humiliation involves the unmasking of pretension
should not imply that it is a judgment made only by superiors resent-
ing the claim of undeserving lower-ranked persons to admission to
their group. Pretension can be recognized and unveiled by lower-
status people. Think of how employees see the truth about their
employers and servants of their masters, much more often than the
employers and masters are likely to discover the truth about their
employees and servants. We could even risk the following propositions: the high are less likely to see the lower as humiliating themselves (mostly because the high often do not even see the low) than
the low are to *feel* humiliated in the presence or on account of the
high. And conversely, but with less confidence, the high are more
likely to *be* humiliated—that is to be seen as humiliating themselves—in the eyes of the low (unlike the high with regard to the low,
the low do indeed *see* the high), than the high are likely to *feel*
humiliated in the presence of the low.[21] One of the pleasures, I would
imagine, that people who belong to minority groupings experience is
seeing the members of the majority culture humiliate themselves with
such insistent regularity. It provides the substance of revenge for the
humiliation they may occasionally *feel* at the hands of the majority.[22]

These propositions seem reasonable only if one admits the possibility of exceptions (I was careful to cast them as likelihoods). The
teacher who gets drunk with students and tries to be one of the guys
can surely be seen to have humiliated himself, but he would also, with
the advent of sobriety, *feel* humiliation, and indeed shame too: shame
for violating the standards of decorous professorial and professional
behavior and humiliation for maintaining the pretense that he is just
one of the guys. But just as often, with higher status comes no small
amount of complacency about how the low see you. The teacher may

feel no humiliation whatsoever, feeling instead rather magnanimous for his willingness to confer on his students the honor of such intimacy. He may in fact feel no humiliation and still feel some shame for having violated norms his colleagues maintain about how far out of role one can allow oneself to be with students. For the higher-status person to *feel* humiliation in the presence of the lower these lower must usually have some kind of connection with him, some continuing relationship, such that part of his definition of self depends on their deference.[23]

Unlike shame, humiliation can run across the closed boundaries of the honor group. In fact, humiliation is the emotional experience of being caught inappropriately crossing group boundaries into territory one has no business being in. *If shame is the consequence of not living up to what we ought to, then humiliation is the consequence of trying to live up to what we have no right to.* Because humiliation often involves boundary transgression, we can feel it in dealings with people with whom we are not competing for honor, even in front of those we deny the capacity for honor. These are not the people, however, we are likely to feel shame in front of. Thus adults only too poignantly feel humiliation before children and adolescents, as do teachers before students.

But the academic in the working-class bar manifestly does not feel humiliated. He may feel awkward, a little anxious, even somewhat apprehensive and fearful, but not humiliated, as a first-order matter. He might feel somewhat humiliated or mild shame for being afraid or anxious, but not for being out of place. The academic would surely *be* humiliated as a first-order matter if he tried a little too hard to fit in, was a little too hearty, a little too vulgar, a little too familiar; and he would *feel* humiliated if he discerned that he was rebuffed in his efforts at rapprochement. The awkwardness he feels initially is partially a function of his awareness of the structural pretensions that his mere presence gives rise to. He hopes that they won't think him prissy, effeminate, or whatever else types like them would be inclined to think of types like him. But the pretension he wills and which could lead to his humiliation is the pretension of thinking he can belong so easily just by dressing down, by talking a little tough, by drinking a lot of beer, or whatever. Do the regular patrons believe that the academic who is out of place is humiliating himself just by being there, even without his making any undignified moves of solidarity? They may, but I suspect not. He may be beneath notice, or if noticed be regarded with some small contempt and loathing, but he also may be observed with distrust, for it may be that the patrons suspect that he is there to slum it, to do research, ultimately, that is, to try to humiliate *them*. In the face of the very real presence of structural pretension, the best strategy in such a dolorous world may be to stay on your own turf or to get in and out of the other's presence as quickly and as inconspicuously as possible when necessity demands forays outside one's own group. Structural pretension is avoidable only if observers and the observed share all of each other's superficial signs and values. By superficial, I mean the commitments we make to such things as styles of personal appearance, modes of amusement, quantity and type of preferred drink, and to the linguistic indicators of education, class, and geography. The "deep" commitments of clearly moral content do not usually carry the same moral and social import in face-to-face encounters as these superficial features do.[24]

Humiliation and Humility

Feeling humiliated, then, may or may not correlate with the state of humiliation. The incorrigibility of certain pompous souls is the proof of the pudding. The very faculty that allows them to humiliate themselves without feeling humiliated, without picking up on any of the signals in the eyes and attitudes of others, to be so impervious to what passes as an honorable character, is not quite tautologically the inability to feel humiliation. The previous sentence illustrates a difference in how we talk about shame and how we talk about humiliation. If someone is incapable of feeling shame, we call him or her shameless. But the pompous or just inept buffoon whose threshold of humiliation is too high ever to deter him from his fatuousness is not thought of as humiliationless. We have no analogous verbal form to *shameless* to describe him and, unlike the shameless person, we still grant him the capacity to offend, which is why we are able to take a not too perverse pleasure in the comic aspects of his state of humiliation.

Freud devoted some attention to words that mean themselves and their opposites.[25] In English, *shame*, if not quite meaning its opposite, comes pretty close to containing within it antithetical claims. *Shame* refers not only to the unpleasant emotion and the state of disgrace involved in situations in which one should feel that emotion but also to the capacity to resist the disgrace that gives rise to the feeling.[26] This is the meaning of shame when we say that someone is without shame or has no shame, or is shameless. Shame as the capacity to resist shame is only rarely if ever attributed positively to someone in modern usage; our usage always laments or condemns its absence. When we wish to indicate its presence we speak of the "sense of shame."[27] The capacity of shame to mean the consequence of viciousness and the virtue that defends against it is not shared by humiliation. The defense against humiliation is not a capacity called humiliation or a sense of humiliation. It is rather the fear of humiliation or perhaps, more subtly, it is humility. Both words—*humiliation* and *humility*—come from the same Latin root, *humilis*, meaning low, lowly, which in turn is derived from *humus*, meaning ground. In their earlier histories both words were intimately connected to one style of Christian moral discourse until well into the eighteenth century, whereas only humility still remains an active part of that discourse today.

There is more that motivates humility, clearly, than the fear of humiliation, although I would not be surprised to find this fear the motivating force of more humility than most have been willing to admit. Humility can protect against humiliation by several mechanisms, depending on how the content of humility is articulated. Humility might be understood as the personal commitment never to pretend to more than what the most ungenerous, but not irrational, public assessment of our merit would allow us as our due. This view is not very satisfactory; it is much too narrow. It reduces humility to little more than a strategy someone adopts to avoid humiliation by never risking the possibility of seeming pretentious or fatuous. Genuine humility, we want to believe, has transcended this kind of strategizing. But humility always finds itself in curious binds. If I wear my hairshirt under my rich garments we have one kind of pretension, the pretension of Thomas à Becket. If I wear my hairshirt openly I am pretentious in another way.[28] In a religious and moral scheme that ranks people by how humble they are, the whole game of status achievement ends up being played out in a kind of inverted and masochistic way, but played out none the less for that, so that eventually people were treated to the spectacle of pus-drinking saints.[29] In that kind of world, humility is no sure strategy to protect people against being or feeling humiliated for the exposure of their pretensions; it can seldom be disinterested and can never be above suspicion; it cannot avoid the suggestion of hypocrisy.

Humility might be supposed to be that virtue which accepts the possibility of suffering humiliation for one's humility but accepts such suffering calmly as one's due. As such, it intimately partakes of patience. If I am humble then I accept status degradation, if it should come, as my due and as something that does not even displease me. Hence I do not *feel* humiliated, only rightly humbled. But this stance gets rid of conscious strategizing only at the price of making the humble masochistic. There must be more to the story.

Most of us know some genuinely humble people. They impress us as decent, patient, strong, even tough, who if they are self-aware are rather limitedly so. They pretend to nothing they do not have and they genuinely do seem to possess a modest way of self-presentation which does not have the least air of the strategic about it. Their humility is often accompanied by a simple decency that can have its own substantial unstudied charm. As long as their humility doesn't descend to the morbidity of obsessively and perversely undervaluing their virtues, people humble in this way have a near airtight defense against being humiliated and, for the most part, against feeling humiliated too, at least for those classes of humiliations which are a function of posturing and pretension. They would not be completely immune, however. We need not suppose them such lifeless stones that they would not feel humiliated for being stood up on a date. And there are still the humiliations that share with embarrassment the capacity to humiliate simply by being in the wrong place at the wrong time, as the victim of accidents over which they have no control.

Embarrassment Distinguished: A Parable

Like shame and humiliation, embarrassment is also an emotion of self-attention and self-consciousness.[30] All three suppose some relation to a social world in which one's actions, one's appearance, one's very being are being judged.[31] All three are unpleasant and all three figure prominently in the social and psychic mechanisms of social control.[32] I have been at some small pains up to now to carve out a realm for humiliation which distinguishes it from shame but at the cost of giving it some features generally associated with embarrassment. If shame's genre is tragedy, and humiliation's is comedy, what could embarrassment be if not also comic? But comedy is a very broad genre and capable of welcoming a variety of emotional styles into its embrace. Humiliation is dark, embarrassment light. Humiliation is rough justice, embarrassment a gentle slap on the wrist. Embarrassment is a very close relative of amusement, for it takes only a very subtle shift in context, distance, or involvement to turn embarrassing situations into causes for mirth both for observers *and* for the person embarrassed. But one senses that if humiliation has anything to do with amusement, that amusement would be dark indeed. The observers would get to indulge their malice, while the victim would suffer his fury and chagrin. The delight we take in the discomfiture of the pompous can never be one of simple mirth. There is always a tinge of brutality in it, the delight of kicking someone who is down, a delight we can indulge in because the justice and desert of the humiliation excuses us from having to make excuses for our failure of fellow-feeling. We can even congratulate ourselves on the labor we devote to the administration of such justice as a service to the community.

To be sure, humiliation is often used in common parlance to indicate an intense form of embarrassment. This is the humiliation of the unzipped fly in front of a class, sweat stains under the arms, falling on the ice, among others. Humiliations of this sort are like embarrassment in that they deal not with the seriously moral, the great and grave standards, but with adherence to the conventions of good manners and proper attention to the body and its excrescences.[33] We also say humiliation to mean intensely felt moments of shame. Such would be the humiliation of being discovered stealing from the offering dish. Here I think we can still distinguish between the sensation of being exposed in a furtive act from the sensation of knowing yourself as a person who does shameful things. The former is an intense humiliation, the latter shame.

But I think that an area of the comic which is peculiar to humiliation and distinguishable from embarrassment can be carved out. I speak now of the feeling, not the state. Consider those situations in which one must accept quite privately that one is not quite at the status level one thought oneself to be. Here is one: I was recently introduced to an academic whose work I knew. He was perhaps a little further along in his career than I was in mine, but not so much that I didn't think that most third parties would consider us roughly equals. We shook hands. He was polite and indicated that he knew who I was, although it was clear to me that he had never read any of my work. I could explain that to myself because we were in different disciplines and I had no reason to think that he should read about saga Iceland. After our introduction we engaged in pleasant conversation for some ten minutes, shook hands vigorously on parting, and gave each other hearty farewells registering our pleasure at finally meeting. These indications were mutual.

Then came a moment some two months later. We were in a similar setting and I looked toward him to catch from him the indication that a greeting was in order. He looked ever so briefly at me with the look of one who desires to avert his gaze quickly because caught impermissibly looking at someone he did not know. In other words, he looked away to avoid what from his point of view was staring at me. My emotion at being so eminently forgettable was one of humiliation. It clearly was neither shame nor embarrassment. I had no defense against it. After all, I had remembered him, and he did not remember me, at least he did not remember what I looked like. Presumably I had lapsed back into the status of someone he knew about but did not recognize.[34]

He had humiliated me in the only way he could have and have made me *feel* humiliated. A conscious snub would have been an insult.[35] It would have engendered indignation or vengefulness in me, but not humiliation. If he had wanted to snub me, he would have had to make a small indication that he indeed recognized me and that that was the reason I was not being greeted. But I observed no signs of recognition at all. Although some snubs can be humiliating, they are less so than being shown to be of no consequence. The insult was not that I was not deemed worthy of insult but that such deeming had never taken place. This could be restated in another way that brings embarrassment into the picture. *I felt humiliated because I knew that he would be embarrassed if he learned that he knew me.* The humiliating thing about this incident after all is that he intended nothing. He could not even have intended not to remember me, because that would involve him in the self-defeating activity of remembering to forget.

My humiliation was not just his doing. I could not have felt humiliated if I had not recognized him.* I felt humiliated because of my private knowledge that he had beaten me in a game of deference and relative status adjustment. He had made enough of an impression on

---

*Suppose a third-party observer, however, who knows that both the first and second parties have met each other, and that neither of them has remembered the other, who then informs the two of them of this fact. Each actor would feel humiliated by the knowledge that the other had not remembered him even though each had done the other the same turn. In fact, the mutual nonrecognition would force them to have to see themselves as being as self-absorbed as the person whose self-absorption they found offensive.

me for me to recall him, but my public appearance had made no such impression on him. It was impossible for me to ignore that I had lost. Humiliation (the feeling) can thus be played out without a real observing other, or an other that intends to humiliate.[36] But am I in a state of humiliation? It seems I feel that I am, thus the feeling. Although there is no actual observer of my state, I am in effect that observer, seeing myself as others would see me, others, that is, who are as ungenerous as I myself am being, others who magically possess my knowledge that the person I remember has forgotten me but who also can see what it is about me that makes me so forgettable. We might, nonetheless, still wish to distinguish between the state of humiliation triggered by a hypothetical observer and that of really being seen as humiliated. For it seems that although the feeling of humiliation always depends on believing oneself to be in a state of humiliation, the subject's judgment might not be confirmed by real observers. The subject could simply be being too hard on himself.

Some would deny that they would feel humiliation in the situation I have just described. Clearly the degrees of self-consciousness and sensitivity to points of honor vary greatly among people. But some of us who deny the feeling might only be indicating the success of certain remedial strategies we employ in order to misunderstand the event so as to keep our self-esteem intact. Consider the move of telling ourselves stories that might excuse the offense. Some stories desperately (and pathetically) try to excuse the other: no wonder he didn't recognize me, I just had my hair cut, or I was wearing a coat and tie that day. Other stories adopt the style of the fox and the grapes and take on a mildly vindictive tone as they seek to redefine the other: he's a real pompous ass (in which case we are trying to see him as humiliating himself for having failed to honor the conventions governing competent interpersonal interaction); I always thought his work was rather dull and uninspired. Soon one finds oneself actually talking that way when the other's name comes up. We may even succeed by such moves in convincing ourselves that the other is of little account and thus eventually pave the way for repressing the whole humiliating event.[37]

On a somewhat smaller scale we all dish out and suffer on a weekly if not a daily basis the lesser humiliations (they are not shames or embarrassments) of unreturned phone calls, the promised call that never occurs (both in and not in dating situations), the noninvitation. Some of these petty things do not raise any emotion beyond a brief bit of wonder or quizzicalness or depressed acceptance. But depending on the precise context, the stakes might be just high enough (and they need not be very high at all to get over the threshold) to make us feel unmistakably humiliated.

These incidents do not embarrass. They hit too deep; they call too much of our being to account and are too deflating; they catch us up in overvaluing ourselves, rather than in just being inept. More exactly, they catch us assuming that others value us as much as we value them or as much as we value ourselves. This is often the very stuff of presumption. These incidents do not make us feel shame either. They do not involve the humiliated one's breach of the kind of norm which drives the feeling of shame. We are guilty only of a minor misjudgment about where we belong in our social world; it is not that we have failed to measure up to important community standards of conduct.

There is yet another way to distinguish this state of humiliation from embarrassment. What causes us embarrassment almost invariably will be looked at by its sufferer at some point as the substance of a funny, if at times, ribald tale. Much of genuinely amusing conversation involves the confession of embarrassing things one has done, or the embarrassing things one has witnessed which caused one to "catch" the embarrassed feeling. Humiliating incidents, however, will cause us pain to recount even years later. These are the things we prefer never to reveal about ourselves, unless we find ourselves in a strangely Dostoyevskian mood.[38] The likelihood of retelling (at least voluntarily retelling) is a very good indicator of whether something has passed from the realm of the embarrassing into the realm of the humiliating on the intensity scale. When we say that we were humiliated by a fall on the ice in front of several bypassers or by unflattering remarks we made about a person to his or her best friend without knowing they were friends, the fact that we will tell these stories within days to the laughter of ourselves and others is a sign we were not humiliated, only embarrassed. Saying we are humiliated in those contexts only indicates the intensity of the embarrassment, not the qualitative change that makes it dark, unutterable, and humiliating.

The Embarrassment of Praise and the Discomfort of Doing Good

One thing that clearly marks off embarrassment, as we understand it, from humiliation and shame is that we can be embarrassed by sincere praise, but it would be a strange person indeed who would be shamed or humiliated by it. At least such is the case when there is agreement as to the norms governing what is praiseworthy and the rules for assigning praise: we can praise a five-year-old for dressing herself, but not an adult without mocking. There must also be agreement on the acceptance of certain modesty conventions. Cultures vary greatly regarding the acceptability of giving and receiving public praise, and in those in which it is expected one would not be embarrassed in receiving it. We can also imagine that a person would feel humiliated by praise if he knew that it was undeserved and he felt that his lack of merit was also known by some of those present. But these provisos aside, the general rule for us is that praise embarrasses but does not shame or humiliate.

If praise for deeds done can embarrass, many people feel painful awkwardness and embarrassment, but not humiliation, *doing* certain kinds of good deeds. We unfortunately live in a world in which doing the right thing can provoke self-consciousness, so that often there is no way to avoid embarrassment for, say, helping a blind person across the street, giving money to a beggar, assisting someone who has fallen on the ice and who either does not have the grace or is too pained to make light of it. Why does helping the blind or an obviously handicapped person cause embarrassment? Its source is more than just negotiating the risk of insult in offering what can be construed as charity to a person who wishes no such meddling kindness, for the embarrassment often continues after you and the person you are helping have settled that matter. You strain to make conversation that tries to deny that help is being given, which is only slightly less awkward than not being able to find anything to say in the first place. Might we also fear looking ridiculous to third parties? Why should we fear looking foolish for nonmeddling assistance, especially when we have been raised to believe such actions praiseworthy? Is it a breach of certain modesty conventions to offer aid when there are others present who are not offering it? Or is it because others are not offering it that we doubt what the norm is that governs the situation? Maybe minding one's own business trumps helping others. The virtue of the Good Samaritan can easily be the intrusive vice of the officious meddler if undertaken a little too eagerly; it can make one look like a professional do-gooder.[39]

I suspect that there are several variables at work here. The type of emergency seems to make a difference. The person who dives into a river to pull out a child who has fallen through the ice feels no embarrassment. The necessary haste of the decision and the risk incurred by the rescuer work to obviate embarrassment. More than severe emergency is involved, however, for helping a child cross the street is not embarrassing either. Children are by definition members of a status that allows and even requires solicitude. They are by definition people who need help and therefore helping them can be accomplished with minimal awkwardness.° Perhaps most of the awkwardness of helping an adult is that adults aren't supposed to need help crossing streets. Adults are by status and definition people able to cross streets without crossing guards. Adults who cannot do these things for themselves confuse, to our evident distress, the integrity of the categories by which we understand the world.

It also seems that certain types of victims are "untouchables": their victimization makes them, in effect, pariahs.[40] The condition of untouchability can be very brief. A dignified elderly man who falls on the ice has it only for a few moments after getting up and rearranging himself. A blind person, however, is more permanently cursed. Our embarrassment, then, seems to be embarrassment at our intimacy with their shame. At some level we feel that their condition should not be presented publicly, just as the shame of nakedness, excretion, spousal squabbling should not be presented publicly. The embarrassment also owes something to the need to touch the other. We would not feel as foolish helping someone by making a telephone call or changing their tire as by picking them up off the ground or helping them across the street. We are embarrassed because their condition puts us on the spot, puts us in a quandary of not knowing what to do. Even a blind person walking toward us on the street creates anxiety and embarrassment. We feel that the very condition of another's distress makes a demand on us, an importuning one at that, no matter how we resolve it. We thus can balance the shame we feel by turning a blind eye to the person in distress against the embarrassment we feel when we come to their assistance. Of course all these sentiments will depend on the race, class, age, gender, and general presentability of both actors. Males helping women, for instance, are always suspect unless the age difference obviates certain sexual anxieties. And so on.

°Helping children who are not your own, however, has recently become a ground for adult awkwardness: being nice to children in need might type you as a child molester. Yet we continue to help, hoping we have developed sufficient signs of normality, decency, and disinterest that we manage to maintain a respectable front. See generally Goffman, *Relations in Public*.

Contagious Embarrassment and Vicarious Emotion

Several writers have noted that embarrassment provides the conditions for generating more of it.[41] Your first embarrassment represents a failure of poise, which failure embarrasses you further, especially if you pride yourself on your self-possession. There are times, however, when the loss of poise is exactly the right move. This might be, for instance, one of the best ways of handling embarrassing praise. Goffman puts it exactly right: "When an individual, receiving a compliment, blushes from modesty, he may lose his reputation for poise but confirm a more important one, that of being modest."[42] Embarrassment can also serve as the best remedy for itself, as when my embarrassability does all the work of apologizing for my faux pas by showing myself as a properly socialized person who recognizes faux pas as faux pas.

It has been frequently observed that embarrassment is characterized by infectiousness; it is catching. It also can be experienced vicariously.[43] These are different phenomena. When you catch embarrassment you are embarrassed by witnessing another's presently felt embarrassment. When you experience it vicariously, you are imagining yourself in the position of the other and feeling her embarrassment as if you were her. In this latter case, it is not necessary that she actually feel embarrassment for you to feel it vicariously; but she, of course, must feel it if you are to catch it from her. Do shame and humiliation behave in the same way? Humiliation and shame are not contagious in the way or to the same degree that embarrassment is. In fact, humiliation, rather than causing humiliation in others, is more likely to cause pity, indignation, embarrassment, or amusement; the precise emotion depends variously on how identified we are with the humiliated one or how much we think he is aware of being humiliated, that is, how much he feels humiliated. The comedian who isn't funny, the teacher who doesn't know what he is talking about, the beauty queen who can't disguise her lack of talent in the talent portion of the pageant, do not humiliate us or make us feel humiliated. They embarrass, amuse, or are pitiable in a nontragic sense. *Our own embarrassment is often our best indication that we have judged others to be humiliating themselves.*

Although we experience vicarious shame and humiliation, we do not usually do so in the easy manner in which we experience vicarious anger, indignation, or embarrassment.[44] The shame many Americans felt at the country's involvement in the Vietnam war was shame of the first order. Nor would my feeling of shame for the actions of Lieutenant Calley be an example of vicarious shame, but of shame as an American. In the close group identifications of Mediterranean-style honor systems, a sister's lack of virtue will be both her and her brother's shame, but the cultural paradigm makes the sister's lack of virtue a cause not of her brother's vicarious feeling of shame as if he were her, but of his own shame for having such a sister and for having failed in protecting her. What of the teenager the very existence of whose parents embarrasses him? The poor soul, constrained to eat out with his parents, experiences the shame he thinks his father should feel but doesn't when the father sends back the steak because it is too rare. Surely, however, the larger component of his discomfort is not vicarious at all but simply the shame of having such shamefully clueless parents. And consider a Jew's possible response to Ivan Boesky's or Woody Allen's newsworthy failings. This shame is vicarious, unless it is motivated by self-hatred, in which case it is a first-order shame of belonging to such a group. And as for vicarious humiliation: parents feel it for their children, recalling similar anguish in their own childhood and adolescence, although concern, pity, disgust, anger, outrage, or whatever often intervenes so quickly as to prevent the experience of vicarious humiliation in the clearly identifiable way vicarious embarrassment is experienced; and children feel it for parents once they have learned to see them as people rather than as enemies. Another example: one of the more excruciating experiences for academics who have maintained close friendships with non-academics is seeing how friends from one camp deal with those from the other. One feels painful humiliation for the nonacademic friend's hypercorrecting and trying to sound "intellectual" and for the academic friend's hypocorrecting and botching it badly as they both desperately try to get on with each other for your sake. It seems to come down to this: shame and humiliation can be felt vicariously, but both (humiliation more than shame) seem to require a closer connection between the parties than embarrassment does. We can feel embarrassed for anyone we observe making a fool of himself, but we usually reserve feeling vicarious shame and humiliation for those we care about.

Embarrassing, Shaming, and Humiliating Another

The focus up to now has been on the person shamed, humiliated, or embarrassed. Let us shift perspective to examine some of the meanings of intentionally acting so as to inflict these emotional states on another. To intend to embarrass someone else has a distinctly different sociology than intending to humiliate or shame another has. These last two suggest the tough work of imposing negative social sanction, or the aggressive and hostile challenge in the game of honor, or the perversity of sadism. To shame is serious business. Shaming someone is usually understood to be more formal, more regularized, more directed to the maintenance of specific community norms than humiliating someone is. If the work of shaming is degradation of status, the work of humiliation (not in the sense of the torture chamber) is deflation of pretension. Shaming operates by stripping someone of a status she had some right to before the particular failing, whereas humiliation destroys the illusion of having belonged at all. Humiliation is what happens to Malvolio, not what happens to Coriolanus. Above all, one does not normally count a humiliator or a shamer as a friend, although the shamer, but not the humiliator, may legitimately play that role as parent, teacher, or other authority figure.

These instances contrast greatly with the raillery, sometimes tasteful and in good fun and sometimes misdirected and inept, which so often accompanies the intent to embarrass. This is the stuff of friendship, amusement, and conviviality.[45] This is teasing, tweaking, razzing. This is the kind of work which makes for laughter and genuine amusement. Some people are adept as teasers, some not. Those who aren't but who lack the self-knowledge not to engage in it will usually suffer ostracism and be controlled, not by being the object of embarrassment but by being the target of humiliation or even shame. Some people are adept at being teased. They are those who subscribe to the norms of being a good sport and accept being embarrassed for the general mirth of the multitude. Those who are not good sports will also be ostracized, especially if they are also teasers, whether adept or inept. The prime motivation for intending embarrassment in this kind of setting is usually understood to be to provide general amusement, not to degrade the object of the teasing. There may be a deeper hostile motivation to this sort of play, but play it is, bearing the necessary markers of unseriousness and all the other signs of conviviality and good will which mark the occasion as an amiable one. In this, it is not unlike gift exchange. Like gift exchange, it demands reciprocity. The embarrasser should take his turn at being embarrassed. But in actual practice, the real skills of being a clever teaser and the sweetness of disposition needed for being a good sport are rather unevenly distributed, so that the good teaser usually teases while the good sport takes it. Reciprocity in this situation requires not that the good sport tease the teaser as much as he gets teased but that when he does score on the teaser the magnitude of resulting hilarity will tend to make up the general unevenness in the account books. We have all noticed that the sallies of the usual butt of the jokes are often granted greater laughter than the actual wit of the remark deserves. The audience is doing some small justice here in making sure that the accounts do not get too out of balance. And if the habitual butt of the jokes is not up to making any comeback, it is not unusual for members of the audience to tease the teaser, likewise often eliciting more laughter than their remarks by themselves deserve. I am assuming a community of equals here. The rules change whenever a higher-status person teases a lower-status person. In these settings the higher-status person's sallies of wit are usually accompanied by formulaic laughter motivated in part by the nervousness of the lower-status person, who fears what it would mean not to laugh (this is the laughter of students or employees for the lame attempts at humor offered by teachers or bosses). Mingled with this laughter is also the more boisterous, even heartfelt laughter of the unconscious flatterer and worshiper of authority. Higher-status people need never be all that funny to get their laughs.

The tone and official intention of banter and raillery are very different from the tone and intention of humiliating and shaming someone. If there is a concern with justice-as-fairness in raillery, that justice is not the dark sanctioning social justice of pretense deflation and status degradation. The style of justice in convivial banter is characterized by the will to do equity, the justice of humiliation by the will to punish. Speaking roughly, we can type the shamer as authority, the humiliator as enemy, and the embarrasser as friend.

One might object that the embarrassment that attends amiable teasing is not embarrassment at all because it is not necessarily unpleasant. But even painful embarrassment bears a very close relation to amusement. I indicated earlier that we will retell even excruciatingly embarrassing incidents that befell us because we discern they have the capacity to amuse others as well as ourselves. Usually one recounts one's humiliation not to entertain but rather to confess, to apologize—themselves acts of abasement and humiliation—or otherwise to punish oneself by reexperiencing the pain. The intended embarrassment of convivial raillery is less painful because we are generally prepared to be embarrassed, if not quite prepared for the particular item that will embarrass us. There is mixed up with so much entertainment not just a little bit of *Schadenfreude* at the mild discomfiture of others.

The close connection of embarrassment with entertainment is also evidenced in the attraction certain competitive spectacles have for us. Take figure-skating competition. We watch because it is graceful dance performed by gifted artist-athletes, but we also watch because the performance is structured as a dare to the performer, a dare not to fall. And when the fall comes we feel we want to crawl out of the room in embarrassment (I assume, clearly, that we are watching on TV), but we don't, and we don't because part of the reason we are drawn to the spectacle is that what really entertains us is the risk we undertake in being embarrassed watching the discomfiture of the performer. A fall in the slalom might give us some vicarious discomfiture but that fall is not the sacrilege it is when the performers are unhelmeted, vulnerable—exposed in skimpy outfits designed with an eye more to eros than to function. The scanty clothing of the skater seems to deny cavalierly that falling is a possibility, when in fact falling is nearly all that we and they are thinking about. What is competitive figure staking but a dare not to fall? But figure skating also claims to be art, dance in the high style, and dance introduces certain pretensions and claims about the grace and controllability of the human body. To fall while pretending to the gracefulness of dance: therein lies humiliation. Figure skating's pretension lies in the implicit claim that the artistry of dance can successfully banish the world of awkwardness, of clumsy solid flesh. The more aggressive unmediated athletic events do not make this denial. It is this that makes a fall humiliate the skater but only embarrass the skier. Of course my claim is baldly stated and ignores all kinds of variables.[46] A skier who falls in the flats coasting in would move in the dark direction; a figure skater who fails a jump no one has ever made moves in the lighter direction. My point stands nonetheless.[47]

The Feeling as Felt

It is not easy to separate out the pure feeling of a single emotion from the emotions that help cause it or are felt simultaneously with it or are felt very quickly after the onset of it. The literature, for instance, often discusses shame along with anger,[48] and humiliation and embarrassment along with rage and indignation.[49] As a preliminary matter it would seem obvious that the constellation of emotions surrounding any particular emotion depends on the details of the eliciting conditions of that emotion. Whether rage rather than despair attends humiliation will depend on who or what is perceived to have caused it, or on who or what can plausibly be blamed for causing it, and on what the possibilities of remedying it may be. We should expect rather wide-ranging cultural variation, depending on the rules and practices regarding blame, the permissible objects of blame, the extent to which blame is appropriately focused inward or projected onto others. Humiliation would thus yield different accompanying emotions, which would vary according to how cultural norms and dispositional traits enable people to recognize a certain justice in their own discomfiture.[50] These practices will be intimately connected with cultural rules governing honor and the intensity with which honor is held as a value; they will also be tied up with the various styles in which remedial work is accomplished, whether, for instance, vengeance is preferred to apology and forgiveness, whether ready-made rituals exist to do the work of ameliorating the state of humiliation or of objectifying the feeling so as either to get rid of it or to preserve it.

But let us put all those complications aside and consider them sufficiently dealt with for the moment by simply having been mentioned. Most of us feel humiliation as different from embarrassment and even shame, although we probably would have a harder time *describing* the difference between them than feeling it. All have been identified at times with blushing and with various intensities of the feeling of wishing to disappear. But there are articulatable differences: in embarrassment we are intensely aware of our faces. The face, after all, is often the culprit, as when one speaks amiss or when spinach is stuck between the teeth or when mucus hangs out of the nostril; the face also indicates embarrassment with blushing and linguistic glitches that indicate fluster. And it falls to the face to do the work of amelioration, again by blushing or by apologizing, that is, by deflecting attention from the other bodily areas that might have been the source of embarrassment: these areas are usually associated with sex and excretion, but need not be. We feel giddy, but the feeling is one of lightness, of things rising, like our temperature, the heat in the ears, even a tingling at the surface of the skin.

With humiliation, the feeling may also lead to blushing and rising temperature, but the center of feeling is the gut. The stomach goes queasy, the bowel contracts. One may even feel the sudden urge to defecate which fear produces with the attendant efforts of tightening in the bowel to prevent oneself from doing so. If embarrassment lingers on the surface of the body, humiliation is located at its deepest center. We may even pale in humiliation rather than blush.

Shame, on the other hand, is less acute than humiliation but less superficial than embarrassment. Shame will linger, suffusing one's whole being with the coldness of despair, the sick feeling that comes with knowing we don't make it. Things shut down, everything points down. One wants to sink, one looks down, slouches down.[51] This taxonomy is all too neat—embarrassment/up, humiliation/center, shame/down—but it captures a rough tendency.

In spite of the difficulty language has with pinpointing sensation descriptively, most people can discern the differences in most of the feelings they have once the feeling is contextualized sufficiently. Yet many unpleasant feelings that we are quite capable of distinguishing from one another during the events that elicit them often appear as an undifferentiable generic anxiety or nervousness when they assault us during insomniacal nights. There is also the fact that people often do not pin a formal name on the emotion they are experiencing until they later reflect on the situation. Certain cultural scenarios take over and tell us what the rightly sentient and properly socialized being should have felt, and these scenarios will have a large effect on how we ultimately come to articulate the feeling. We do not, however, have to wait for moments to recollect in tranquility for these scenarios to influence our perceptions of the event; they also give us road maps suggesting how to feel in the very middle of the emotion-generating activity.

Rituals of Humiliation and Shame

Even if we have now carved out an area for humiliation independent of shame and embarrassment, the three share, as I have indicated at the outset, significant points of contact, and on occasion our usages do not distinguish all that precisely among them. Yet these three words are hardly synonymous, and common usage gives each a very different feel. They can even be used more formally to capture real differences among certain ritualized practices. In what follows I distinguish between two kinds of humiliation ritual on the one hand—rituals of self-abasement and rituals of initiation—and shaming rituals on the other. Consider, for instance, the following cases and how they variously make use of combinations of shame, humiliation, and embarrassment to effect their ends.

The Indian ritual of sitting dharna is a classic instance of a humiliation ritual of self-abasement, variants of which can be found in many cultures. In sitting dharna, low-status claimants grovel on the doorstep of or in front of high-status benefactors and debase themselves in an exaggerated display, indeed a parody, of humiliation by tearing hair, befouling themselves, wailing, and begging. The ritual is a grotesque comedy and plays off the ability of people who are humiliating themselves to engender embarrassment in others. For the potential benefactor, the embarrassment is generated by watching someone disgrace herself, but the ritual also generates the embarrassment of being put on the spot.[52] The substance of this latter embarrassment is the fear of being shamed for not conforming to the norms of generosity and *noblesse oblige* by granting the request of the groveler.[53] This ritual functions, in effect, by threatening to shame. Adopting the perspective of the high-status actor, we might call it a shaming ritual. But if described from the lower-status claimant's point of view, it is a ritual of humiliation, because it is she who must play the fool by violating the norms of decorous public comportment. There is good reason to privilege that perspective because, for one thing, the shame, if generated, is parasitic on the display of humiliation; and for another, it is the lower-status claimant who determines the timing, location, and object of the ritual. It is her ritual.[54]

The Icelandic sagas, as usual, supply a wonderful and typically tough-minded variant, one that I have written about elsewhere at great length. It involves dismembering corpses for use in a ceremony that compels a higher-status person to take vengeance for the corpse. In that ceremony the threat to shame is made explicit by the person (usually a woman) bearing the pieces of the dead man: "If you don't take revenge, you will be an object of contempt to all men."[55] The humiliation is as much that of the corpse (it suffers mutilation as well as public evidence of its own insufficiency to motivate revenge without being mutilated) as of the beseeching woman. This is the ultimate in grotesquerie, but the grotesque and the dark comic world to which it belongs is, as I have been claiming all along, the defining substance of the humiliating. Other examples abound in the Bible and elsewhere.[56] Penitential practices, for instance, can be understood as adopting this style,[57] whether they be forced on someone as with Henry at Canossa or voluntarily adopted as with flagellant rites.

But let us move to a more familiar practice—apology, perhaps the most frequent ritual of humiliation we have recourse to. In the paradigmatic performance of the ritual we abase ourselves in front of the party we have wronged. The abasement takes the form, conventionally, of submissive posture, of words of unconditional admission of fault and error designed to display contrition, remorse, or regret.[58] The structure of apology requires that the apologizer posture as the inferior and invest, for however brief a moment, the wronged person with a higher status. The assumption of the lower position, the position of the beseecher, is the substance of the compensation paid to the other party. It is what does the work of repair. The apologizer, however, need not feel humiliated, or contrite either; in fact, she might just be going through the motions because the occasion demands them. But the feeling is not that important, because it is forever inaccessible to others; it is the display that matters, and she knows that others will perceive her to be in a state of humiliation, even if ever so slightly. If an apology does not look somewhat humiliating to the wronged person or to third parties, then it isn't one and it would be utterly ineffective in accomplishing the remedial work it is supposed to do. We have all given, witnessed, and received surly apologies that are intended and received as new affronts requiring more apology.[59]

But though an apology must be seen as humiliating it is not seen as shameful in those situations in which it is deemed acceptable to give or receive one. Quite the contrary, it is seen as the appropriate behavior of someone who has a proper sense of shame. The sincere apology, of course, may very well be accompanied by feelings of shame, but the shame will be a consequence of the violation that created the need for the apology, not a consequence of the apology itself. Thus the paradigm case. Apologies as we all know are manipulable and capable of multiple meanings. It is possible, as always, to turn the ritual on its head and use it to humiliate the recipient, as when we apologize with obvious insincerity. Then too there is the class of apology which is designed to nip big offense in the bud and thus prevent the elicitation of grand emotions. These are the quick "sorry"s for the incidental contacts and interruptions of daily life; they only mimic a show of humiliation, if that.

Not all rituals for which the designation "humiliation ritual" feels appropriate depend on voluntary self-abasement as do the ones I have just mentioned. Practices such as hazing—some would include the tenure process—and other forms of testing prior to final integration into some group can be seen as humiliation rituals and distinguished further from shaming rituals such as scarlet letters, dunce caps, charivari or rough music, stocks and pillories, which involve ostracism and exclusion from the group as a form of sanction. Both of these types of rituals—initiation and shaming rituals—are imposed by an authority that has the power to demand compliance with the terms of the ritual. This characteristic distinguishes them both from humiliation rituals of self-abasement. But they can be distinguished from each other in a significant way that meshes with one of our major themes despite their similarity in their relations to authority. The humiliation of initiation rituals borrows from the world of comic ordering, the shaming rituals from tragic ordering. The initiation ritual conceives of humiliation as a test, a rite, prior to and indeed allowing for the attainment of honor as a group member of good standing. Shaming rituals, on the other hand, only hold the opportunity for reintegration at a new status lower than previously held, if they will allow reintegration at all. The shaming ritual typically carries with it a double whammy. The first is the feeling and state of humiliation of being seen in the stocks or wearing the scarlet letter; the second is being remembered as the person so humiliated after the ritual. The status degradation of shaming rituals, if not formally disabling, is often informally so as an effect of communal memory.[60] Humiliation rituals have as an original assumption something of the hierarchical in them: a person is being put low either as a prelude to being raised on high or as a redefinition of continuing relations of dominance, whereas shaming rituals initially assume a community of equals from which one is expelled by the communal authority.

The designation of these two types of rituals as either humiliating or shaming makes no certain claim about the feeling of the person performing or subjected to the ritual. The shame and humiliation in the classification adopt the point of view of the observer—not of the performer, as in rituals of self-abasement—and describe the quasi-juridical state of the person performing the ritual. Here too we can imagine the feeling of the person in the stocks as more closely approximating humiliation or embarrassment than shame, and the feeling of the person going through ritual hazing ranging anywhere from purposeful to apprehensive to hostile as well as (if the ritual is doing what it claims to do) intense moments of shame, embarrassment, and humiliation. The emotional economy of all these rituals involves a complex play among humiliation, shame, and embarrassment, whether as actually felt or as publicly displayed. And though these rituals confirm how closely connected these feelings and states are, they also are not readily comprehensible in all their varied richness unless we can distinguish among them.

Humiliation with a Big H Distinguished

I have described a domain of humiliation which stayed within the bounds of the normal and the familiar: no concentration camps, no torture chambers, no sexual sadism. Yet we are wont to describe the victims in these latter settings as humiliated. It may seem pure authorial fiat on my part to find in our usages of the word *humiliation* a real social and experiential domain at the level of common social interaction but then to exclude from that domain the perverse, sick, and sadistic practices that provide the context for so many actual uses of the word. It is not that the sphere of commonplace humiliation— the comedy of pretension deflation, of unwittingly playing the fool or the grotesquerie of self-abasement or of just botching things badly— has nothing to do with the horrific domain of brutal and systematic cruelty. Surely such acts of horror, Humiliation with a big **H,** can be described as the grotesque run amok. The humiliation in that horrific world can still be subsumed within the notion of pretension deflation which defines so much of comic humiliation. But the pretension being deflated in that upside-down sadistic world is different. It is not the unmerited claim to a higher social status in the moral and social world than one justifiably merits; rather, the claim of the torturer, the concentration camp guard, the ideologues of ethnic, racial, and religious genocide, is that the humanity of their victims is a pretense.

Pretending to be human represents a difference in kind from commonplace pretensions to unmerited rank and esteem. Look what happens to the word *pretense* when it is suggested that a human is pretending to be human. We immediately locate a power in others to declare whether or not someone is a member of the species. Yet these others need not be hostile. Groups always enforce certain standards and regulations of inclusion. But I am referring to a situation in which the stakes are higher, situations in which hostility is openly and unambiguously the basis of decision. Here a distinction should be made between the hostility of primitives and the hostility of modern totalitarian or terrorist regimes. The primitives divided the world into us and them, group members and strangers, to which the first was accorded humanity and the second a kind of ambiguous status that could lead to their being summarily killed as strangers, summarily coerced into being wives and mothers or slaves, or summarily honored as guests. If a stranger wasn't exactly human, he wasn't nonhuman either. He was simply ambiguous. This view is very different from that of the modern regimes of torture which take a perverse delight in denying a set of moral norms whose force they understand. Their sadism lies in this understanding. They know that the people they torture are humans (there is no ambiguity) and that is why they torture them, in the hope that they can reveal them as not being what they know they are. There is no thrill in making a rat act like a rat. The thrill is in making a human a rat. And a human who acts like a rat justifies his torture for two contradictory reasons: because he disgraces his humanity by acting like a rat and because as a rat he is pretending to humanity, a most disgraceful and arrogant presumption for a rat.

Elaine Scarry[61] has written on this subject better than I can hope to, but let me add just a few more thoughts. Does the torturer suppose that he is making the victim actually feel humiliation? This he cannot know. He can know only that the victim is humiliated as a social fact, as matter of status. I would even suppose that victims' feelings range from fear (mostly), to disgust (depending on the form of torture), to boredom, the kind of fatalistic lassitude which sets in when people are numbed sufficiently by having the living daylights kicked out of them long enough. Under continued torture affect begins to disintegrate. Scarry makes this point. The emotional universe falls apart in the presence of so much physical pain.

There is a paradox in the torturer's making someone *feel* humiliated. He must make sure that the victims continue to retain an image of themselves as worthy of respect, because the feeling of humiliation depends on some part of the self's ability to see things with an undegraded sensibility. So what does the torturer want? To break down the victim completely so that he will really be the rat the torturer's ideology tells him the victim is? Or does he want to preserve just enough of the victim's self-respect so that the victim can feel degraded? Humiliation of this sort, unlike the world of conventional humiliation, is perversion. It appalls and sickens, but it also gives rise to a justly vengeful and ironic paradox. For the humiliators do indeed succeed in reclassifying some subset of humans as nonhumans, but it is not their victims who are thus transfigured; it is themselves.

Humiliation with a big **H** denies the social world of normalized encounter. In fact, it humiliates by virtue of this denial. It tells the victims that all social norms are suspended in dealings with them because they are not human. Day-to-day humiliation, the humiliation of you and me, operates by reaffirming and confirming social norms and is the very stuff of normal social interaction. It is the risk we all take just walking down the street, just talking to one another. It is the unavoidable pain attendant on the discovery of the divergence between how we see ourselves and how we see ourselves as others see us. I give priority to commonplace humiliation. This is the farcical and dark comic world we are all familiar with. It is clear that Humiliation with a big **H** is part of the concept of humiliation only by imaginative extension of the normal experiential domain of the discomfort of self-assessment and self-attention. The normal funds the horrific, not the other way around.

But how do I deal with the humiliations of sex? By cold decision, little at all. Sex gets more than enough attention throughout the entire range of academic discourse, from the most avant garde to the most conventional. So I do not apologize for treating it as an afterthought. But where would I put it if I were to deal with it—with torture or with the normal? Sexual violation within the structure of something already clearly marked as torture belongs with the former, as does gang rape, coerced nakedness, and other brutalities forced on women usually, but also on men. The categorizing of sadomasochistic practices depends on whether a colorable claim can be made that the humiliated one is actually consenting to be humiliated. I assume that the consenter to humiliation in these settings is playing a strategy not all that dissimilar to the one adopted by the underground man whom we will meet shortly. It is not only "I am humiliated therefore I am" but also "I am humiliated therefore I am better than you."

It is not in sado-masochistic practices that normal sexual humiliation takes place, however; normal sexual humiliation is a risk of normal sex, just as falling is a risk of figure skating. To the usual intermittent bodily dysfunctions I must add the most usual experience of commonplace humiliation there is: the humiliation of sexual rejection.[62] And although the comedy of this can elude us when we are the victims, it is not elusive at all when it happens to others: thus much of the attraction of such television shows as *Studs* and *Love Connection*. But if watching people humiliate themselves or be humiliated embarrasses us and embarrassment is an unpleasant emotion, why do these shows attract such large audiences? Here again we see an intimate connection between amusement and embarrassment. The titillation of openly confessed seduction—which is titillating both because of its sexual nature *and* because it is accompanied by the breach of norms of propriety regarding the public confession of such things—generates both amusement and embarrassment simultaneously, each feeling feeding back to elicit the other. The viewer also experiences the *Schadenfreude* of seeing others rejected; this pleasure too is inextricably bound up with the embarrassment the rejection engenders. No one gets all that much pleasure from witnessing the erotic successes of others when such others are not movie stars but simple vulgar souls we feel should not be so lucky; on the other hand, the *Schadenfreude* of witnessing a rejection is often not by itself sufficient to offset the excruciating discomfort it can occasion. The shows are thus structured on the belief that the titillation of successful seduction needs to be balanced about equally with rejection, neither by itself being sufficient to maintain viewer interest.

Humiliation is also richly gendered as feminine, so richly that the few remarks I confine myself to here will probably annoy everyone, both for the infinitude I leave unsaid and for the things I have chosen to say. Let me deal with this gendering briefly with one anecdote and then some general observations. I teach a seminar for which the catalogue carries the name Legal Anthropology. Over the years I have used it as a shell for whatever content I could reasonably include under that rubric which dovetailed with my research interests. One year it was called "Legal Anthropology: Violence." The next year, obsessed with humiliation, I decided to make the subject of this chapter the core of the seminar, which got posted during preregistration simply as "Humiliation, Prof. Miller." In the violence seminar there were two men for every woman; in the humiliation seminar there were six women for every man. Even before the seminar met, I had gotten as useful a piece of information out of it as I could have hoped for. Women can admit to an interest in humiliation without loss of face.[63] Men suspect that they can only lose face. Either they type themselves feminine if they admit to being humiliated, or they type themselves immoral, as sadists, if they admit to humiliating. They fear, I suppose, that the subject concedes all the moral high ground to the women in the class.

The gendering of humiliation as feminine is intimately connected to vulgar views of the sexual act. In this view, men poke, prod, pierce, penetrate; their actions rely heavily on verbs that cause deflation. And what is being deflated if not the pretension of women to moral equivalence with men? Women are on the bottom, on the *humus*; they are brought low, done dirt, subjected to a host of metaphors which capture the root sense of humiliate. In this view of sex, a view held by some feminists,[64] the sexual act can only humiliate women in the eyes of men and often in their own eyes as well.

The issue is more complex than the simple gender typing of the vulgar account is capable of getting at. For if the sex act itself is by that account perceived to be humiliating to women, the search for women thus to humiliate is humiliating to men. Courtship and humiliating oneself seem to be intimately associated. Whether boorishly aggressive or shyly retiring, men find it nearly impossible to avoid looking foolish to the women who finally accept them. It might well be that a woman's decision that the man so humiliating himself is "cute" is a complex mediation of her contempt. The aggressive boor never seems to feel his humiliation, while the shy retiring soul feels his ever so acutely. He knows that the chances of not looking foolish in this complex mating ritual depend on desiring a woman who is too undiscerning to interest him, his very desire for whom also gives him reason to feel humiliated. But he also sees himself as a higher more refined mutation and is dismayed that reproductive success favors the boor, who never seems to have trouble finding women to forgive his foolishness. Underground man, whom we are about to deal with more closely, were he to opine on this topic, might note that humiliation (of males) is a necessary condition to the reproduction of the human species.

Reprise: Strategies of Humiliation Avoidance Revisited— Underground Man

In usual social interaction, most of the settings that give rise to embarrassment could also generate shame and humiliation, the particular outcome dependent on various intentions of the actors and observers, the various degrees of skill they have in remedying glitches and breaches, the various roles they assume, and the particular structure of the interaction. Dostoyevsky's underground man, for example, shames himself by his callous humiliation of the young prostitute Liza but then humiliates himself by confessing his shame to us. A rough correlation can be discerned here: if the humiliator's act is shameful, his confession of it will produce embarrassment or revulsion in third parties as it humiliates himself in the telling; if the person he is humiliating is pompous and pretentious, the humiliator's retelling of the act will produce amusement or a sense of satisfaction that justice has been done, as long as the humiliation is proportionate to the presumption of the person being humiliated.

Confession, like apology, to which it is closely related, involves ritualized humiliation, which if voluntarily entered into can function as an act of self-abasement, or if imposed by an authority, can be assimilated to shaming rituals. I am more interested in it as a self-imposed act of humiliation. Confession reveals that what one appears to be is not what one is and as such it declares one's unconfessed self to be a pretension to a dignity not deserved. The intimate connection between confession and humiliation is what we think of as the signature of so much of Dostoyevsky's work.[65] Both the underground man and Raskolnikov, among others, are obsessive confessers, and where else but in a Dostoyevsky novel would the guests at a soirée decide to amuse themselves by making a parlor game out of telling the worst thing they had ever done?[66] It is in Dostoyevsky that we find anatomized humiliation as identity, humiliation as the substance of a kind of perverse spiritual hierarchy in which people are ranked by how obsessively self-torturing they are. In one way, this quest for humiliation is merely an extension of the pride in humility I discussed earlier as one of the pitfalls of Christian morality, except this is pride in humiliation and there is a difference betwixt the two. Humiliation absolutely requires making a fool of oneself or being made to make a fool of oneself. Humility can be achieved without being foolish, although if one is seen as foolish in the course of being humble that experience too should be suffered with quiet dignity, not with painful anguish.

What drives the underground man to humiliate himself all the time, or better, to put himself in situations that require that he be humiliated and contemned by others in public settings? He could just play humiliating scenes in his head, inasmuch as he is more than capable of torturing himself by his hypersensitive self-consciousness. It seems that the underground man is not just a masochist; his is a complicated psychology not so easily cabined by such an easily available term. Above all, his very being depends on his ability to maintain his belief that he feels things more precisely and more deeply than others do because he thinks things out not only with greater consciousness of self but with greater attention to the consciousness of others. For him to be humiliated and to be an object of contempt is also a source, as indeed he says, of pleasure,[67] and this is not masochistic pleasure at all but one of status and rank. He distinguishes himself from those direct and confident men, those oafs of action who feel nothing very deeply, who are untroubled by the foolishnesses they do, who do not even perceive their failings and pomposities. These people swell the ranks of the complacent and secure, whose security comes at the price of lacking the imagination to see themselves as he sees them. He can only too well imagine the self-doubt and self-loathing he would feel if he were in their places; he, in fact, imagines himself situated like them all the time, but he cannot imagine himself as they imagine themselves. To do so would be an act of imagination which would require killing his own imagination: he would not want to lose himself in a fully contained fantasy of being them *and* thinking like them. For it is his inability to think like them which is the source of his belief in his superiority to them. If they are men, then he is to his own mind a mouse,[68] an insect, a fly, but a mouse or insect or fly of the most exquisite sensibility, a sensibility so keenly aware of the possibility of humiliation, that that very awareness actualizes every one of those possibilities into the fact of feeling humiliated. His ability to experience humiliation, to find it where others would not, is precisely the source of his superiority and thus his pleasure.

But there is a catch here. Underground man cannot be satisfied with imagined humiliation no matter how keen the feeling of his humiliation is in those imagined settings. He is too smart not to know that his own feelings of humiliation might not be confirmed by others as a recognizable state of humiliation.[69] Without real humiliation in which he is and feels humiliated by a real Other he would never engage to test his superiority. He needs real competitors as well as imaginary ones. He needs them because he needs them to find him worth humiliating and to provide the justification for the hatred that drives his imagination. He thus seeks to get thrown out of a tavern window by an army officer or to be bumped into on the Nevsky Boulevard. He wins either way. If others refuse to recognize him sufficiently to find him offensive, then he is humiliated by their failure to see him, or, if they do take offense and beat him or knock him down, then he will be humiliated by his own cowardice and impotence in taking revenge. Either way, however, he provides himself with the moral justification for having fantasies of revenge. And it is in fantasies of revenge that he exercises his imaginative talents to their fullest. Yet it is these fantasies, because they are fantasies and will remain only fantasies, which prompt an even more intense sensation of humiliation. They show him better than any insentient oaf could that humiliation lies in his inability to act or, if not exactly to act, then to act in such a way that won't itself be an even greater source of humiliation. But then it is that very humiliation which displays again his superior sensibility to the oaf and so on in an infinite regress. This is the *Untermensch* as *Übermensch*.

Earlier I dealt with some of the pitfalls of certain strategies of humiliation avoidance. If you adopt a style of consummate self-possession or of dignified aloofness, those very styles of self-presentation, because easily construed by observers as haughtiness, pompousness, or pretending to the world of cool, leave you open to being seen as the fool, the object of deflating laughter. Humility brings with it the risk of being prideful of one's humility, which in turn leaves one open to the humiliation of being revealed a hypocrite. All too painfully aware of the counterproductivity of such strategies, underground man perversely develops the strategy of seeking humiliation to preempt some of its worst aspects. It is more than just a matter of claiming the dignity of choosing your misery rather than having it imposed upon you: what underground man succeeds in doing is never allowing others to see him as humiliating himself *before* he sees himself in that way. And seeing himself in that way is the necessary condition for *feeling* humiliated. What makes the buffoon a buffoon, the pompous ass a ridiculous figure, what, in effect, is the enabler of their state of humiliation, is their obliviousness to how contemptibly foolish they are to the discerning eye of someone like underground man. Because they cannot imagine being seen as humiliated they cannot feel it. This inability is the substance of their ineffable foolishness. Like these fools, underground man will look foolish in the eyes of observers, but it is his genius to understand that looking foolish is an inescapable fate of social existence. He would not want to avoid being seen in that

way even if he could. He needs it to justify his superiority, the foundation of which is that he *feels* humiliated before or simultaneously with
being seen as humiliating himself. Or, alternatively, because humiliation is the lot of us all, the nobility in such a world are those who
possess that knowledge, using it as the basis for an elaborate parody of
the human condition.

Let me not overstate his case. Underground man's exquisite attention to the humiliations of social interaction are unlikely to make him
better company than the oafs he despises. His strategy for the avoidance of humiliation succeeds (if such a strategy even allows success to
have its conventional meaning) only at the level of the introspective
and psychological; the costs of his success are borne largely by everyone who must endure him in social settings, for he is obnoxious, ill-
mannered, quarrelsome, oversensitive, and obsessively self-involved.

Most of us are unwilling to accept the bleakness of underground
man's take on the inescapability of looking foolish, nor are we so
unsocialized as to adopt his strategy systematically. Yet we also discern
that he is on to something, even if we reject the hyperbolic parody of
his self-presentation. Like him, we recognize that it is a sign of greater
sensitivity to the demands of social intercourse, to the critical sense of
the figure we cut, that we do not have to wait until the act of recollection after the offending events to first come to see ourselves as fools
and thus to feel humiliated later than we should have. This is the
humiliation of the morning after, which can also, given the right
circumstances, generate misery for as long as memory does not fade.
John Keats, as usual, captures the sensation perfectly: "the most un-
happy hours in our lives are those in which we recollect times past to
our own blushing—If we are immortal that must be the Hell."[70] The
pain of painful recollection is worse in many ways than the pain of
awareness of the truth during the actual humiliating event. For the
feeling alerts us to the need for remedy. It allows the chance to
ameliorate the situation, or at least to control the damage. As with
embarrassment, the visibly apparent signs of distress often are the
very cure required to reestablish oneself as someone who feels what a
respectable and competent person ought to feel. With recollection,
however, comes, in addition to the pain of seeing oneself as the
consummate fool, the recognition that one's foolishness was so great
as to have let the best opportunity for making amends slip away. This
is part of the reason that recollection most often paints us a harsher
truth than the truth witnessed by the people before whom we felt so

discomfited. They are usually willing to be more forgiving of us than we are of ourselves, and no wonder, for so long as the incident was not an answerable assault on their self-esteem our humiliations do not quite displease them.

5
Humiliation— Part II: Historicizing Humiliation

> Melantha: Truce with your *doceurs,* good servant; you see I am addressing to the princess; pray do not *embarrass* me—*Embarrass* me! what a delicious French word do you make me lose upon you too!
>
> —John Dryden, *Marriage à la Mode*

Philology and Humiliation

Our emotional vocabulary would be greatly impoverished if we lacked the words *embarrass* and *humiliate.*[1] Such words as *awkward* or *uncomfortable* could, I suppose, fill in partially for *embarrass,* and *shame* or *mortify,* though sounding a bit formal and old-fashioned, could do service for *humiliation.* But we would feel we had lost two very useful words for getting at important features of our emotional life. It should then come as a surprise that both words were rather late additions to English in the sense indicating the uncomfortable emotions we are all very familiar with. According to the *Oxford English Dictionary* the earliest recorded use of *to humiliate* meaning to mortify or to lower or depress the dignity or self-respect of someone does not occur until 1757.[2] Its usual sense prior to the mid-eighteenth century is more closely related to the physical act of bowing, of prostrating oneself as in "Such a religious man may not . . . humiliate himselfe to execute the rite of homage" from 1602. The metaphoric underpinning of *humiliate* connected it more to humility and making humble than to what we now think of as humiliation. The *OED* nowhere actually defines humiliation or related words as an emotion but brings it into the orbit of the emotions of self-attention by linking it to mortification and the lowering of self-respect.[3] Under *humiliation* the listed usages tend to be examples of displays of humility or of humble condition clustering around religious devotions. As with the entries under *humiliate,* only the last example from 1866 clearly distances humiliation from humility or being humbled: "I think 'humiliation' is a very different condition of mind from humility. 'Humiliation' no man can desire." It is under *humiliating* that we get our earliest instances of uses that strongly imply the emotion. In 1776 Adam Smith can describe bankruptcy as "perhaps the greatest and most humiliating calamity which can befal [sic] an innocent man."[4]

Smith takes us into the world of finances and hence to the intimate association of eighteenth- and nineteenth-century embarrassment with money matters, either too much or (usually) too little. What linked an embarrassment of riches to being pecuniarily embarrassed was a shared notion that embarrassment's root sense meant something that encumbered or impeded. Unlike *humiliation,* which was floating around in English in devotional senses from the fourteenth century on, *embarrass* in its various forms in any sense made its presence felt only in the seventeenth century. Dryden gives an indication of its strangeness in the quotation that provides the epigraph for this chapter. The *OED* finds it in the late seventeenth century referring to the state of being perplexed, but it is not until almost exactly to the year that *humiliating* means what it does to us that *embarrassment* does too: perplexed, yes, but with particular reference to awkwardness about the propriety of certain actions.[5] The first instance given by *OED* is from Burke in 1774: "If my real, unaffected embarrassment prevents me from expressing my gratitude to you as I ought . . ." The *OED* gives earlier instances of *embarrassed* meaning perplexed, but the first examples that evidence awkwardness and constraint are from the 1760s, one of which comes from Laurence Sterne, a writer who would have had to invent the word if it did not exist.[6]

Let me add another bit of information. Take these two collocations: (1) I feel + emotion term (e.g., guilty, embarrassed, ashamed, humiliated, sad); and the similar one (2) I am + emotion term. I do not want to discuss why some are nearly synonymous as, say, I feel or am sad, and why others are not, as I feel or am guilty. What I do want to note, however, is that as far as I can tell (I supply the basis for my claim in note 7), the construction with feel + emotion term is relatively recent in regular usage, in fact becoming common only in the nineteenth century. After that, both the *be* and *feel* constructions were available for most emotions; before, the *feel* construction is encountered only rarely.[7]

I don't want to make too much of this shift. It does not provide a secure basis for grand claims about the effects of romanticism, industrialization, and capitalism on the articulation and conceptualization of the individual and the self. These "isms" are the usual unsavory suspects rounded up when real explanation fails us. But even so, this is a rather remarkable piece of evidence possibly indicating a change in the imagining of the self. One could hazard the claim that as late as the seventeenth century the self did not feel emotions at all; instead the emotions were borne almost as a quasi-juridical status or as allegorical personae that the subject put on masklike. When one *was* sad, one became the character Sadness in a moral and social drama, with its behaviors thus constrained by the role. But when one could at last *feel* sad, sadness became a feeling, a perturbation of the nerves coupled with the effects of the thoughts one might have about that perturbation. The new self could thus be something more than its feelings; it could be more detached from them, more ironical, perhaps more restrained, and definitely more self-conscious. And this last characteristic—self-consciousness—might also tend to make this new self more likely to feel such emotions as humiliation and embarrassment than heretofore. This claim may seem a bit mystifying, but it is not without some reason. It is reasonably consistent with some of the drift of Norbert Elias's work.[8]

What are the causes of this different way of articulating the relation of the self to emotions? We might start to find them by looking closely at changes in styles of religious devotion and the changes in language as a consequence of enthusiastic religion. In this regard, mortification, too, with its long association with religious self-abasement and the denial of the pleasures of the flesh came to indicate the unpleasant feeling of humiliation and chagrin roughly concurrently with the semantic changes we have already parsed for humiliation.[9] This concurrence provides another small piece of fodder, or at least is not inconsistent with the idea that what was occurring was a secularization or recontextualization of devotional diction which attended major shifts in the styles of devotion in the seventeenth and eighteenth centuries. To this change in religious discourse might also be added the effects of the closer looks at the inner life, whether in the philosophical and medical treatments of the passions, the novels of Richardson and Sterne, or the extraordinary attention to manners and the emotions supporting them in elite social circles.

A more modest story could also be told. It might only be that the verb *to feel* got extended to mean *to be* in the environment of emotion words. Nothing changed, in other words, except the terrain occupied by the verb *to feel*, a minor and purely linguistic matter not at all connected with great psychosocial transformation. This may have been the case, but even if *to feel* was doing some new grammatical work only as a copula or quasi-auxiliary, it would also carry with it some semantic baggage from its more "sensual" senses. *To feel* plus emotion can never be quite the same as *to be* plus emotion as long as *feel* continues to carry with it its fundamental association with tactile sensation. Nevertheless, this more modest argument has some claim to truth. It is a reminder that although linguistic change may not be tightly constrained to effect only linguistic matters, it can still be part of the story of what is going on and provide a nice brake on the pomposity of finding explanation only in big abstractions.

This information and especially the late arrival of *humiliation* and *embarrassment* to the lexicon raise rather emphatically the question of the relation between the emotions we feel and how we express them and in turn how these expressions are related to changes in social and cultural arrangements. We touched on this relation briefly in Chapter 3, but I wish to expand on it here. Were people not feeling humiliation and embarrassment before 1700? Did they have no need to name them because there was nothing to name? Or did they feel them but not talk about them? Or did they feel them but talk about them in different ways, using other words and phrases or lengthier circumstantial accounts? If so, what were the ways?

Some of the answer must lie with the philological, social, and cultural history of shame. Unlike *humiliation* and *embarrassment*, both of Romance origin, *shame* was always around in English, rooted in the Germanic past. It clearly referred to the emotion that still goes by the same name. I do not mean this last sentence to be controversial. Old English *shame* (*sceamu*) described both the sensibility that would avoid shameless behavior and the unpleasant emotion that accompanies the status degradation attending the failure to live up to the moral norms and standards accepted by social equals. Beowulf was said to have no cause to suffer shame for the quality of the gifts given him for killing Grendel (1025–26), but his craven thanes felt shame acutely for abandoning their lord in his time of need (2850). At least from this time (the eighth century), shame was intimately associated with blushing. In Old English, *shame* glosses Latin *rubor* and *erubesco*.[10] Six centuries later Chaucer's Canon Yeoman's cheeks waxed red for shame (*Canterbury Tales*, G 1095). And many will recall Hamlet to his mother:

> O shame! where is thy blush? Rebellious hell,
> If thou canst mutine in a matron's bones,
> To flaming youth let virtue be as wax
> And melt in her own fire. (3.4.83–86)

The association of shame and blushing continues into present times, although we are now more likely to think of blushing as an incident of embarrassment and shyness than of shame; the latter is likely to be indicated somatically by a defeated slouch and downward gaze aversion.[11]

Shame then clearly seemed to occupy much of the ground we would now call embarrassment and most all the ground we would call humiliation. Thus it is that Chaucer's Troilus "wex a litel red for shame" (2: 645) when he heard his praises sung before the people. Coriolanus is likewise "shamed" to hear of his own exploits (2.2.63–66). This for us is the world of embarrassment, whereas what we perceive as Malvolio's humiliation is thought of as "a notable shame" by his humiliators in *Twelfth Night* (2.5.5).

But I am imposing our categories on them. Before 1700, these incidents were not so many embarrassments and humiliations; they were shames. And that must tell us something about the conceptualization of emotional life, especially about the emotions of self-attention which have to do with the successful presentation of self and the adherence to community moral and social standards. As I have mentioned in Chapter 3, the notion that shame culture gave way to cultures of guilt with a kind of evolutionary logic has been greatly discredited.[12] It seems that anthropologists credited the wrong emotion with driving shame out of its dominant position among the emotions of social control. Embarrassment, not guilt, would have been a better choice. In the English-speaking world, at least, we have moved from a culture of shame to a culture of embarrassment. A woman whose moral existence would have been threatened by a wind-blown revelation of an ankle and who would have blushed with shame in consequence gives way to the embarrassment of the woman whose skirt rides up too high when she sits down so that she must do the remedial work of readjusting herself and give the necessary signs that indicate no flirtation or desire to exhibit was intended. Modesty here can be preserved without a blush; a businesslike shift in posture is all that decorum demands. Rom Harré makes this point and attributes the phenomenon to the expansion of the sphere of manners at the expense of the sphere of morals, a shift that he notes has had marked effects on the social position of women.[13]

Harré identifies a transformation that merits more attention. It was not just women who were affected. Back then, men too were more likely to experience shame than embarrassment, not over bodily display so much as over any interaction that might call honor into question. In the feuding culture of saga Iceland, honor was always at stake among the class of men who feuded. In one's presentation of self lay one's claim to reputation and respect. Tripping over someone's outstretched leg at a feast was thus only with the greatest difficulty understood as an embarrassing accident rather than as an intention to shame on the part of the person whose leg was tripped over. In the world of Beowulf embarrassment had little or no place. Bragging and self-assertion were required, and the failure to make good on one's grand claims meant shame, not embarrassment (e.g., 1465–72).

In the heroic world of Germanic epic or of the Icelandic sagas it could be argued that there was only a very weak desire (I hesitate to say ability) to distinguish finely between levels of seriousness of shame. There were just two rough categories: the shame that was absolutely irremediable and the shame that could be repaired. The first is the shame of betraying trusts. This was the situation of the brother-killer or the abject coward. The Norse had a special name for this type of shame (níðingsverk), a term borrowed from them by the Anglo-Saxons.[14] The second shame included the whole range of shamings which one could set aright by taking revenge. Some of the events that elicited this shame would continue to shame us today, but many we would find at best to be the stuff of "mere" embarrassment. In saga Iceland, for instance, one's honor suffered little more for a failure to avenge the death of a brother than for a failure to avenge laughter when one was accidentally hit by a piece of turf.[15] I am somewhat oversimplifying. Third parties, the class of people who had an interest in making peace, were able to conceptualize an argument that some shames should be treated as less than big deals. But even peacemakers had no very consistent view as to which types of shame were by their very nature "mere" shames. They would simply argue that any shame could be the basis for accepting compensation as well as for taking vengeance,[16] not that a bruise on the forehead was less serious than a dead brother. The anthropologists may have gotten it wrong when they contrasted shame and guilt, but they hit the nail on the head when they coupled shame and honor.

When we move to the world of romance, the world of Chaucer and the *Gawain* poet, the style of courtly love, a world of conscious concern about "refinement" (a concern largely unthinkable in heroic society), we see emerge the ability to think of degrees of shame and even to make jokes about people who thought their honor to lie equally in the little shame as in the big shame. In other words, it started to become possible to think of some shames as the basis for comedy.[17] The comedy of fabliaux introduced the sometimes dark and uproariously funny world of humiliating cuckolds and farting at pretentious fools. The psychologizing of love allowed for the blushing of embarrassment. These distinctions were only emergent and still did not dispense with the language of shame and honor. As the *OED* indicates, no one as yet thought it necessary to redefine *humiliation* and import *embarrassment* into the lexicon.

But just because an emotion is not distinguished at the level of the word does not mean that nuance is not attainable in talk about emotions. The emotion may be there, but it has to be expressed indirectly; it is in the "feel" that the particulars of context convey; it occupies various levels of consciousness, ranging from the knowledge we have without knowing we have it to that which we talk about by recourse to phrases and paragraphs rather than to particular words that condense the knowledge of those paragraphs. Above all, it was in the particulars of context that nuances in the broad category of such emotions as shame were understood to reside before they were understood as essentialized in unique lexical categories. Certain emotions started to cluster around defined social statuses and to be developed discursively in the literary genres purporting to describe and define those statuses. *Pity* thus articulated what the high felt and only the high were able to feel for the high who had fallen from atop Fortune's wheel: "for pitee renneth soone in gentil herte."

Have mercy on oure wo and oure distresse!
Some drope of pitee, thurgh thy gentillesse,
Upon us wrecched wommen lat thou falle.
For, certes, lord, ther is noon of us alle,
That she ne hath been a duchesse or a queene.
Now be we caytyves, as it is wel seene,
Thanked be Fortune and hire false wheel. (*Canterbury Tales* A 919–25)

People understood that the shame of the noble in high-styled tales of love or war was not the shame of a carpenter or a greedy cleric who got his comeuppance. There was in the official literature and confirmed in laws[18] an institutionalized contempt by the high for those lower who aped high fashion and style. It was in the keenly honed fear of contempt (*despit* in Middle English) that we can discern much of the contour of our humiliation, the deflation of pretension. The comic literature depicting social climbers portrays their shame as the shame of not being able to elicit the deference they pretend to deserve. Pretentious householders have their pretentious wives and innocent daughters swived literally in their presence, amorous young townsmen aspiring to women beyond their merit get their faces farted in or hot colters rammed up their anuses, and intellectually pretentious friars are stumped by such churlishly posed questions as how to divide farts into twelve equal parts.[19]

The wit of these ribald tales depends on a lot more than the hilarity of farts. It depends on keen attention to status differentiation, to social, moral, and intellectual pretension, and to the styles of discipline used to keep offenders against the social order in their place. The social climbers will be dealt assaultive contempt by their social equals and contemptuous disregard by the superiors with whom they are seeking to ingratiate themselves. These pretenders are more than shamed. They are dealt with "dispitously," contemptuously. This style of contempt is close to our humiliation indeed, but played out in a society in which rank was distinctly demarcated, not as precisely in the world of practice as in the world of ideology, but much more clearly than in the official rankings we admit to in our world. For us, pretension comes in all kinds of styles, because in a highly differentiated society we can pretend to many things. But in the Middle Ages pretension was more limited as to content. There were the hypocrites, who had religious pretensions, and there were the social climbers, who offended against dress codes and speech "classolects."[20] As much as high-status people wanted to think that the boundaries of their status were impermeable, it seems that many of the low acted as if they were not. At some level of consciousness the high also knew that they were not. They saw the low rising from time to time, but more disconcerting was the fact that they saw themselves falling down and out of their rank. The cultivation of contempt and the fear of contempt and ridicule (our humiliation) was the thumb in the holes of the porous dike separating the nobles from the lower orders. The fabliaux literature that spares the upwardly mobile no ignominy is the stuff of the nobility's wishful thinking.

The Wonderful Case of Sir Gawain and the Green Knight

I need to ballast the assertions I have been making. I can do this only by asking you to enter the world of *Sir Gawain and the Green Knight*, an anonymous fourteenth-century poem whose sense depends on the conceivability of certain conceptual cuts in the category of shame which correspond rather closely to what we would call humiliation and embarrassment. To make the points pertinent to our general theme I must tell you the story, one of the best stories ever told. I shame to think of what I must do to translate and truncate it, but I nonetheless have provided an account full enough to make the following discussion easily accessible to someone unfamiliar with the poem.

Gawain involves the surprise resolution of two and even three interlocking games, the surprise in fact being the revelation to Gawain and to us that the games are complexly interdependent so that a move in one is actually, but not known by the player to be, a move in the other. Besides generating an almost infinite regress of ironies about the supposed boundedness of the magical world of Arthurian romance from the familiar world of hospitality, conviviality, courtly behavior, and about the separation of the world of games from the wider social and moral order, the interpenetration of these spheres makes for the very real and almost certain possibility of having to see oneself or to be seen as playing the fool. This is even more the case when the games are by design intended to shame and, as I will argue, to humiliate and embarrass, all being part of an elaborate plot to puncture the pride (and pretension) of Arthur's court and its leading knight.

The tale begins with an account of New Year festivities in Arthur's court at Camelot. Arthur had vowed that he would not sit down to eat unless he heard tell of or saw something unusual. The entry of the Green Knight into the hall satisfies the vow. The knight is a very large man equipped all in green, riding a green horse, and green himself from head to toe. He carries an enormous ax and is a master at denying deference, refusing to recognize who might be the king— "'Where is,' he asked, 'the governor of this gyng?'" (225)[21]—and by refusing to consider anyone worthy of formal battle—"There are about on this bench but beardless children" (280). Refusing hospitality, he craves instead a game: that someone will take the large ax he offers and strike at his head in return for receiving the same from him in a year and a day. The request is greeted with a rather nervous and stunned silence, which prompts more words of blistering contempt: "What, is this Arthur's house . . . ? Now is the revel and the renown of the Round Table / overwalt [overturned] with a word of one wye's [person's] speech" (309, 312–14). And it is said that he laughed so loud that Arthur was angered. The "blood shot for shame" into the king's face (317).

Arthur's shame is the stuff of honor and challenge. It is the shame the honorable man feels and is the usual emotional accompaniment of status preservation, a prelude to violence. Arthur takes the ax, intending to give the Green Knight what he had been asking for, but Gawain intervenes, asking that he be allowed to take up the game instead. His request is granted. The Green Knight always maintains the mocking style of one who knows more than those with whom he speaks and who feels confident about dictating terms, especially delighting in the irony of terms that seem so obviously suicidal to himself. After he has Gawain rehearse the terms, he adds the further stipulation that Gawain undertake the burden of seeking him out for the return blow. "I wot [know] never where thou wonies [dwells]," says Gawain, rather unschooled, it seems, in the range of the possible in the romance world (399). And the Green Knight's response, which I render loosely: "Don't worry about it. I'll tell you after the blow and if I can't tell you, then all the better for you" (406–9). The Green Knight kneels down and Gawain chops off his head, which goes rolling on the floor and is kicked in horror and disgust by the people gathered around. The Green Knight then quickly reaches out and grabs his head, holds it on high, and it tells Gawain to meet him in a year at the Green Chapel. The whole scene treats with delightful irony the psychological assumptions one must make to live in a world of green men who bleed red and who can talk through severed heads. The Green Knight is a master at revealing the limited ability of "real" people, like the men and ladies of King Arthur's court, to accept the terms of all that Celtic weirdness which is part and parcel of the literary genre they find themselves in.

The seasons pass to the accompaniment of some of the finest verse in the English language, and Gawain sets out to seek the Green Knight in early November. He instinctively heads for North Wales, but no one he encounters has heard of the Green Chapel. He freezes in his armor in cold forests "With many birds unblithe upon bare twigs / that piteously there peeped for pain of the cold" (746–47). Finally in despair on Christmas Eve, he prays to Mary and soon discovers a large and well-appointed castle. He is welcomed there by the lord of the castle and his beautiful wife. The numerous members of this provincial household also welcome the opportunity to have in their midst the most skilled practitioner of refined courtly manners. From "that fine father of nurture" (919) they hope to observe and learn the highest style of courtliness, courtesy, "the tasteful terms of talking noble" (917), and the latest in "love-talking." Gawain spends four days in Christmas festivities and resists his host's attempt to keep him longer, citing a New Year's Day appointment at a place called the Green Chapel. The lord of the castle tells him to stay and rest, for the Green Chapel can be reached by midmorn from his castle. The host then proposes that Gawain stay and rest in the castle for the next three days while the lord goes hunting and, further, that they make a game of it by exchanging with each other whatever winnings they happen to come by.

Each of the next three mornings the lord hunts. On day one he kills a number of deer, on day two a wild boar, on day three a rather ragged fox, and each evening he returns to the castle and renders his gain unto Gawain. In the meantime Gawain is himself hunted by the amorously inclined lady of the castle. On the first day, as Gawain slumbers in his curtained bed, he is awakened by a little noise at his door. He lifts the curtain just enough to see the lady, "loveliest to behold" (1187), drawing the door shut behind her and moving toward the bed. Gawain "*shamed* and laid himself down lightly and let as [pretended that] he slept" (1189–90). What is the content of this shame? It is clear that it is not big Shame, the stuff of self-abasement. It is not the shame of challenge and riposte among men. It is not the failure or lack of honor. It is the blush, pure and simple, of embarrassment. There is no word for it other than shame at this time, but the context makes clear that this is not the shame of the sort that Arthur felt when he flushed red at the contemptuous challenge of the Green Knight. If these two incidents can give rise to shames of one sort or another, it is fairly clear we are dealing with an emotion term of very general applicability whose more precise senses must be abstracted from the local details surrounding its use. The challenge of the Green Knight to Arthur produces the kind of shame which is attended by and justifies rage, while the anticipation of some not quite proper and perhaps importuning attempts at seduction produces the kind of "shame" whose substance is nothing more than awkwardness, confusion, and annoyance, but otherwise manageable social dis-ease.

The lady "cast up the curtain and crept therein / and set herself softly on the bedside / and lingered there selly [very] long to look when he waked" (1192–94). Here we have a man pretending to sleep while being watched by someone who has already taken enough liberty with certain kinds of proprieties to signal boldly that a new game is being played, one that goes hand in hand with the possibility of embarrassment—no, one that *requires* embarrassment. We do not need a special word to describe the uneasiness of what it feels like to be looked at as we pretend to sleep, especially when the feigned sleep (as it usually is) is an attempt to avoid demands made on us which would be difficult to avoid without giving offense or augmenting the amount of uneasiness already in the air.[22] In three lines the poet is able to flesh out the circumstances that generate a feeling in Gawain infinitely richer and more subtle than shame, the only emotion word in the scene. We do not have to imagine what Gawain felt and risk the ahistoricism of substituting our experience for Gawain's, for enough is given to reconstruct a good portion of it: "The lad lay lurking a full long while, / compassed in his conscience what that case might / mean or amount to . . ." (1195–97). This is psychologically astute writing and it is done with a rather impoverished emotional vocabulary dedicated precisely to describing it. I do not mean to suggest that emotion talk was foreign to the people of high and late Middle Ages. They, after all, basically invented the romantic way of talking about love as an inner state. And they also described love as something intimately connected to feelings that bore some resemblance to what we call embarrassment. The blushes of love after all were both something less and something more than plain old shame. The context made that clear. The shame of the love game in its courtly manifestations was just not the shame of the bloodfeud or of the pure point of honor.

I wish I could present you with the delicious seductiveness of the lady, her wittiness with its pyramids of double-entendres, the suggestiveness that stops short of vulgarity by virtue of its being so verbally smart and accomplished even as it leaves nothing to the imagination. Poor Gawain is caught in a bind, and more than one at that. He comes to this provincial court with a reputation for being an accomplished lover, making it all the harder for him to decline erotic invitation without giving offense, especially since the norms of courtly love did not take much heed of the marital status of the woman. For three days Gawain must walk the narrow line between not insulting the lord by laying with his wife and not insulting the wife by spurning her suggestions to do so. The setting is the very stuff of what we would call an embarrassing situation, but of what they understood more as moral battle, testing the soul in its perpetual war against the flesh. But the *feeling* of such microcosmic battle occupied only one level of their consciousness; at another there was the actual business of meeting the demands of courtliness, of good manners, of refined love and seduction, of how not to offend and of how to salvage the situation when one had offended. They might not have called it embarrassment, but this poet and Chaucer too would not have made much sense in the fourteenth century unless embarrassment was indeed felt in certain restricted settings, settings that some poets were adept at creating. They didn't need the word. It was subsumed within the very way they talked about love and courtship.

There is the unintended embarrassment that arises from the situation itself and then there is the embarrassment that is deliberately created as part of a design to embarrass. The lady intends to embarrass; she teases Gawain, not just sexually but in a way designed to undermine the seriousness of his self-presentation. She suggests that he isn't quite what his reputation has him cracked up to be. I translate: "You can't be Gawain. Gawain could not have lingered so long with a lady and not craved a kiss" (1293, 1299–1300). And Gawain is greatly disturbed "lest he had failed in the form of his casts [words]" (1295). He gives her a kiss.

The lord returns from the hunt and, by the terms of their game, he gives Gawain all the butchered carcasses from the day's hunt (the poem is always "innocently" forcing Gawain to think about corporal dismemberment, this, too, part of its consistent strategy of humiliating poor Gawain, even if ever so tastefully and mildly). Gawain also gives up his winnings: he grabs the lord around the neck and "kisses him as comely as he could devise" (1389). The next day things go as before. The lady is a bit more direct than on the previous day. Yet in the end she only manages to kiss Gawain twice; he, in turn, gives them to the lord, after having received from him the head of the boar he had killed that day.

On the third day, the day before Gawain must receive his stroke, the lady arrives in extreme décolletage, "her breast bare before and behind too" (1741). Gawain almost loses his resolve and she loses what little is left of her indirection so "that need him behooved / either to latch on to her love, or loathly refuse it" (1771–72). The lady finally gives up her quest for sex and craves of him only some small token. Gawain refuses, citing the inappropriateness of anything he has with him on this journey that would do her or him sufficient honor in the giving. She then offers him her ring, which he also refuses, alleging his inability to repay so rich a gift. She is still not deterred and offers him her girdle of green silk adorned with gold, which, because it is not so valuable as the ring, would oblige him less.[23] Gawain again says he cannot accept and will not consider accepting anything until he gets through the mission that brought him there. (Gawain has spoken very generally about his quest, giving no details and only revealing that he must be at the Green Chapel on New Year's Day.) I paraphrase her: "Are you refusing this silk because it is so simple? I know it is not much, but if its virtues were known it would be valued more highly" (1847–50). It so happens that anyone who wears the girdle can't be "hewed under heaven." Whatever scruples Gawain had about accepting it suddenly disappear, and when she asks him "for her sake" never to reveal the gift to her husband he agrees. When the lord returns, all he has is a foul fox skin to give Gawain, while Gawain has three kisses to give him; the girdle he packed away. The scene is obviously repleat with the ironies imposed by the competing demands of gift exchange, the formally undertaken demands of the exchange game with the lord of the castle, and the explicit promise to the lady not to reveal to the lord the gift of the girdle.

The next day Gawain must meet his appointment. In spite of the girdle he spends a sleepless night. This may be the world of romance, a world in which one should trust magic girdles, but for medieval people the fantasy of romance was less the fantasy of replaceable heads and green skin than the desire for wealth, health, beauty, and good company—things which, though hard to attain, did not require suspension of disbelief regarding their existence. Gawain, in other words, is not immune to the stresses of normal humanity. He dresses himself, and the poet reminds us that Gawain surely did not forget "the lace, the lady's gift" (2030). One can discern here a rather insistent strategy of the poet and his characters to undermine Gawain's courage, to call it into question, to make him scared, or if not scared, to make him nervous in the way that mocks the convention of the fearless unquestioning courage of knights of less self-mocking and self-doubting romance. Even the servant sent from the castle to point him the way tries, before abandoning him, to tempt Gawain to flee and to trust him (the servant) to hide that he did.

The Green Chapel turns out to be nothing but an old barrow with no Green Knight immediately in sight. Gawain hears then from the other side of a brook the sound of a grindstone sharpening metal (another detail whose sole purpose is to make him more anxious). The Green Knight, as before, is a master of subtle degradation. He greets Gawain with only a harsh "Abide!" as if said to a servant, making Gawain wait until he finishes sharpening his ax. He commends Gawain for showing up and they immediately get down to business. Gawain takes off his helmet and kneels down baring his neck. The Green Knight lifts his enormous ax, takes aim, swings down hard, but jerks the blade up short of the neck. Gawain flinches. "You are not Gawain . . . That so good is held /. . . Such cowardice of that knight could I never hear" (2270–73). The Green Knight reminds Gawain that he had not flinched when it had been his turn to suffer Gawain's blow, and Gawain reminds him in turn that, unlike the Green Knight, if his head falls off he can't put it back on. Gawain promises that he won't flinch, and the Green Knight takes aim again and again withholds his hand at the last second just to see, as he says, whether Gawain would actually lie still.

The Green Knight takes aim a third time and brings the ax down but only so it nicks Gawain in the neck, shedding a little blood. Gawain sees his blood on the snow and knows himself alive. He springs up, puts on his helmet, pulls his sword, and claims that he has fulfilled his bargain and will resist violently any attempt to suffer any more blows. The Green Knight just leans on his ax, looking rather amused, and then speaks "merrily." He tells Gawain to relax; you are quit. I will translate closely. The speech contains the startling revelation of the Green Knight's identity, even more startling for the casual way in which it is delivered: "I could have given you a deathblow if I had cared to. The first blow was feinted, I drew no blood. I dealt with you justly on account of the agreement we made the first night. And you held it truly when you gave me all the gain that you received like a good man. The other feinted blow likewise drew no blood because the kisses you got from my wife you gave back to me. But you faltered the third time and that's why I tapped you. You see, that's my girdle

you are wearing. I know all about the wooing of my wife. I planned
the whole thing. I sent her to test you and truthfully I find you to be
one of the most faultless of men that ever lived. But you lacked a little,
sir, some faithfulness was wanting. But that wasn't for any frivolous
matter, but because you loved your life. All the less to your blame"
(2342–68).

The revelation of the Green Knight's identity forces us and Gawain
immediately to have to reconstruct new meanings for all the prior
action of the poem. And Gawain is furious. "All the blood in his breast
blended in his face / and he *shrunk for shame* . . . " (2371–72). He
curses his "cowardice and covetousness" for destroying his virtue. He
berates himself for forsaking his own nature which was to be true and
faithful. "But now am I faulty and false" (2382). The Green Knight
can't take Gawain's self-castigation very seriously and just laughs. He
tells him to consider the small cut as a penance. Gawain is very
distraught now. He stops blaming himself and like a good fourteenth-
century man he lights into womankind instead. As Adam by Eve, so
was he beguiled by a woman (2414). Our story ends with Gawain's
refusing the Green Knight's offer of hospitality but accepting a gift of
the girdle as a sign of his misdeed so that he can always recall with
remorse the "fault and the faintness of crabbed flesh / how tender it is
to entice taints of filth" (2435–36). He returns to Camelot, tells his
tale in the manner of a confession and penance for his moral failing,
to the renewed experience of shame and blushing.

> He tened [was chagrined] when he should tell,
> He groaned for grief and gram [wrath, mortification],
> The blood in his face did mell [mix],
> When he it should show, for shame. (2501–4)

But the court treats this public display no differently than the Green
Knight had treated him: they laughed, not cruelly but as a gesture of
"no big deal" and they all decide to wear a green garter in solidarity.

The poem raises a myriad of issues that are extraneous to our
purpose. I thus ignore its humane moral vision, the gentle mockery of
rigid and uncompromising moralism even as the account suggests
that moral life cannot be confined to bounds narrower than all of
one's life. Games are thus not neatly cabined and separable from
broader social and moral concerns. We will not indulge ourselves in
exploring the wonderfully suggestive "what ifs" the poem raises. What
if, for instance, Gawain had slept with the lady? Would he have paid it

over to the lord? Or is the lord adding another inducement to keep this famous ladies' man chaste in his household? What if Gawain had rendered the host his girdle? Would he have lived? The poem is always mocking the world of romance but it still is a romance, and girdles in that world can keep one's head from getting chopped off. Is it certain that it wasn't the girdle that saved Gawain?

But let us get to humiliation, for that is what I think is driving much of the story once we put the big questions about the possibility of a perfect moral life aside. Just telling the story in the context of a discussion of humiliation, as I have done, will have made much of my case already. Gawain, of course, is set up for a fall, not as big a fall as he wishes to claim, but a fall nonetheless. There was no way he could know that the moves in the castle exchange game were really moves in the beheading game, that the test was only superficially one of courage, failings in which would justifiably elicit shame in this warrior culture, rather than a test of the general quality of one's moral *and* social life, failings in which could also produce shame but often produce something less, like humiliation or embarrassment. He is subjected to a continued, insistent, and wonderfully clever assault on his self-esteem. His tormentors are relentless. "You are not Gawain," "This can't be Gawain," is almost a refrain, as it is constantly suggested by the lady and the Green Knight that the Gawain they see is not quite up to the expectations engendered by his reputation. What feeling are these taunts supposed to elicit in Gawain? They are not designed to make him feel Shame with a big **S;** these are the tactics of pretension deflation, not a judgment of total status degradation. In the end, Gawain's actual position in the social universe he occupies is enhanced by virtue of his quest, even if, especially at the end, he must still suffer the mortification, chagrin, and humiliation of posturing a little too pompously.

Gawain's real pompousness lies in his overvaluation of the fault he committed by cheating at the exchange game. He wants to make it the basis for Shame, but no one will let him get away with that. To both the Green Knight and the entire court of Camelot, Gawain's fault was a peccadillo.* It was the stuff one atoned for by feeling embarrassed and maybe momentarily humiliated, but it was not the kind of

---

*It may well have been proper for Gawain, as an initial move, to claim Shame for himself. After all, it is not for him to absolve himself *before* others indicate that they were not judging him harshly. But once they give every indication that he is overvaluing his own failing, it is bad form for him not to give up on that strategy of self-presentation.

failure which justified Shame. The point about shame is made explicitly in the poem. For the Green Knight, the fault of cheating at the exchange game was fully amended ("I hold it hardily whole" [2390]) by the scratch on Gawain's neck and by the courage with which he met his obligation in the beheading game, which, after all, was completely rigged in the Green Knight's favor. The Green Knight is really quite impressed with Gawain and he lets him know it, confirming his admiration with an invitation to return to the castle ("I think you one of the most faultless of men that there ever was, as a pearl is more in value than a white pea" [2363–64]). This is not a man who is in a state of shame that requires the negative judgment of the other; if he *feels* shame he is being consistently reminded by those about him that to do so is inappropriate to the circumstances. But it is in precisely the effort of others to deny Gawain his shame that they continue his humiliation. For shame is pretentious in this setting. It is the pretentiousness of that kind of moral punctiliousness which refuses to admit degrees of seriousness and importance among rules. It also bears special remarking that Gawain experienced no shame for the private realization of his fear and untruthfulness (there was no breast-beating when he hid the girdle from the lord); only when he discovers that this knowledge is public does he "shame."[24] This is not as yet the shame that engages the inner self. This shame concerns one's public persona. It is precisely its public nature that gives the Green Knight and the people in Camelot the power and the right to judge Gawain and to determine what he should feel. This affair is not a matter for his conscience alone, and they, for their part, suspect that any such claims are self-indulgent.

The entire plot, but especially the conclusion, is deprived of much of its finely calibrated moral and psychological nuance if we fail to discern that shame in the narrow and high tragic sense is being found inappropriate to its eliciting circumstances. We cannot suppose that Modern English *shame* has the same contours and boundaries as Middle English *shame* has; the shame of the *Gawain* poet encompasses a much wider range of feeling than we presently accord it. The word seems to apply to any feeling that might provoke a red face that isn't also clearly anger, although anger is often mixed with shame. It includes the embarrassed and shameful blush as well as the humiliated flush. But I do not mean to say that Gawain's emotional world was identical to ours but for the lack of two emotion words. It surely must make a difference that the only sphere in *Gawain* in which we see something like embarrassment is in the world of courtship, where the language of love, seduction, modesty, and blushing is capable of describing the sensation. Embarrassment has a long way to go, as Elias suggests, before farts, snot, belches, and scratching one's crotch will embarrass. Even a particularized humiliation distinct from shame must await a secularization of the sense of what it means to be brought low.

Yet because this is not the world of heroic epic either, the shames of Gawain are only partly the shames of the epic hero. Emergent in this world are the shames that are the substance of comedy. Gawain is already adept at surviving and appreciating the blushes of erotic encounter. But there is dispute as to what the appropriate response should be to being the butt of an incredibly brilliant joke, staged as a complicated sting operation. Gawain responds as an old hero would, with fury and shame. But he is a hero in a comic romance that won't ratify his response. It is not that he shouldn't feel shame, but once shown that the laughter of those who witness his breast-beating is not hostile, not itself designed to humiliate but rather only to assuage his sense of shame, he should then get his genres right. This is the stuff that should lead to laughter, even eventually his own. But as long as Gawain refuses to join the laughter, that laughter can only further mortify him. Yet part of the reason Gawain gets it wrong is that he has no readily available vocabulary to distinguish the cuts we are making and that the poet, his author, must make by suggestion and implication. With the feeling of shame comes shame's archetypal world, the world of honor, of challenge and riposte, where being the object of laughter is always serious business.

These observations jibe rather well with Harré's point that embarrassment depends on a keen distinction between morality and manners. The only area of a largely autonomous manners relatively distinguishable from morality which does not engage a man's entire claim to honor is the turf of refined seduction, the art of "fine talking," the game of courtly love. To be sure, there was a morality of love, but it was a morality that derived from men's dealings with women, and women and only women could judge how well the men were performing. As such, the world of courtly love marked out a sphere different from the one in which the game of aggressive honor between men was played out. In that heroic world women were a means for men to get at other men, either by competition for a particular woman or by connection through the woman to her male relatives. In the new autonomous realm of love a man could picture a woman as an end in herself. In the male-female relations of this world, a new morality is constructed out of acting well, out of acting with softness. In short, this is the first small creation of a sphere of manners, a context within which embarrassment becomes more normal than shame. Men could fail miserably in this sphere and still be respected by other men. Yet in one way the poem seems to lament this separation of morality and manners. What other conclusion can we draw from the interconnection between love talk and the beheading game? But in another way the poem is even more strongly delighting in the possibility of gradations in shame. How else can we explain the laughter that accompanies Gawain's self-indulgent moralisms?

The poem is really a handbook of character deflation and its various styles. Just look at what Gawain had to endure. First, he must see himself as the sophisticated courtier outsmarted by the local provincials. Provincials can subject one to a type of humiliation which could never be perpetrated by one's equals or superiors; it depends on a naive humiliator who should be adoring and accepting and in fact may still be trying to be so. It's the humiliation of the inadvertently uttered "Oh gee, I thought you would actually be taller than that." As has been mentioned before, it is Gawain's misfortune to have to struggle always to fulfill the expectations created by the exaggerations of his own literary reputation. Second, there is the humiliation of being the butt of a joke with no notice that a joke is being staged. This situation is very different from the raillery of teasing, which assumes reciprocity and implied consent. The kind of humiliation Gawain endures depends on the complete absence of consent and is also independent of the content of the joke. What matters is that the joke by being a "joke on" the other represents a refusal to accord the other a certain respect and dignity.

Third, there are the humiliations exacted by the substance of the joke itself. These are the public discoveries of Gawain's untruthfulness occasioned by his fear. Gawain is most conscious of this humiliation, but another may be even more demeaning. The flattery and attentions of the lovely lady, he now realizes, were contrived and part of the plot. Imagine how foolish Gawain feels having to revise his understanding of how he was being looked at by a woman he had until then assumed to be a star-struck devotée; now he must endure the humiliation (the feeling) of the discovery that he was seen as humiliat-

ing himself (the state) in her eyes. We have all suffered the discovery
that our momentary self-satisfactions were based on total mispercep-
tion: the man who thinks a woman is looking at him and puffs himself
up only to realize that she was looking at someone else in the same
line of vision; the unattractive high school boy who is asked out by a
very popular girl, not knowing that she is doing so because she lost a
bet. It was not that a woman tricked Gawain into cheating at the
exchange game, but that she fooled him as to the motivation of her
amorous intentions that explains his only genuinely distasteful act—
excusing himself by blaming the lady (and all womankind) for his
failing.

These substantive humiliations of the preceding paragraph engage
Gawain's being much more deeply than do the first two types of
humiliation, which are a function more of situation and structure than
of person. Gawain is thus sympathetic and indeed quite charming
right up to the moment of revelation. We do not see him making a
fool of himself, just as he cannot see himself as a fool, until we and he
have the knowledge that he was set up, a knowledge that both we and
Gawain must wait to acquire from the Green Knight. Before that
knowledge he experiences only the embarrassments and minor discomfitures of having to pay for others' exaggerated opinions of himself. After it, Gawain sees himself as a fool and responds with the
pompous self-indulgence that makes him a little foolish to us. For
we are in accord with the Green Knight: Gawain performed as well as
could be expected given the impossible circumstances. Shame not
confirmed by the judgment of others is self-indulgence. To the humiliation of seeing himself made a fool of, Gawain must add the humiliation of being considered foolish for claiming a continuing sensation of
shame for moral failings that were not failings at all. If the embedding
of the games suggests that games are life and thus very serious, the
final judgment is that Gawain's failings are excusable because life is a
game and thus accommodating to indulgent laughter.

It seems reasonable to assume that the richness of one's emotional
life depends to some extent on the richness of linguistic resources
available for the expression of emotions, yet language does not need a
rich lexicon of specifically dedicated emotion terms to fund this richness. The *Gawain* poet was able to nuance shame delicately, making,
in fact, a good part of the story revolve around the different senses
shame could have.

Conclusion to Unfinished Business

As is so often the case when we use words like *shame* and *humiliation*, even *embarrassment*, it is not clear whether we are referring to specific feelings we imagine someone experiencing or to a social fact, to what might be referred to as a quasi-juridical status. Nor is it always possible to make the distinction. For since the middle of the eighteenth century it became very hard not to suppose that the state implied the feeling, either as something that was actually felt or as a normative judgment that it should be felt given the setting. The feelings serve two kinds of functions: the fear of them or the imagined or hypothetical feeling of them keeps us from getting into the predicaments in which others deem we should feel them. This aversion is the defensive function of the emotion. On the other hand, the feeling is often the demanded inner state that makes repair possible, the dues one must pay for social and moral failure. This is the remedial function of the emotion. Both functions serve as part of the useful raw material of social control.

Scholars have troubled themselves greatly about the extent to which the particulars of our emotional life are transportable across centuries and across spatial boundaries. Ricks argues strongly that embarrassment, at least, is a very English phenomenon and one mostly fitting in the English nineteenth century: "One could suggest that English life and literature have had the advantages and disadvantages of embarrassability, and that the French have had the advantages and disadvantages of unembarrassability."[25] I have been less particularist than Ricks, but still not essentialist about the matter. One begins to suspect that different cultures share more than the social constructionist orthodoxy would allow, but that we surely share a lot less than the constraining and complacent universalism of the positivist sciences unquestioningly assumes. The constructionists are closer to getting it right but they ignore the rather insistent cross-cultural association of certain concepts and behavioral patterns: the widespread presence of something recognizable as the heroic ethic from the cold North Atlantic to the Arabian desert is but one example, and the continuing easy accessibility of heroic literature is another. As a polemical matter, constructionists privilege difference at the expense of sameness. Difference is thus what makes the other culture belong to those other people; sameness becomes an illusion because what looks like sameness cannot be the same, tied as it is to different structures of meaning. Yet this view supposes a confidence that our ability to discern difference is much more reliable than our ability to discern sameness.

Difference thus becomes an essential category immediately knowable, paradoxically, because unknowable. We never trouble ourselves that Arabic is different from English or that the English of the northwest midlands is different from Modern English. But what do we do with eighteenth-century English? Is that the same as Modern English? Or do we just delude ourselves into thinking it is because the vocabulary is so familiar and the spelling conventions are virtually the same? And if we argue that it is more different than it seems, and haul out some silly observations from recent readings of Adam Smith which assume that such words as *sensible* and *condescend,* because familiar, meant to him what they mean to us, then what? If eighteenth-century English is not the same, is nineteenth, and if not nineteenth then just when does language become identical to itself if it is always undergoing change and the culture in which it is being spoken and the things being referenced in it are also changing? We are talking degrees here clearly, but it is not always obvious that it will be easier to understand those quite near to us in time or space than those far removed. With distance comes, I think, a certain methodological humility. We cannot make complacent assumptions about the sameness of their words, categories, and values to ours because we cannot make any sense of them at all until we can read what they say. Words we render as *old, family,* and *read* meant different things to them than to us and self-evidently so. Terms referring to social categories or social practices advertise their difference, but emotions are harder to get at. Not only do language and culture intervene, but so do all the imperfections in the knowledge we have of ourselves and the other. All we can hope to do is to check and crosscheck the other's words and expressions against ours, then try to ascertain the meaning of those words in their structures of meanings, even as we must contaminate the process by filtering that meaning through our words and sensibilities. These observations are well known, and hardly merit stating. If I sin in erasing difference I think the sin lies more in the fact that I have made us look a little more like Gawain or like inhabiters of heroic culture than I have made them look like us. Thus does my incurable romanticism play havoc with my misanthropy.

But maybe the real assault on my arguments will be not against the historical claims I make about emotion vocabulary and my read of

Gawain but in my pretension of thinking that my reading of humiliation corresponds to the general experience of the American educated classes, both male and female, and perhaps beyond. I have presumed to speak for people who can still speak for themselves, and perhaps they have none of the underground man in them at all, and wouldn't care to know if they did and would be committed to disagreeing that they did even if they did. People may suspect that I haven't localized my claims sufficiently. I wonder how I could localize them more. They are clearly the reflections of an academic on the psychology and sociology of certain social practices common to those who occupy comparable social niches. Certainly I am aware that modesty conventions, so intimately connected to the eliciting conditions of humiliation and embarrassment, vary greatly across class, gender, and time. Boasting, for instance, is more acceptable among urban black males than among suburban white women, among Beowulf and his comitatus than among his rural descendants who settled Minnesota and northern Wisconsin. Still, dedicated localists might suspect an implicit universalist claim in the fact that I draw on historical examples, anthropological examples, and a neurasthenic nineteenth-century Russian anti-Semite. But even so impeccably credentialed a social constructionist and linguistic determinist as Richard Rorty accepts one social-psychological universal independent of the languages which may or may not contain the concept: the *humiliatability* of human kind.[26] He would make it our tragic essence; I would make it the style of comic accidence. But there we are.

I have discussed a change through time in the conceptualization of the emotions of self-attention which is more than a change in vocabulary. Yet I also supposed that something very close to embarrassment was feelable and discussable within the terms of the refined eroticism associated with *courtoisie* and more than evidently manifested in *Sir Gawain and the Green Knight*. Clearly this was not "our embarrassment" under a different name, for it would not have had the same range of nuance, association, and privilege. Because discussable only by varied description rather than by reference to a ready-made and available word, it could not have the conceptual power to drive other meanings. But at the behavioral and somatic level it does not appear all that different from ours, as the blushes and minor distresses of the characters indicate. As for humiliation before the word *humiliation*, it is found in epic as part of the ecology of shame. One of the necessary

conditions I supposed for eventually conceptualizing a difference between shame and humiliation was social differentiation and hierarchy
sufficient to give rise to epidemics of hypocrisy and social climbing.
The comedy of pretension could play only a very small part in the
heroic world because there was only one noteworthy ground of pretension: pretending to be courageous when one was really a coward.
In a differentiated and hierarchical society the possibility of pretension grows geometrically. The comedy of humiliation, as noted earlier,
is already present in Chaucer's fabliaux and in Shakespeare's *Twelfth
Night*, but articulated in terms of shame, despite, and contempt.

Then why the very late emergence in English of the words for
embarrassment and humiliation? Part of the answer must come, as I
indicated earlier, with the takeoff in interest in the general psychology
of motivation which characterizes important aspects of the work of
certain key seventeenth- and eighteenth-century philosophers: Descartes, Hobbes, Hume, and Adam Smith.[27] Outside the philosophical
tradition there were Robert Burton, the anatomist of melancholy, and
also a rich medical literature of the passions;[28] there were the French
courtly moral psychologists and memoire writers: La Rochefoucauld,
Madame de Sévigné, La Bruyère, the Duc de Saint-Simon all make
manners, the folly of pretension, the microscopic particulars of self-
presentation and self-advancement not just a topic, but the central
topic. Elite culture was still sufficiently transnational that we need not
trouble ourselves too much that the moralists were mostly French. It
was not, however, that the English were without candidates for this
group: Jonathan Swift, Samuel Johnson, Samuel Richardson, Laurence Sterne, and others can take their places among them. If the
elite culture then was pressuring the conceptualization of emotions
from above, I am guessing that there was a corresponding push from
below from the religions of enthusiasm which took off during the
same time and which were characterized by their intense focus on
emotions. Emotions were in vogue among the high and the low. Many
people began to make finer and finer cuts in articulating their contours and styles. In this kind of ferment it should not be surprising to
find the vocabulary of emotions getting richer. This view, of course, is
offered as a hypothesis, but a reasonable one even though it still needs
to be proven.

Undoubtedly, as a historical matter, the realm of embarrassment
expanded and continues to expand at the expense of shame in spite of

what the new psychotherapy of shame is claiming. Harré provides much of the reason: the category of morality has shrunk relative to the category of manners and convention. In my terms, this change has increased the possibility of comedy at the expense of the possibility of tragedy. Try as we might to invest our lives with the possibility of the tragic, our social lives play themselves out in the comic world. Sometimes the comedy is benign; just as often it is quite dark. Instead of Antony and Cleopatra, we have Prince Charles and Princess Di, who though English also play before an American audience. Yet before we get to Diana we have to confront Hester Prynne and Dimmesdale. If there was a move to manners from morality it did not move inexorably toward greater freedom and less constraint. What the upper classes deemed to be matters only for embarrassment the middle classes still sacralized for a considerably longer time.

As I noted in the discussion of violence (see Chapter 2) the standard historical account of state formation in western Europe is of the progressive pacification of the countryside, the greater rationalization of government, all coupled with the inexorable civilizing of the population. People repressed their more aggressive behaviors and the emotional arrays that supported those behaviors and started to become well-mannered repressed capitalists. I also indicated that some believe another story that basically subscribes to a law of conservation of violence. Suppose a feast in an English lord's hall in the thirteenth century. By one account you could belch, pass gas, wheeze and hack, spit, vomit, and blow your nose in your hand and your status remained secure. But if someone tripped over your foot, tempers rose and serious violence could occur. In short, some little matters (mostly regarding bodily functions) provided no basis for anxiety, but other "little" matters (accidental clumsinesses) put honor and life on the line. Move to a dinner in a Henry James novel dealing with roughly the corresponding rank of people which we just left in the thirteenth-century hall. There were no little matters at all, only "little" matters (i.e., big in spite of themselves). The wrong fork, the wrong serviette, the wrong placement of the fingers on a cup handle all became serious ways of determining character and social and even moral standing. And if these mistakes could ruin you, imagine what running noses, passing gas, burping would do to your reputation. True, you did not have to kill or be killed, and to this extent the stakes were surely smaller, but every move had now become a possible basis for glitch, for embarrassment, for mortification and humiliation. Although James was not an ordinary observer, the key point is that his kind of gaze was possible; a lot of people imagine only too well being subjected to it. So in which venue was the level of anxiety the greater, the thirteenth-century hall or the Jamesian dinner party of the early twentieth century?

Epilogue

Malvolio: I'll be revenged on the whole pack of you.
                                 —William Shakespeare, *Twelfth Night*

Strange, but it may well be that a writer is not any better qualified than a moderately attentive reader to write a conclusion to his or her book, for all writers have at once said both more and less in their books than they think they have said. Concluding words are thus hard to write, especially when, as in this book, no single question was begged at the beginning which was indeed answered at the end. Moreover, each chapter in this book moved, I think, toward the discovery of complexity, variety, and richness of meaning rather than toward constraining material into the confines of an overarching theory. But I have asked Malvolio to come to my aid to provide a little twist to tighten the various strands I have been weaving throughout the course of these essays. He is no stranger to us: in addition to being one of world literature's best-known comic villains, he even made a cameo appearance in Chapter 4 as an example of the close association of humiliation and the comic. Malvolio reminds us that the theme I began with, the grip of the norm of reciprocity, of paying back what we owe, is intimately connected to the violence of revenge, which in turn was motivated by the fact of his having been cruelly (but rather deservedly) humiliated. Malvolio's humiliation also reveals its intimate association with presumption and pretension, for they were his chief character flaws, and his humiliation was to be tricked into exaggerating precisely those flaws so that he would finally be perceived the fool by everyone. And by the mere fortune of having been created some four hundred years ago he raises the problem of the translatability of emotional experience across time. Even in his name, ill will in Italian (and a bad pun on mine too), we find not only his ill treatment justified, but also a suggestion of the darkness of the comedy of humiliation. As pathetic as is his refusal to join in the laughter at the end of his play, his desire for revenge shows him to be a man deeply wounded in his honor. Yes, Malvolio considered himself a man of honor even as he is presented as a person of the narrowest and meanest self-interest. He, poor soul, is the most modern character in the play. Yet he too, like us, cares viscerally about giving and getting back, evening things up, requiting favors and disfavors in the specie he feels they deserve. Malvolio, in the end, confirmed a power of a norm of reciprocity which he had heretofore denied. All these themes are immanent in the discussion of gift exchange in the first chapter, where it was suggested that the norm of reciprocity is maintained by something very akin to an ethic of honor which has as its emotive foundation humiliation, shame, and embarrassment. The possibility of humiliation and embarrassment lurks in every aspect of the most benign gift exchanges, just as getting even, or in Malvolio's case the fantasy of getting even, is one of the most predictable consequences of having been humiliated.

What I want readers to come away with is a sense of the social and psychological complexity of the most innocuous of our daily encounters. I suggested that the reason such simple interactions are fraught with danger is that we still feel the demands of something like honor very keenly. This honor involves two basic ideas: (1) that we pay back what we owe, whether it be good or bad, and (2) that it matters deeply to us (more perhaps than we are usually willing to admit) that we acquit ourselves well with the people we encounter. At the most fundamental level our minimal desire is only that we do not lose esteem or undo the basis for maintaining self-esteem from the interaction. Most of our disposition with regard to honor is defensive rather than offensive, preserving rather than acquisitive. This characteristic distinguishes us from the denizens of heroic culture, who not only had to be very defensive about losses of honor but also had to keep pressing to prey on the honor of others not so vigilantly defended. These public dispositions of defensiveness can be supported by different emotional apparatuses in the two types of culture. In heroic culture, shame did the major share of the work defending honor; among us, the tasks of defense have been assumed by humiliation and embarrassment. Envy, so intimately linked with the competitiveness of honor-based society and the means by which people were kept from getting too big for their breeches (a pun on breaches would enrich the meaning), still moves us but not so greatly as to lead us to challenge the envied. We are more civilized and more repressed. Our envy does not drive grand action; it usually bides its time waiting for the delights of *Schadenfreude,* those effortless gains we acquire solely by the failures of others who expend all the effort. Nevertheless, the live-and-let-live attitude supporting the aura of noncontentiousness which characterizes routine social encounter among us can give way rather quickly to a desire to even the score when we feel wronged, to reassert and reestablish our claim to respect. These tendencies help to show how much the emotions of honor remain with us and thus help to explain our receptiveness to tales of honor and revenge.

The move from shame to humiliation and embarrassment is the emotional side of a conceptually more general move from epic to farce, from tragedy to comedy, if I can continue to use literary genres to label the "feel" of a culture. This move seems to have been a partial consequence of a slow trend that saw the separation of manners from morals. The shrinking of shame's domain also had a linguistic aspect. The semantic range of shame was much greater when there were no specifically dedicated words to describe the emotions or states we now call humiliation and embarrassment. *Shame's* semantic range was rezoned into a smaller area once the words *humiliation* and *embarrassment* made their appearance in their modern sense. I suggested that something very much like humiliation and embarrassment existed within the wide semantic boundaries of shame before the words to describe them came into English. I also sought to demonstrate in the discussion of *Gawain* that people could distinguish various shades of shame very much like humiliation and embarrassment within the large domain of shame.[1] But even in arguing that proposition I also noted that affective life was not static either, and not only because of shifts in word boundaries. Literary genres and anthropological work give the impression that certain moral systems favor the likelihood of some emotional experiences at the expense of others. I thus supposed that embarrassment operated in the most restricted of ways in the in-your-face world of hypermasculine honor, but that in romance it had already widened its domain as a consequence of refined "love-talking." Similarly, humiliation's domain could expand as a consequence of the peculiar types of anxiety generated by a social universe in which hypocrisy and pretension were perceived to exist in epidemic proportions and in which personality was envisaged as the donning of a mask.

Several emotions figure centrally in this book, but humiliation has the lead role, and thus imparts a kind of darkness to the tone of the book. But if humiliation is dark, it is not, as I have argued, tragic for all that. Humiliation plays itself out in the comic world, and in this it is like its close cousin embarrassment. I have made humiliation depend on pretension and presumption. But it might be justly noted that to write a book is to pretend to have something to say. It also is to presume on the time and patience of the reader. The writer thus incurs considerable risk of experiencing humiliation when for whatever reason the book is either not read at all or read and dismissed. To some souls, humiliation may come as a consequence of being read and disagreed with. Somewhat counterintuitively, there are more souls who will experience something akin to humiliation when they are read and agreed with. Agreement, for instance, might be based on misunderstanding the argument, which can hardly be a cause for self-congratulation, or worse, on understanding it. Such is the strangeness of the academic world that it is not at all unusual to take being understood as a sign that one was not subtle enough, was too simple, too reductionistic, or just too dumb to see the real complexity that is discoverable in anything. For it is few of us indeed who do not so fear the humiliation of appearing too slow to comprehend the difficult that we are not willing to risk the lesser humiliation of finding the obfuscatory and obscure brilliant.

A last parting observation: if what distinguishes humans from animals is the ability to feel humiliated (thus Rorty[2]) then to be humiliated and feel so is what humanizes. We are back to the underground man. The elite are those who know that they are humiliated and feel the humiliation keenly. As I have said earlier, humiliation is a normal risk of normal interaction; it is an unavoidable feature—indeed, as I have argued, one of the key features—of civilized emotional life. That's a pretty grim view of the universe unless we can find solace in supposing that humiliation need not require humiliators, that it can be deemed merely a consequence of the structure of things, not the malign intent of sadists. But humiliation has its brighter side: sensitivity to it helps socialize us, and it also enables one of our subtler pleasures—*Schadenfreude*. By being humiliated we take turns providing a kind of illicit mirth for others which isn't really all that morally unsettling. By one account, *Schadenfreude* is not evoked by just anyone, and we do not generally feel it, if we are properly socialized, when the other's losses reach beyond a certain threshold. *Schadenfreude,* as La Rochefoucauld noted more than three centuries ago, is what we feel for our friends and cordial competitors when they fail to do too much better than we are doing;[3] it is thus less culpable than either callousness or cruelty. What ultimately reduces the moral offense of this gray sentiment is that it is readily capable of equitable distribution. For just as our humiliations provide others with the basis for their *Schadenfreude,* so do their humiliations provide us ours. Such a nice gift, we believe, could hardly do without an equally nice return.

Notes

Introduction. Burning a Witch

1. To create and maintain a culture of aggression and punctiliousness of honor just might take a richer and more intrusive normative order than is needed to maintain a culture of long-suffering and mild-mannered souls. See Herdt, "Sambia Nosebleeding Rites": "Aggressiveness is not an easy condition for humans to *create and sustain*. Freud should have visited New Guinea" (394, emphasis in original). My own writing also shows the elaborate cultural mechanisms and work needed for men to maintain the point of honor in the face of their own reluctance to expose themselves to risk. See, e.g., Miller, "Choosing the Avenger" and *Bloodtaking and Peacemaking*.

2. By "official" I mean to indicate a position that claims a certain privilege for itself independent of whether in fact that position represents an accurate description of motive or behavior. The official claims the ground of legitimacy, a legitimacy often backed by public institutions. Its style is often aspirational, sometimes hortatory; it also claims for itself the realm of the moral as that is defined by the society's dominant institutions. Official discourse can be complacent in tone, the kind of thing we understand as represented by the paying of lip-service. Yet it would be wrong to think of the official as a kind of sham. The official represents those kinds of public statements of values in which a culture images itself, and as such it bears no small role in reproducing the culture that produces such official discourses.

3. Honor did not require the discharge of debt to everyone, but only to those people held to have the capacity for honor.

4. I don't wish to overstate the case. An official ideology of the justifiability of revenge, of the honorableness of paying back what was owed, did not mean that people always lived up to those ideals in practice, or that they were without marvelously subtle strategies for avoiding the dangerous demands of honor even as they managed to maintain honor. See my *Bloodtaking and Peacemaking* and Chapter 3.

5. The Christian attack on the sinfulness of honor and pride was of long standing. To this we find beginning in the sixteenth century attacks on honor

as irrational, foolhardy, and unproductive. But it is really not until the eighteenth century that these arguments begin to win the day. Honor never disappears. It still plays a significant role in the nineteenth century, but it is driven underground and becomes ever more an illegitimate motivation, one that should embarrass the person so motivated rather than justify his actions.

6. See Parry, *"The Gift,* the Indian Gift, and the 'Indian Gift.'"

7. Comedy can be pretty rough business for its victims and scapegoats, although the fact that people get hurt does not mean that the genre is mislabeled. It only means that comedy is not fun for all of the denizens who occupy its world.

Chapter 1. Requiting the Unwanted Gift

1. Egil's history is told in *Egils saga.* Convenient and readable translations exist for most of the sagas, and I include references to them in the Works Cited. I cite the sagas parenthetically in the text by chapter because the chapter divisions of the Icelandic texts are maintained in English translations and the chapters are mercifully short, seldom longer than several pages. Translations from Old Norse are my own.

2. Egil is clearly extreme, but not incomprehensible. No contemporary would have thought him justified if he had killed Einar, but neither would people have been surprised if such a gift had ultimately led to a coldness between the men which in turn developed into a feud when a more suitable pretext presented itself.

3. Mauss's essay is much commented on. For an exceptionally astute reading of this very difficult book see Parry, *"The Gift,* the Indian Gift." See also Sahlins, *Stone Age Economics* chap. 4, and Weiner, *Inalienable Possessions* 44–65. A more popular general account of gift culture can be found in Hyde, *The Gift.*

4. *Bloodtaking and Peacemaking,* esp. chaps. 3 and 6.

5. *Hávamál* ("The sayings of the high one") sts. 42, 145. Odinn's sayings should not be construed to mean that there was an automaticity to the return. People felt the pull of the norm to make return, but the norm was opposed by very strong desires to retain for oneself. Gift exchange was not, in other words, easy business. See Weiner, *Inalienable Possessions.* Mauss begins *The Gift* by quoting Odinn in *Hávamál.* According to the usual view, Mauss is credited with the theory that gift giving is interested and strategic, but that knowledge was already possessed by the Vikings (and many others too). Jonathan Parry (*"The Gift,* the Indian Gift," 458) has a subtler read: "[Mauss's] dominant proposition . . . is that in our kind of society gifts come to *represent* something entirely different. *Gift-exchange*—in which persons and things, interest and disinterest are merged—has been fractured, leaving gifts *opposed* to exchange, persons *opposed* to things and interest to disin-

terest. The ideology of a disinterested gift emerges in parallel with an ideology of a purely interested exchange. . . . So while Mauss is generally represented as telling us how *in fact* the gift is *never* free, what I think he is really telling us is how *we* have acquired a *theory* that it should be" (emphasis in the original).

6. Heroic society understood immortality to be memorable words of praise. Thus *Hávamál* st. 77: "Cattle die, kinsmen die, you yourself will do the same; I know one thing that never dies: the dead man's reputation."

7. There is a close parallel with the significance of timing in matters of vengeance. See Chapter 3.

8. See the wonderful short narrative known as *Audun's Story (Auðunar þáttr)*, which tells of the adventures of a poor farmhand who takes it into his head to make gifts to kings. When asked by King Harald how King Sveinn repaid the polar bear Audun had given him Audun replied, "First, he accepted my gift."

9. See Miller, *Bloodtaking and Peacemaking* 107–8.

10. See the account of Eyvind's treatment of his poor kinsman in *Hrafnkels saga*.

11. On the violent possibility of seating arrangements see Chapter 2.

12. *Bloodtaking and Peacemaking* 77–109, 182.

13. Bourdieu, *Outline of a Theory of Practice* 5–10.

14. My suspicions are that most of the broader claims I will be making are generalizable beyond upper-middle class boundaries, but the details (and it is the details in which the realm of the interesting often lies) will be quite different and hence the precise significances of certain moves will vary also. Those with knowledge of other practices can make the necessary adjustments in this account.

15. We don't understand parents to be gifting children their education or initial stake for setting up a household.

16. A more detailed account of honor systems would show that there were niggardly and avaricious people who still managed to do very well for themselves in the game of honor. Egil is an example. I am presenting here a somewhat idealized model of heroic culture. The actual practice revealed contradiction, shortcomings, and failures.

17. There were also gifts made to children by doting kin; see *Egils saga* chap. 31. We do not know whether women had their own exchange cycles, although they might have. The sagas show them rewarding servants and aiding poor kin, but as a general matter women's giving did not especially interest the saga writers unless men were the recipients.

18. Caplow, "Christmas Gifts and Kin Networks," 387. This article is useful only for the rough data it presents.

19. The distinction between consumables and durables is a rough one. Food and drink have the capacity to fit in both categories. When they are

served and consumed at the time of the exchange by giver and receiver they are consumables. The gift of cheeses, jelly, whiskey, however, that is gift wrapped and not immediately consumed by giver and receiver, is a durable.

20. This intenser obligation arises because gifts of consumables are also necessarily demands for time *with* the other.

21. Marxian theorists of gift exchange distinguish commodities, which are alienable, have a determinable exchange value, and are exchanged between independent transactors, from gifts, which are inalienable, bearing as they do the person of the giver, have rank ordinal values, and are exchanged between interdependent transactors. Commodities are related to each other by price. Gifts relate people to each other. See Gregory, *Gifts and Commodities*, and also Werbner, "Economic Rationality and Hierarchical Gift Economies"; for a critique of Gregory's model calling attention to the rich range of possibility in the different values associated with gifts and commodities across cultures see Parry and Bloch, "Introduction," and Parry, "On the Moral Perils of Exchange."

22. Greeting cards are not gifts of words; they are gifts of the card as a memento of the thought that led to its being sent. The words are seldom read unless the card bears the clear sign of a punchline of a joke on the inside.

23. Caplow's evidence ("Christmas Gifts") finds that nearly 80 percent of Christmas gifts are received by relatives of the donor.

24. Again, parents are not understood to be making a daily gift of food to their kids in the same way as they are understood to give toys.

25. On the differences in how various social classes deal with food in a French setting see Bourdieu's rich discussion in *Distinction* 179–93.

26. Caplow (390) is adamant that Christmas gift exchange has nothing to do with potlatch: "There is simply no room for competitive gift giving to determine status as it may (or may not) have done among the Kwakiutl Indians (citing Heath, *Rational Choice and Social Exchange* 148). Caplow's surprising notion seems to be partially a function of the inability of his questionnaire-based empirical research to get at matters of nuance and subtlety and partially a function of the blindness of routine rational-choice theory to the richness of social practice. His views demonstrate rather effectively the grip of the ideology of the free gift on him. Children at Christmas or Hanukkah look as much to see what others got as what they got themselves, and a good portion of their pleasure (or chagrin) depends on how their gifts stack up against their siblings' and friends'. From the giver's perspective judgments of rank and status inevitably inhere in the gifts we buy.

27. Having to reciprocate excellent kosher or vegetarian meals raises similar issues. The kosher person imposes on the indebted person the certainty of inadequate recompense, whereas the vegetarian puts the nonvegetarian

host to a burden that does not figure in the accounting of adequate recompense.

28. Miss Manners firmly believes these "extra persons" should be banished from company until they are "forced to do their social share." Miss Manners takes reciprocity very seriously; see Martin, *Miss Manners' Guide for the Turn-of-the-Millennium* 433.

29. The norms and expectations vary according to gender and sexual orientation of the teacher and student. The significance of a heterosexual professor inviting an opposite-sex student for dinner would give rise to other meanings. Likewise homosexual professor and same-sex student. Hence the *en famille*.

30. Goffman (*Behavior in Public Places* 105) also sees the risk of similar impositions in mere conversation: "Words can act as a 'relationship wedge': that is, once an individual has extended to another enough consideration to hear him out for a moment, some kind of bond of mutual obligation is established, which the initiator can use in turn as a basis for still further claims; once this new extended bond is granted, grudgingly or willingly, still further claims for social or material indulgence can be made."

31. I am speaking about the surprise generated by the act of giving itself. Once a gift is expected, however, some amount of surprise as to the content of the gift is what can make of the predictable situation a truly joyous event. See further above, p. 46.

32. See Gregory, *Gifts and Commodities* 45–48, and Werbner, "Economic Rationality," 279. Compare Simmel, who believes the initial gift can never be fully recompensed. For him the first gift has a voluntariness that can never be adequately repaid precisely because the return is constrained by the obligatoriness of making a return. The first gift thus demands permanent gratitude; see Simmel, "Faithfulness and Gratitude," 392–94. I think Simmel underestimates the extent to which the return gift can recapture the high ground and how negotiable the very concept of firstness is.

33. Elizabeth Bowen distinguishes between manners and manner: "In what is called our freer modern life, manners have come to count for a good deal less, which makes sheer manner count for a good deal more." From her *Collected Impressions* 67, cited in Goffman, *Behavior in Public Places* 209. Goffman, in his early work, distinguished between substantive and ceremonial rules of conduct ("The Nature of Deference and Demeanor," 53–56), the former comprising law, morality, and ethics, the latter comprising the domain of etiquette. See also Harré, "Rules in the Explanation of Social Behaviour."

34. For a typically perspicacious account of remedial practices in face-to-face encounters see Goffman, "On Face Work," 19–23, and *Relations in Public* 95–187.

35. Like the Prisoner's Dilemma, the valentine exchange requires moves

to be made without knowledge and without communication with the other player. Unlike the Prisoner's Dilemma's, its payoff structure is such that it is not rational for either player to defect. The payoffs make cooperation an equilibrium if the players can coordinate their behavior. In this case social norms do the coordination work.

36. The view of money presented here is hardly universal, but it is of long standing in the West. In other cultures money need not be felt to be impersonal. For examples and discussion of views of the morality of money see Parry and Bloch, "Introduction."

37. Personalization cannot be supplied by giving money in the form of a check. The donor's signature can be seen to be as much an emblem of how little time the giver wants to put into giving as a sign of personalization. It is, after all, much easier to write a check than to go to the bank or teller machine to get cash. Moreover, by virtue of the check the donor has also "gifted" that labor to the recipient who must now go to the bank and stand in line to deposit the check. This labor can be a labor of love if the check is big enough. If gifts of money are going to be made there is an understanding that above a certain amount a check is the proper way to effect the transfer. But there can be no doubt that recipients are more likely to find a gift of ten dollars less risible if made in cash rather than by check.

38. A gift of new bills also indicates that special time was devoted to the gift because to obtain the bills one would have to make a trip to the bank.

39. See Bloch, *Feudal Society* 206: "And in this society, which was essentially based on custom, every voluntary gift, if it became at all habitual, was eventually transformed into an obligation."

40. There is a recent and able literature on the history and anthropology of gifts to God. Among medieval historians see especially Geary, "Échange et relations entre les vivants et les mort"; Rosenwein, *To Be the Neighbor of Saint Peter*; White, *Custom, Kinship, and Gifts to Saints*. Gifts to God function differently than gifts exchanged between equals. For competing anthropological accounts of the meanings and mechanisms of these gifts see Gregory, "Gifts to Men and Gifts to God," and Parry, "On the Moral Perils of Exchange."

41. Thus the data of Caplow, "Christmas Gifts," 386.

42. Caplow's evidence ("Christmas Gifts," 386) shows that Christmas gifts of money are rarely given to parents or grandparents even from adult children who are considerably more affluent than their elders and who also contribute to their support.

43. On wedding gifts see Cheal, *The Gift Economy* 127–41.

44. See, e.g., among many, Malinowski, *Argonauts of the Western Pacific*, and Strathern, *The Rope of Moka*.

45. This is really more complex than I am making it. The class of givers is not an unvaried class. Thus the minimum amount might bear no shame at all

for someone greatly removed from the recipient in moral distance. One is only judged relative to givers situated like oneself. Nevertheless, the registry makes it impossible to ignore the competitive aspects of the situation.

46. Children, during the earliest years of valentine exchanges, do not have the competence in these norms to feel the obligations imposed so precisely, but it seems that by the third or fourth grade, that is at roughly eight to nine years of age, they have become painfully aware of the stakes involved.

47. On the ideology of the free gift see Parry's discussion ("*The Gift*, the Indian Gift," 466–69). By linking the rise of the ideology of the free gift to the demise of the legitimacy of vengeance and the punctilious sense of honor that fueled vengeance I am adding a twist to Parry's account. Parry sees the rise of the ideology of the pure gift to be connected with advanced state development, division of labor, and the rise of markets coupled with the presence of world religions in which "social behavior is systematically ethicized" (467). Please understand that I am not claiming here that gifts are really governed by self-interest. Like most all social activities, interest, disinterest, rationality, irrationality come mixed up together inextricably in proportions that vary from microsecond to microsecond.

48. See Gouldner, "The Norm of Reciprocity."

49. See the discussion in Parry, "*The Gift*, the Indian Gift," 459–63, and "On the Moral Perils of Exchange," 64–77. Parry is aware of the practice of buying salvation and constructs his elegant discussion taking the practice into account. His argument is a careful one and rather than detail it here I urge the reader to consult this superb piece. Parry looked to India and not to us for the free gift because what we have is not the free gift but the ideology of the free gift, something that became possible only once we had an autonomous economy, politics, state, and self, and the large political role of gifts in stateless societies was assumed by the state. According to Parry, the ideology of the pure gift claimed the gift as a sphere of complete disinterest contrasted to the sphere of market transactions of complete interest, when in fact both spheres accommodate a mixture of interested and disinterested behaviors. See above n. 5.

50. Similarly Parry, "*The Gift*, the Indian Gift," 466. See also his discussion in "On the Moral Perils of Exchange," 82–89.

51. States bear an uncertain relation to cultures of honor. The usually accepted view is the one associated with Norbert Elias: with the state comes the ability to repress the ruder emotions and behaviors commonly associated with honor. See also Blok, "Rams and Billy-Goats." Sometimes the relationship can be quite complex. Consider the case of a Libyan tribe that claimed blood money from the central government for men that had fallen during the Libyan incursion into Chad. The tribe evidently took Qaddafi's writings about the nation as a segmented lineage system more seriously than the government would have liked (reported in J. Davis, "Family and State in the

Mediterranean," 29). See also Wormald, "Bloodfeud, Kindred, and Government."

Chapter 2. Getting a Fix on Violence

1. Foucault, *Discipline and Punish* 3–6; see also Spierenburg, *The Spectacle of Suffering*.

2. Greenblatt, *Learning to Curse* 11–15. Greenblatt's expressions of self-doubt about the propriety of presenting the gruesome text show just how difficult it can be to achieve convincing moral outrage when it is coupled with an unadmitted delight in the lurid.

3. See Miller, *Bloodtaking and Peacemaking*, esp. 1–3, 10–12.

4. See the discussions in Heelas, "Anthropological Perspectives on Violence," also Heelas, "Anthropology, Violence, and Catharsis," and in Riches, "The Phenomenon of Violence." A good portion of sociological, psychological, as well as anthropological work on violence has been carried out under the rubric of aggression studies. The advantage or disadvantage, as the case may be, to this way of fixing the subject was to make it easier to pretend that there was an essential aggressive action or behavior that was independent of perspective or cultural determinants.

5. For reasons I gave in the Preface I style my victims and victimizers as *he*.

6. On the complexity of such sympathetic identifications in horror film see the remarkable study by Clover, *Men, Women, and Chain Saws*.

7. Consider the shamelessness of some claims of victimization. A correspondent of Primo Levi's preserves an account of a German soldier who complained of his arm hurting from shooting so many Jews, the very pain of the rifle's recoil becoming the justification for killing more Jews. See *The Drowned and the Saved* 194.

8. Again the norm of reciprocity powerfully asserts itself. See Chapter 1.

9. It would be interesting to see how various nationalist ideologies arrange themselves on the issue of victimizing vs. victimhood, which ones claim for themselves the image of the conqueror, which the image of the avenger of wrongs and harms suffered.

10. See Shklar, *The Faces of Injustice*.

11. The notion of force makes hurricanes violent, but exempts famine and drought. Our sense of relative amounts of violence is thus often only loosely connected to the quanta of human misery involved.

12. See Anderson, *Imagined Communities* 171–78.

13. See, e.g., the recent attempt to explain violence (only interpersonal violence) as a function of various shame states by Scheff and Retzinger, *Emotions and Violence*.

14. "We usually hate those we have caused to suffer" (Simmel, *Conflict* 26).

Simmel's observation highlights the justificatory function of emotions. The link between violence and the emotions is a rich subject, and the peculiar psychic and moral economy of each emotion and its connection to violence would require each its own essay. See, for instance, the various writings of Michelle Z. Rosaldo, e.g., *Knowledge and Passion* and "The Shame of Head-hunters."

15. See Arasse, *The Guillotine and the Terror* 37–42, for an insightful account of the debate surrounding the guillotine's horror or benignity. A contemporary noted in 1794 that "execution by the guillotine is among the most dreadful, both in its violence and its duration" (37). Arasse explicates (39): "For . . . the guillotine forces into articulate discourse an impossible statement, the unspeakable 'I am dead' which can only be expressed as a metaphor. The guillotine produces this monster, a head without a body which possesses in fact and not fiction the unthinkable consciousness of its own death." The decapitated head, however, is condemned to think "one thought only: 'I think, but I am not.' The guillotine slices in half the reassurance of the Cartesian *cogito*."

16. See generally Adam Smith, *The Theory of Moral Sentiments*, for detailed treatment of the grounding of moral and emotional life in the sympathy of the impartial observer. See Tocqueville for a discussion of the relation between the limits of sympathy and social and political organization (*Democracy in America* vol. 2, pt. 3, chap. 1).

17. Dangerousness is intimately connected to what we think of as violence. And most violence is included within the broader notion of dangerousness. The risk of illness or infection may be dangerous without being violent, but violent actions will be, as a consequence of their violence, risk increasing. Because violence is almost invariably risk increasing it is likely to constitute a danger, or if not quite constituting danger, it pushes things in that direction. On the development in law and psychiatry of the concept of the dangerous person see Foucault, "About the Concept of the 'Dangerous Individual.'"

18. Killing an old man for the crimes of the young man is also unsatisfactory because it again reveals the impotence of the party of the original victims which took so long to bring the criminal to justice. Satisfaction cannot come in depriving an eighty-year-old of three more years of life. Death (or imprisonment) has to cost the criminal more than that.

19. See *Eichmann in Jerusalem*.

20. Much of the motivation behind Israeli toughness and Israeli violence, behind a style that is almost a parody of the confidently violent, is undoubtedly meant to overcome the curse of the feminized Jew. I do not mean to suggest that Israeli style is solely motivated by the curse of a stereotype. Given the geopolitical realities of the region, practicality might generate the same type of style. In any event, practical political concerns certainly help

justify a style that may have had its roots in a reaction to the humiliations of Jews in the previous millennium in Europe. One might note that Jews in the Diaspora, in the absence of overt threat and without the education in pioneer idealism, have felt no great urgency to adopt a hypermasculine style. Quite the contrary.

21. There are, of course, easy cases. Historians can get at restiveness, they can get at formally articulated grievance, and an occasional astutely self-knowing diarist might even allow them to get at the finer points of individual psychologies. But the chief problem with the "happy slave" phenomenon is that people adapt to lack of freedom and do not think to complain at all, being by virtue of their adaptiveness incapable of imagining a radical improvement in the present state of "nature."

22. Lofland, *State Executions* 312, cited in Giddens, *The Nation-State and Violence* 188.

23. Poison still seems less violent than a silenced gun. The silenced gun punctures the body and causes blood to flow. The silence of poison is part of its nature; the silence of a gun is unnatural. This makes the silencer more a disruption of normal expectation, thus helping to confirm a sense that the violence of a silenced gun is greater than that of poison.

24. *Ine*, chap. 43. The translation is my own.

25. Scarry, *The Body in Pain*. Her point was previously made by Jean Améry; see *At the Mind's Limits* 33–40.

26. Adam Smith makes this astute observation: "Pain never calls forth any very lively sympathy unless it is accompanied with danger. We sympathize with the fear, though not with the agony of the sufferer" (*The Theory of Moral Sentiments* 30).

27. Does it make sense to talk about three units of pain? Presumably there is some level of sensation below which the stimulation could not be said to be pain, but simply unarticulatable sensation. Assume for the sake of argument that we can talk about units of pain here.

28. On views on the variation in pain thresholds by class, ethnic group, and race see the interesting account in Pernick, *A Calculus of Suffering*; see also Nietzsche's politically incorrect views on this matter in *On the Genealogy of Morals* 2.7.68 and the discussion in Améry, *At the Mind's Limits* 37–38.

29. "For it seems that the name of virtue presupposes difficulty and contrast, and that it cannot be exercised without opposition. Perhaps this is why we call God good, strong, liberal, and just, but we do not call him virtuous: his operations are wholly natural and effortless" (Montaigne, "Of Cruelty," 307).

30. *Newsweek* 1 April 1991: 46.

31. Some of the essays in Armstrong and Tennenhouse, *The Violence of*

Representation, avoid these exaggerations. See, especially, the excellent piece by McGowan, "Punishing Violence, Sentencing Crime," which discusses how the nineteenth-century penal reformers marked out the category of violent crime and may even be understood to have invented the problem of violence. See elsewhere the interesting discussion by Greenhouse in "Reading Violence."

32. Choices in styles of killing were also available in saga Iceland. Some weapons dishonored the persons they killed. Being stoned or drowned typed the victim as a witch or sorcerer; axes and swords were for one-on-one combat between warriors.

33. See my "Choosing the Avenger." For differences in Catholic and Protestant preferences in matters of corpse abuse see N. Davis, "The Rites of Violence," 179.

34. See, e.g., Huizinga, *The Waning of the Middle Ages* 167; see also Bahktin, *Rabelais* 349–50, and Geary, *Furta Sacra*.

35. Marder, "The Young and the Ruthless."

36. In one version of Milgram's famous experiment in which the "victims" of electric shocks were neither seen nor heard by the subjects, two-thirds of the subjects were completely obedient and administered the strongest shocks (*Obedience to Authority* 35). Milgram was forced to add victim groans and screams and finally the victim's tactile presence to get some spread in his results.

37. Holmes ("The Secret History of Self-Interest," 271) briefly develops a category of "selfless cruelty" to indicate cruelty in pursuit of an ideal, rather than undertaken for narrowly self-interested advantage. The point being made is that disinterested behavior does not necessarily lead to moral action. Holmes does not appear to distinguish violence and cruelty. Once something is typed cruel it is being condemned morally. This is often the case with violence too, but not to the same insistent extent. We can imagine using the word *violence* purely descriptively; I do not think that is possible with cruelty.

38. Primo Levi suggests also that cruelty is useless violence (*violenza inutile*), and thus necessarily disproportionate to the ends it intends to achieve (*The Drowned and the Saved* 106).

39. See Montaigne, "Of Cruelty," 315–16: "I could hardly be convinced, until I saw it, that there were souls so monstrous that would commit murder for the mere pleasure of it. . . . For that is the uttermost point that cruelty can attain. That man should kill man not in anger, not in fear, but only to watch the sight." The implicit claim is that interest and delight make violent actions cruel and hence unjustifiable, whereas anger and fear make otherwise cruel acts somewhat justifiable as violence. We should also distinguish the pleasure in another's pain which is cruelty from *Schadenfreude*, the

pleasure in another's misfortune. *Schadenfreude* has bounds, it occupies the ground of the normal and acceptable; cruelty admits few bounds and should never be acceptable. See further, in Epilogue.

40. See Ross, "Internal and External Conflict and Violence" and "The Limits to Social Structure."

41. It was noted about a certain Viking named Olvir that "he did not catch babies with a spearhead as was the practice of other Vikings; for this reason he was called 'childfriend'" (*Landnámabók* 379). But when the dispute is local we have: "there will be no killing women or children, even though this child shall become the death of us all" (*Guðm. dýri* chap. 18).

42. Evans-Pritchard, *The Nuer* 151.

43. Tocqueville comes close to making this point in *Democracy in America*, vol. 2, pt. 3, chap. 1.

44. We belong to the former; for the latter see Malinowski, *Crime and Custom* 78.

45. On the violence of law see Cover, "Violence and the Word," and the collection of essays inspired by Cover's important article in Sarat and Kearns, *Law's Violence*. For an excellent account of the violence of masters toward servants see Fairchilds, *Domestic Enemies* 122–29, 140–50, 172–85.

46. One might hypothesize that it was better for children and maybe women too to have more than one man per household, even if the men were all violent. Laterally extended households, that is, those in which siblings and their families lived together, provided more opportunities for protection and alliance against some of the rougher forms of abuse. Children could thus have the benefits of indulgent uncles, while truly excessive behavior would bring censure from people capable of stopping it. Cf. Levinson, *Family Violence in Cross-cultural Perspective* 54–65.

47. The deviance of violent men is one of excessiveness within type. The deviance of violent women is one of appropriation of an inappropriate type. The result is that violent women are "incomprehensible" in a way that violent men are not. On this see the excellent Dutch film *A Question of Silence*.

48. See Cockburn, "The Patterns of Violence in English Society," 93–98, and also my "Beating Up on Women and Old Men."

49. Recall the furor over the appearance of the essays in Hay et al., *Albion's Fatal Tree*, presenting the case of law as violence and law as spectacle; see also Cockburn, "Patterns of Violence," 99–101.

50. It is not uncommon for definitions of violence to assume its illegitimacy. See, e.g, Wolff, *The Rule of Law* 59.

51. See Archer and Gartner, *Violence and Crime in Cross-National Perspective* 64. A 1969 survey showed that 57 percent of interviewees believed that police shooting of looters was not an act of violence. "Most textbooks on violence and aggression, however, rarely treat police homicides, capital pun-

ishment, crowd and riot control, or war. In part, this may be because govern-
ments often play an important role in defining the 'problem' of violence and,
in many instances, these definitions omit the acts of government itself."

52. Misery is often the consequence of violence, but need not be so. Like
cruelty, it is intimately involved with violence but analytically distinct from it.

53. See, e.g., Stone, "Interpersonal Violence in English Society."

54. See Elias, *History of Manners* and *Power and Civility*. For a critique of
Elias's caricatured view of the Middle Ages see Krieken, "Violence, Self-
Discipline, and Modernity."

55. See Girard, *Violence and the Sacred*.

56. The treatment of animals is a rich topic. On the connection between
the civilizing process and English fox-hunting practices in the eighteenth
century see Elias, "An Essay on Sport and Violence."

57. See Collins, "Three Faces of Cruelty."

58. See, e.g., Sharpe's reaction ("The History of Violence in England") to
Stone's "Interpersonal Violence in English Society"; see also Stone's "A
Rejoinder."

59. This is a less outlandish claim for precapitalist states than for postindustrial states, but it still captures a certain truth nonetheless.

60. I do not mean to deny that the state might not have other good
reasons for wanting to control revenge. Revenge did not often bring closure
to a dispute, but simply put the ball back in the first party's court. Escalation
often went hand in hand with lack of closure. Disputes expanded to include
more parties, and whole regions could become unsafe as a result.

61. See, e.g., Bartlett, "The Impact of Royal Government in the French
Ardennes"; also N. Davis, *Fiction in the Archives* 28.

62. The information presented here is taken from Knauft, "Reconsidering
Violence in Simple Human Societies." See also the various comments on
Knauft's piece by Betzig, Dentan, and Otterbein, "On Reconsidering Vio-
lence in Simple Human Societies."

63. See Herdt, "Sambia Nosebleeding Rites," in which he describes the
incredibly intrusive, invasive, and brutal socialization of Sambian boys.

64. One might try to define the problem away by arguing that what the
Gebusi are doing is not properly homicide but rather capital punishment—
thus Otterbein, "On Reconsidering Violence." Besides privileging the victimizer's definition of the action this view introduces Western legal
categories—homicide and capital punishment, which depend for their differentiation on the existence of a coercive state—to a small face-to-face
society in which the distinction between homicide and capital punishment
bears no significance. The Gebusi, it seems, would distinguish between (1)
those who kill by evil thoughts and (2) those who must kill by physical
intervention those who have killed by evil thoughts. These physical killings
are considered legitimate by those carrying them out, and this legitimacy of

course will affect their sense of the violence of the action. Yet it has been argued that even in state societies most nonpredatory homicide is accompanied by a sense of justice, by a belief in its own legitimacy. See Black, "Crime as Social Control," Katz, *Seductions of Crime* chap. 1, and Weisberg, "Private Violence as Moral Action."

65. The lack of a sense of violence or of untoward numbers of killings could also be attributed to the small numbers involved. Perceptually there would have to be a big difference between a homicide rate of 500 per 100,000 in a society of 450 people and in one of 4,500,000 people. It is the difference between 2.25 bodies and 22,500 bodies each year.

66. Anthropologists are always looking for such idyllic communities, but they seem to evaporate on closer inspection. See, e.g., Briggs, *Never in Anger,* and Dentan, *The Semai,* and especially the discussion by Knauft, "Reconsidering Violence in Simple Human Societies," 475–76. The gentle Semai, it turns out, made brutal soldiers in the government's campaign against Communist troops. Also see Clifford, "On Ethnographic Allegory," 103.

67. Although, in saga Iceland, physical and verbal wrongs were equally offending, when it came time for the return move physical vengeance was greatly preferred to verbal vengeance. Verbal insults were much more likely to be responded to by physical reprisal than physical violence was by a verbal countermove. This is the advice contained in the Icelandic proverb "they live long lives who are only slain with words." Given the assumptions of honor and feud this proverb cannot be read as the equivalent of "sticks and stones might break my bones but names will never hurt me." Unlike the counsel of sticks or stones, which assuages the victim of verbal insult by denying the seriousness of the wrong, the Icelandic version counsels lethal reprisal: better to kill your insulter than to swear at him.

68. Our recent notion of abusiveness, as it is embodied in abusive spouse or abusive parent, is also held to encompass the behavior of a person whose offensive actions are wholly linguistic: yelling, insult, and verbal threat.

69. See Ker's classic, *Epic and Romance.*

70. The *Iliad,* the *Book of Samuel* have kings as actors but they are not styled as heads of a state. The substance of both epics is that certain key retainers refuse to accept those claiming overlordship as any more than another challengeable equal.

71. See Chapter 3.

72. See, e.g., *Njáls saga, Ljósvetninga saga,* and *Laxdæla saga.*

73. *Ljósvetninga saga* 198–99 of the Andersson and Miller translation.

74. For an interesting account of the intimate connection of threat to violence see Boulding, "Perspectives on Violence."

75. The last clause is meant to distinguish predictions from most threats.

76. The cartoon seems to provide the archetype for the contemporary action film in which the violence is what James Twitchell refers to as preposterous (*Preposterous Violence*). Arnold Schwarznegger, even James Bond, owe their celluloid souls more to that sadsack coyote and Daffy Duck than to real soldiers, spies, and cops.

77. A certain style of anthropologized cultural history tends to minimize ritual violence, to rationalize it and excuse it, to the extent it can be seen as functional or as having symbolic and ritualized aspects. For a friendly but astute critique of this style see Desan, "Crowds, Community, and Ritual."

78. See Copet-Rougier, "'Le Mal Court,'" 50.

79. *Le sens pratique* 217.

80. Foucault, *Language, Counter-Memory, Practice* 51.

81. See generally Archer and Gartner, *Violence and Crime in Cross-National Perspective,* and Heelas, "Anthropology, Violence, and Catharsis."

82. See Tilly, *From Mobilization to Revolution* 248, and also the work of T. R. Gurr. See also Rule, *Theories of Civil Violence.*

83. Yet even homicide has its problems in this regard. See the discussion in Cockburn, "The Patterns of Violence," 75–76, 105, and further Hay, "Time, Inequality, and Law's Violence."

84. Likewise Cockburn after his exhaustive study of four centuries of crime rates in Kent: "It is in fact not at all clear that homicide rates are a reliable measure of the overall level of violent behaviour in a particular society" (105).

85. Cockburn (102) suggests that if increased medical skill has critically suppressed modern homicide rates compared to prior centuries (Cockburn is speaking of England, not the United States), then homicide statistics for the twentieth century should be adjusted "to include some cases of attempted murder." See also Katz, *Seductions of Crime* 32: "Contemporary writers on homicide and assault routinely note that whether an event ends in a criminal homicide or an aggravated assault depends on such chance factors as the distance to the hospital; the quality of medical services available; whether a gun was used and, if so, its caliber; whether 'a head reeling from a punch strikes a rail or concrete floor'; or whether the knife chanced to hit a vital organ."

Chapter 3. Emotions, Honor, and the Affective Life of the Heroic

1. Brown, "Society and the Supernatural."

2. The middle classes, however, have traditionally tended to have a rather dim view of what they perceive as the amorality and looseness of the upper or noble classes. Nevertheless, even the middle classes see the profound

emotional movement of the tragic to be more appropriate to kings and queens than to insurance salesmen, *Death of a Salesman* depending ironically on that point.

3. In the sagas it is almost a conventional indication of lack of astuteness for a person to mistake a laugh or smile for a sign of fellow-feeling and good spirit. See, e.g., *Víga-Glúm* chap. 18, and *Nj.* chap. 11.

4. Commentators have frequently noted the lack of indulgent or even direct depiction of emotion in the sagas. See, e.g., among many, Steblin-Kamenskij, *The Saga Mind* 86–95.

5. See, e.g., *Bloodtaking and Peacemaking* and "Justifying Skarpheðinn."

6. The anthropological literature through 1985 is reviewed nicely in Lutz and White, "The Anthropology of Emotions."

7. People have puzzled over the universality of mental and psychological states other than the emotions. See, for instance, Needham's detailed demonstration of the cross-cultural nongeneralizability of the mental state represented by the English word *belief* in *Belief, Language, and Experience*. Needham, however, was not as pessimistic about the possible universality of certain emotions, especially those closely tied to facial expressions and other bodily changes (see 136–46).

8. See Kagan, "The Idea of Emotion in Human Development." For a recent mapping out of the main positions in the emotion debate in the psychological literature see Ellsworth, "Some Implications of Cognitive Appraisal Theories of Emotion." One view posits some eight or nine hard-wired emotions that are intimately connected with the facial expressions associated with them. Another posits only two basic emotions—feeling good, feeling bad—which we then interpret to produce a kind of illusion about the complexity of emotional life. The third general view is that cognition precedes affect or at least proceeds together with it so that the emotions are generated by various cognitive appraisals of stimuli. This view suggests the possibility of richly varied emotional existence and thus seems the most congenial, but present manifestations of it largely ignore the constraint that linguistic categories and diction may exert on the supposed infinitude of emotional ranges. See also Hochschild, *The Managed Heart* 201–22.

9. See Wierzbicka, "Human Emotions: Universal or Culture-Specific?"; see also the discussion in Gibbard, *Wise Choices, Apt Feelings* 140–47.

10. See Wierzbicka 591, citing Hiatt, "Classifications of the Emotions." For the very different world of Maori emotional concepts see J. Smith, "Self and Experience in Maori Culture."

11. Kagan, for instance, proposes different names for feelings often lumped under one category name: "The state defined by an undetected ten-beat change in heart rate to a mild insult should be treated as different from one in which the same cardiac change to the insult was detected" (42), and

cf. William James (cited by Kagan 39): "If one should seek to name each particular one of [the emotions] of which the human heart is the seat, it is plain that the limit to their number would lie in the introspective vocabulary of the seeker, each race of men having found names for some shade of feeling which other races have left undiscriminated." See also my discussion of fear in Chapter 2.

12. See Smith and Ellsworth, "Patterns of Cognitive Appraisal in Emotion"; see also Lutz, "The Domain of Emotion Words on Ifaluk."

13. Richard Rorty, who sees our beings deeply constituted by language, comes pretty close to saying that crude vocabularies lead to crude inner lives. In his view the elite, the ironists, the intellectually playful, read a lot, know a lot of words, and have more ways of using the ones they know. See, e.g., *Contingency, Irony, and Solidarity* 80–81.

14. Emotions clearly have a justificatory aspect, and the fact that they do is intimately connected to our views of the appropriateness of emotions to their settings. See Hochschild, *The Managed Heart* 56–75, and further below.

15. These views are often associated with the work of Paul Ekman and Carroll E. Izard among many others who trace their inspiration to Darwin's *The Expression of the Emotions in Man and Animals*. See, e.g., Ekman, "Biological and Cultural Contributions to Body and Facial Movement in the Expression of Emotions," and Izard, *The Face of Emotion*. See also the accessible discussion in Frank, *Passions within Reason* 114–33.

16. This is the strong form of Ekman's position.

17. It may be that we know others better than we know ourselves; this view is surely an implicit claim of the therapist's role in various psychotherapies.

18. Some displays are relatively unambiguous, but still might be fakable. Surprise and shock, for instance, are clearly indicated by a certain movement of the brows, but that movement can be reproduced voluntarily. The usual expression for shock or surprise in Old Norse actually refers to the movement of the brows: *bregða í brún*, literally, to be startled in the brows.

19. *Lax.* chap. 48. For discussions of the practice of goading see my "Choosing the Avenger," *Bloodtaking and Peacemaking* 211–14, and Clover, "Hildigunnr's Lament," and cf. Jochens, "The Medieval Icelandic Heroine."

20. Is there a physiological distinction between blushing and flushing? Darwin seemed to have wondered much the same, concluding tentatively that flushing and blushing are not the same; see *The Expression of the Emotions in Man and Animals* 334.

21. Note the convergence of certain moral emotions. Shame and humiliation frequently are accompanied by anger or various styles of anger: indignation, outrage, vengefulness, or resentment. Skarphedinn is also manifesting the outward signs of what the Norse called *víghugr*, literally killing mood,

war mood. In the sagas it can be signaled by fits of laughter; see *Víga-Glúm* chap. 7; cf. chap. 18. Compare the closely related *vígreiðr* or killing fury, killing rage (*Nj*. chap. 147).

22. One might surely see the old Njal's lying down to die amidst the flames engulfing his house as a conscious attempt to combine the meaning such behavior would have in the new Christian dispensation with the meaning it had in the culture of vengeance. Njal was thinking about both meanings, for moments before he had been talking about martyrdom ("God will not let us burn in this world and the next") but also about being too old to take vengeance ("I am an old man and little able to avenge my sons") (Nj. chap. 129).

23. On the relation between grief, anger, violence, and personhood see M. Rosaldo, *Knowledge and Passion* 157ff., and "The Shame of Headhunters"; also R. Rosaldo, *Culture and Truth* 1–21. See also Aristotle, who makes revenge a necessary feature of anger: "anger [is] a longing, accompanied by pain, for a real or apparent revenge for a real or apparent slight. . . . Anger is always accompanied by a certain pleasure, due to the hope of revenge to come" (*Rhetoric* 2.2.1).

24. See Lutz, "The Domain of Emotion Words on Ifaluk."

25. See the career of Vodu-Brand in *Ljós*. chaps. 8–12; see also Hrafnkel in the saga that bears his name.

26. One would expect that views of the fluidity or permanence of character have moral implications. To the extent we can change or improve ourselves we can be held accountable; we can make amends by emending ourselves. But from another viewpoint, fluidity of character can be used to justify avoiding accountability: "That was not me who did it, it was a stage I was going through; that was not the real me," etc.

27. See the discussion in Shweder and Bourne, "Does the Concept of the Person Vary Cross-Culturally?" Shweder and Miller, "The Social Construction of the Person," and Shweder et al., "Culture and Moral Development."

28. There is a great risk in talking about a culture's sense of personhood, or sense of self or individuation. The risk is to assume that all people within a culture are governed by the same view. This is not so, even among us. In saga Iceland, heads of households were clearly more individuated than their servants, men were more individuated than women, the rich more than the poor. The same might be said about us. In the text to which this note is appended I am talking mainly about the theory of personhood governing men (and sometimes women) of honor.

29. Some aesthetic emotions depend on an absence of emotion in the fictional character. The apprehension we feel, for example, because we know that the character is blithely ignoring absolutely certain warnings of doom depends on the character's feeling no apprehension at all.

30. *Bloodtaking and Peacemaking* 191–92.

31. See Sveinsson, *The Age of the Sturlungs* 76–82.

32. For well-taken criticism of the dichotomy see Piers and Singer, *Shame and Guilt*. Even though Ruth Benedict was not the first to formulate the shame-versus-guilt culture distinction she is usually given the credit for calling wide attention to it; see *The Chrysanthemum and the Sword*. Benedict seems to have been the inspiration behind certain literary and cultural historical attempts to get at emotions and values in earlier cultures; see, e.g., E. R. Dodds's classic *The Greeks and the Irrational*, and Jones, *The Ethos of the Song of Roland*. See also the discussion in Williams, *Shame and Necessity* 89–95.

33. See the excellent discussion by Taylor, *Pride, Shame, and Guilt* 55; see also Goffman, who distinguishes pride, which is self-referential, from honor, which involves a relationship to wider social units ("On Face Work," 9–10). Nozick makes the mechanism of self-esteem operate similarly to honor by operating comparatively (*Anarchy, State, and Utopia* 243). Compare, however, Neu, "Jealous Thoughts," 440–41. For an able discussion, in the Icelandic context, of the public nature of honor and its connection to the public display of verbal artistry see the account in Bauman, "Performance and Honor in 13th-Century Iceland."

34. In this respect the Icelandic honor system was not unlike one view of honor systems centered in the Mediterranean; see, e.g., Gouldner, *Enter Plato* 49–51; Brandes, "Reflections of Honor and Shame in the Mediterranean," 121–22; Pitt-Rivers, *The Fate of Shechem* 92. I am suppressing some nuance in the desire to paint a rough and serviceable picture in a reasonable space. There were, for instance, frequent attempts by third parties to persuade combatants that both sides could win honor if they settled amicably. Part of the ideology of peacemaking, in other words, held out the possibility that honor could be more than zero-sum. Cf. Elster, "The Norms of Revenge," 867, and see my discussion in *Bloodtaking and Peacemaking* 30–34, 75. There were also those ambiguous settings in which it was not quite clear as to who had gained and who had lost honor. The actual politics of honor acquisition was played out over time. Events could be reinterpreted at later dates so that what might have been accepted as admirably prudent could be later seen as cowardly and what was at first deemed justified vengeance could be later understood as shameful assault.

35. Snorri figures prominently in many sagas, but his skillful strategizing, his remarkable negotiation of the world of honor, is best revealed in *Eyrbyggja saga* and *Laxdæla saga*.

36. On this point see also Bauman, "Performance and Honor," 141–42.

37. See the discussion by Taylor, *Pride, Shame, and Guilt* 57–68.

38. See Bourdieu's discussion of the *amahbul* in "The Sentiment of Honor in Kabyle Society," 199–200, and also *Outline of a Theory of Practice* 12.

39. If not shame, the person, however, may feel embarrassed for violating norms that others hold dear but that he or she does not. It would be the embarrassment of failing to do in Rome as the Romans do.

40. There is an enormous literature on honor in the Mediterranean basin. See the essays, especially those by Pitt-Rivers and Bourdieu, in the classic collection *Honour and Shame: The Values of Mediterranean Society*, edited by Peristiany, 19–77, 191–241. See also Pitt-Rivers, *The Fate of Shechem*, and the well-known contribution of Campbell, *Honour, Family, and Patronage*. The classic honor/shame model of these texts has been subjected to criticism and revisionist pressures in the last decade or so. See, for instance, Herzfeld, "Honour and Shame" and "'As in Your Own House.'" The usefulness of the honor/shame paradigm survives Herzfeld's attacks, but he provides a needed reminder that the exact content of honor varies greatly within the Mediterranean basin. The model has also been refined and given greater nuance by sophisticated gender analysis; see, among others, Delaney, "Seeds of Honor, Fields of Shame." For a recent and able review of new work on Mediterranean honor and shame see Gilmore, "The Shame of Dishonor," who concludes by defending the value of the classic model as reconceived via gender analysis and who in his "Honor, Honesty, Shame" demonstrates that the content of Andalusian honor allows for more than just confrontational competitiveness. See further the discussion in Cohen, *Law, Sexuality, and Society* 54–69, on the applicability of the classic model to Periclean Athens. For studies on honor and feud in the Mediterranean making use of historical materials see Black-Michaud, *Feuding Societies*, Boehm, *Blood Revenge*, and Wilson, *Feuding, Conflict, and Banditry*.

41. See, e.g., Pitt-Rivers, *The Fate of Shechem* 78–80; Campbell, *Honour, Family, and Patronage* 199.

42. The extent to which Mediterranean women were actually sequestered has been called into question (see Cohen, *Law, Sexuality, and Society* 133–70), but no amount of questioning can undo a very strong sense of the difference between the official (and actual) limitations on free women in the saga world of medieval Iceland when compared to their less fortunate Mediterranean sisters; see Gilmore's discussion, "The Shame of Dishonor," 8–16. On the conceptualization of gender in the northlands see especially Clover, "The Eternal Effeminate."

43. The sagas do not readily reveal the obsessive fears of the feminine which characterize the hypermasculinity of Mediterranean cultures. The separation of women and men was not anywhere near as systematic in saga Iceland as in the south. There were no villages to speak of in Iceland to support the café or marketplace masculine spaces that characterize the Mediterranean. As a matter of ideology, though, woman's space was still indoors and man's outdoors, but in reality the men were underfoot more often than not. If it is true that saga men were less obsessively fearful about

masculinity than were Mediterranean men, there might be some confirmation here for those who would seek to explain the fragility of manhood in the Mediterranean by the absence of adult men for the formative years of their male children (see the discussion in Gilmore, "The Shame of Dishonor," 9–15). On the other hand, the Icelandic evidence shows that an honor-based culture can still socialize its boys to be particular about their honor and shame even if their fathers were around the house. Recall that it is Skarphedinn's mother who demands his aggressiveness.

44. *Skömm, virðing,* and *sæmð* are cognate respectively with English *shame, worth,* and *seem,* as in seemliness. Shame was also indicated by *sneypa* (a legal term), *klæki,* and *(h)neisa.* The terms are largely synonymous and they are often paired with each other for purposes of emphasis. E.g., *skömm ok klæki, sneypu ok svívirðing (Gísli* chaps. 32, 29), *skömm eða neisu (Heið.* chap. 22), *svívirðing ok skömm (Lax.* chap. 48; *Band.* chaps. 8, 9; *Hrafnkel* chap. 3). This last cite appears as *skömm og sneypu og svívirðing* in the newest and best edition of the saga, ed. Bragi Halldórsson et al. (Reykjavík: Svart á Hvítu, 1987) 2: 1403.

45. The person who fails to rescue a drowning infant at little or no risk to him or herself has done a shameful thing, but not (in the United States) an illegal or a violent thing. See Chapter 2.

46. See, e.g., the actions taken by Bjarni of Hof against his gossiping servants in *Þorstein.*

47. The interconnections between feud and gifts and the logic of requital and of getting even are the central themes of my *Bloodtaking and Peacemaking;* see also above Chapter 1.

48. Avenging: *Nj.* chap. 44; *Drop.* chap. 3; *Eyrb.* chap. 13; *Gísli* chap. 27 (in the Svart á Hvítu edition); *Græn.* chap. 8; *Korm.* chap. 15. Paying: *Nj.* chap. 139; *Þorgils sk.* chap. 18.

49. See especially the speech of Njal (chap. 91) concerning the indignities and dishonor one must endure before one can be justified in retaliating.

50. See Bourdieu, *Outline of a Theory of Practice* 14.

51. On the emotions that regularly accompany shame see Burton, *The Anatomy of Melancholy,* pt. 1, sec. 2, memb. 3, subs. 6, who gives a prominent role to grief. One way of distinguishing the heroic ethic from other more forgiving styles would be to compare the emotions most likely to attend shame. In the heroic ethic these would more likely be anger, indignation, and a sense of duty than remorse, guilt, or sorrow.

52. *Eyrb.* chap. 47; *Hall.* chap. 4 (Svart á Hvítu ed.); cf. *Nj.* chap. 98.

53. *Lax.* chap. 48. On goading see the references above n. 19.

54. Blushes and shame have been recognized as intimate associates by poets for centuries and by scientists since the last century. It is typical of Skarphedinn's desperate effort to restrain his emotions that he can manage to keep part of his face from participating in the involuntary response of

facial reddening. The received view is that blushes (or flushes) cannot be faked. See Darwin, *The Expression of the Emotions* 310; also Edelmann, "Embarrassment and Blushing."

55. See further Chapter 4.

56. See *Bj. Hít.* chap. 4; *Nj.* chap. 129; *Svarf.* chaps. 4, 5.

57. Remorse is the feeling Hrafnkel has for killing the boy Einar (*Hrafnkel* chap. 3), and it is what Bolli feels after he has killed Kjartan (*Lax.* chap. 49). In each case remorse is indicated explicitly, but also confirmed by action. Hrafnkel follows up the killing by offering an extraordinarily generous gift to the father of the boy, while Bolli cradles the dying Kjartan in a pietà-like tableau.

58. I gloss *skammask* as "feel shame" rather than "to be ashamed" as do Cleasby and Vigfússon, *An Old-Icelandic Dictionary* s.v. skamma, II. Gabriele Taylor notes that feeling ashamed need not in English usage be the same as feeling shame (*Pride, Shame, and Guilt* 52). When we say we feel or are ashamed we are often talking about remorse or regret, which are not emotions that depend on one's standing in a community.

59. According to the unpublished concordance of the family saga corpus, there are some three and one-half times more occurrences of the various grammatical forms of shame (including combined forms) than forms of envy (*öfund*).

60. See *Bloodtaking and Peacemaking* 277, 301–2, and the bibliography noted there on 370n31.

61. This is the meaning of Old Icelandic *öfund*, which is consistently used in contexts that show people grieving another's pleasure and success. Of the 28 uses of *öfund* in the saga corpus, whether in substantive, verbal, or combined forms, only two or three might more precisely indicate begrudging rather than envy. I take begrudging following both Rawls and Nozick to indicate the preference that another not also have what you have, which is distinguished from envy where you prefer that neither of you have it to the other having it and you not; see Nozick, *Anarchy, State, and Utopia* 239. Modern English usage must borrow German *Schadenfreude* to distinguish the sentiment of pleasure in another's misfortune, which is sometimes included in some uses of spite, malice, and envy. Chaucer's Physician included *Schadenfreude* within the concept of envy: "save Envye allone, that sory is of oother mennes wele, and glad is of his sorwe and his unheele" (*Canterbury Tales* C 89–194), and 250 years later Robert Burton (*The Anatomy of Melancholy*, pt. I, sec. 2, memb. 3, subs. 7) would do so too: "envy is naught else but sorrow for other men's good, be it present, past, or to come: & joy at their harms, opposite to mercy."

62. Nozick, *Anarchy, State, and Utopia* 239. This sense of spite accords with common notions that the spiteful person is willing to harm himself in order to harm another, often without reference to whether he thereby harms

the other as much as he harms himself. (I add the latter proviso to except rationally motivated scorched-earth policies from spiteful motivation.) In at least one translation of Aristotle spite is used to indicate *Schadenfreude; The Nicomachean Ethics* 2.7.106; likewise Hume's malice; *A Treatise of Human Nature* 2.8.425.

63. Maxim #95.

64. See generally the penetrating treatment of envy, envy enjoyment, and envy provocation in Elster, *The Cement of Society* 252–63.

65. Gluckman, *Custom and Conflict in Africa* 96.

66. *A Treatise of Human Nature* 2.8.425–26. Aristotle makes the same point. "And since men strive for honour with those who are competitors, or rivals in love, in short, with those who aim at the same things, they are bound to feel most envious of these" (*Rhetoric* 2.10.241).

67. "Verses on the Death of Dr. Swift," vv. 13–14.

68. This is hardly a new idea. If the connection between honor and shame is an ethnographical commonplace, the connection between envy and honor is a moral philosophical one. See, e.g., Aristotle: "Nearly all the actions or possessions which make men desire glory or honour and long for fame, and the favours of fortune, create envy" (*Rhetoric* 2.10.239).

69. See generally *On the Genealogy of Morals*.

70. *Ethics* 2.6.102, but see the much more nuanced view he presents in *Rhetoric* 2.9–10.231–43.

71. See *Piers Plowman*, B: 5.83–85, 91–92, for a delightfully comic and grotesque caricature of an allegorical Envy.

72. See *A Treatise of Human Nature* 2.8.420–29. Recent theorists of emotions continue the tradition. See Solomon, *The Passions* 306–9; Taylor, "Envy and Jealousy," and Lyons, *Emotion* 188: envy is not only "not useful," but "socially divisive."

73. See, e.g., Schoeck, *Envy*.

74. Nietzsche, "Homer's Contest" (55):

The whole Greek antiquity thinks of spite and envy otherwise than we do and agrees with Hesiod, who first designates as an evil one that Eris who leads men against one another to a hostile war of extermination, and secondly praises another Eris as the good one, who as jealousy, spite, envy, incites men to activity but not to the action of war to the knife but to the *contest*. The Greek is *envious* and conceives of this quality not as a blemish, but as the effect of a *beneficent* deity. What a gulf of ethical judgment between us and him. (emphasis in the original)

The passage supposes a close connection between envy and competition. But clearly for envy to fuel only productive competition and not destructive "war to the knife" we need either effective normative constraints that make feud unthinkable and impractical or in the absence of such self-regulation we need constraints imposed by force. The state becomes necessary.

75. Rawls, *A Theory of Justice* 531–34. Rawls distinguishes between particular and general envy. Particular envy depends on a rough equality between envier and envied and is played out in competition for office or for specific things. It is envy as we usually think of it and behaves like the envy of Aristotle and Hume (see above n. 66). General envy behaves somewhat differently in that it depends, not on the social proximity of envier and envied but on their distance. This is the envy the least advantaged have for the better situated. It is general because it is not envy for any particular objects but for the kinds of general goods they are favored with, like wealth and opportunity. General envy, when occasioned by great differences in distribution, can be excusable, its excusability being very much related to the failure of the conditions for particular envy, i.e., a rough egalitarianism shared by competitors in the same game. In Rawls's system excusable general envy signals a failure of justice.

76. There is nevertheless an ancient tradition that also sees emulation as a source of anguish. See Burton, *The Anatomy of Melancholy*, pt. 1, sec. 2, memb. 3, subs. 8.

77. See *A Theory of Justice* 533, 539.

78. *A Theory of Justice* 539.

79. Classic honor societies also seem to be characterized by large amounts of male leisure time. The coffee houses of the Mediterranean, the markets of North Africa, the farmhouses of Iceland, the streets of the ghetto are evidence.

Chapter 4. Humiliation: Part I

1. Karen, "Shame," *Atlantic Monthly*. This very accessible internalist and friendly guide to the recent spate of shame literature itself shares some of the problems of the texts it reviews; for a less sanguine view of this literature see Lasch, "For Shame," *The New Republic*.

2. Shame in this literature starts to coalesce with guilt, differing only in rather formal ways. In the subtlest of these schemes, for example, guilt is contrasted with shame in but one particular: the totality of self-blame involved. Specific self-attributions of fault define guilt, global self-blame defines shame. See Lewis, *Shame: The Exposed Self* 65, 72–73. The social psychologists Scheff and Retzinger, *Emotions and Violence* 104–5, treat guilt as a subset of shame. Guilt is a "shame-anger" sequence directed against the self. For competent performances in the new shame genre see Lewis; see also S. Miller, *The Shame Experience*, and Broucek, *Shame and the Self*. For a fuller bibliography see Lewis.

3. See Massaro, "Shame, Culture, and American Criminal Law."

4. See Goffman, "Embarrassment and Social Organization." Among philosophers see the excellent piece by Harré, "Embarrassment," and Taylor, *Pride, Shame, and Guilt*. There is a voluminous literature in social psychology; for comprehensive performances in this discipline see Edelmann, *The Psychology of Embarrassment*, and more recently the collection of essays in Crozier, *Shyness and Embarrassment*.

5. It is not clear that embarrassment has yet systematically extricated itself from shame in the social-psychological literature either. Only recently has Carroll Izard, a leader in the hard-science approach to the psychology of emotions, seen fit to distinguish them and then mostly as a matter of intensity; see Izard and Hyson, "Shyness as a Discrete Emotion"; cf. Izard, *Human Emotions*. See also Scheff and Retzinger, *Emotions and Violence* 26. Once blushing starts to figure prominently in discussions of embarrassment, shame comes tripping in along with it. Darwin, for that matter, never mentions embarrassment in his study of blushing and the emotions of self-attention. But his shame and modesty often look more like what we would think of as embarrassment than shame; see *The Expression of the Emotions in Man and Animals* 309–46.

6. See Silver et al., "Humiliation." See similarly Rorty's understanding of humiliation in *Contingency, Irony, and Solidarity* 89–95.

7. See Simmel, *Conflict* 20–21: "much of what we are forced to represent to ourselves as mixed feelings, as composites of many drives, as the competition of opposite sensations, is entirely self-consistent. But the calculating intellect often lacks a paradigm for this unity and thus must construe it as the result of several elements."

8. A person may not hold a particular value very dear but still feel shame for failing to measure up to it both because she cares about what others who hold that value think of her and because of a commitment to the belief that what the community she belongs to values is of concern to her whether or not she is committed as an intellectual matter to the particular value at issue.

9. See, e.g., Taylor, *Pride, Shame, and Guilt*, and also Williams, *Shame and Necessity* 89–95.

10. Piers makes shame a function of tension between the ego and the ego ideal, not between ego and superego as in guilt. Guilt is generated when a boundary set by the superego is transgressed and shame occurs when a goal presented by the ego ideal is not reached. Guilt accompanies transgression; shame failure. The threat implied in shame is the anxiety of abandonment; in guilt it is of mutilation (castration). See Piers and Singer, *Shame and Guilt* 23–24.

11. For reviews of the literature see Broucek, *Shame and the Self* 11–17, and S. Miller, *The Shame Experience* 9–18.

12. For attempts to reinvigorate shame within the paradigm of psychoanalysis see Wurmser, *The Mask of Shame*, and also Hultberg, "Shame—A Hidden Emotion."

13. See, e.g., Scheff and Retzinger, *Emotions and Violence* 3, in which the social is reduced to seeing oneself from the viewpoint of others. Helen Lewis, the matriarch of the new shame psychology, ends up making guilt more social than shame. Shame focuses on the self, guilt on concerns about the other (discussed in Michael Lewis, *Shame* 71). It is hard to deny Christopher Lasch's point that the new shame literature is little more than an avatar of the feel-good movement in which low self-esteem figures as the fount of all ill.

14. "To a Louse," vv. 43–48.

15. In her fine discussion of shame Taylor (*Pride, Shame, and Guilt* 68) also makes humiliation depend on presumption: "It is that she aspired to the high position when she had no business to do so, and it is this thought, that she is regarded as presumptuous, which is essential to humiliation as it is not to shame." Taylor thinks of shame and humiliation as distinct emotions ("the difference between the two emotions [shame and humiliation] is one of emphasis"), but because she makes the difference only one of emphasis, humiliation ends up as a vestigial appendage on shame's corpulent body. My view is that the difference between shame and humiliation is somewhat more than just a matter of emphasis.

16. I mean comic in a very broad sense, taking it to include the most savage satire, the bitterest irony, the most ribald farce, as well as the gentler more intellectualized smiling at folly which George Meredith takes the essence of the comic to be; see "An Essay on Comedy," 42–48. Still, Meredith's comic Spirit has for its general subject the deflation of pretension in all its forms and as such is intimately connected to what I am taking the essence of humiliation to be.

17. There is of course a pretentiousness in hypocorrection, involving a quest for "cool" by upper-middle-class whites.

18. A whole different set of discomforts arises when a maintenance person is present in an academic office while the academic is talking shop with a colleague. In that setting the attuned academic experiences acute embarrassment, even a kind of self-loathing, as she hears herself as she imagines she is being heard.

19. In this regard one might note that the "sick joke" still thrives, but it is legitimate only if it is told by a member of the group that is its subject. By calling such humor sick we seek to excuse our laughter by a confession of impropriety. Grotesquerie for us lives a restricted and unhealthy life compared to its robustness in earlier times; see generally Bakhtin, *Rabelais*.

20. The pretender who does not botch the job is (1) either not then a true pretender or (2) an artful fraud, a con artist, who makes infinitely greater fools of others when exposed by them than they make of him by exposing him.

21. This is more complicated than I am making it here. The likelihoods of being humiliated and feeling humiliation would depend on the makeup of the audience before whom it is played. The low and the high are not judging these things by the same set of norms.

22. Both these propositions underlie much of *The Red and the Black*, and the character of Julien Sorel is a wonderful example of how they might motivate a person.

23. The paradigm here is Hegel on master and slave, which my discussion implies is applicable only to a rather circumscribed set of human interaction, not even as extensive as the one under inquiry here.

24. Darwin, among others, has also noted this tendency; see *The Expression of the Emotions* 345.

25. Freud, "The Antithetical Sense of Primal Words."

26. Other languages differentiate at the lexical level between the unpleasant emotion and the capacity to avoid it—e.g., French: *pudeur/honte;* German: *Scham/Schande* (both however coming from the same Primitive Germanic root).

27. See Schneider, *Shame, Exposure, and Privacy* 18. This nice book, written somewhat in the style of a pastoral guide, ranges widely and takes risks.

28. For witty and subtle discussions of pride in humility and the hypocrisy of humility see Franklin, *The Autobiography* pt. II: "For even if I could conceive that I had compleatly overcome [pride], I should probably be proud of my Humility" (90); see also Stendhal, *The Red and the Black* I, chap. 26; and Montaigne, "Of Not Communicating One's Glory," 187. This kind of pride in humility is readily distinguishable from the mandated humility of the low-status person in a rigid class society who presents his humility in such a way as to make clear to his superiors that his pride is as great as theirs. Thus can Julien Sorel affect an air "orgueilleusement humble" (II, chap. 9).

29. For example, Catherine of Siena; see Bell, *Holy Anorexia* 5–12 *passim.* On the public style of humility in the context of early medieval supplication rituals see Koziol, *Begging Pardon* 59–70.

30. The most consistently insightful works I have read on embarrassment have been those of Goffman, Ricks, and Harré, from the disciplines of interpretive sociology, literary criticism, and philosophy. The work of social psychologists, even when good, suffers from the limitations "science" imposes on insight when it attempts to deal with the morass of motivation encountered in face-to-face interaction.

31. The social nature of these emotions does not mean that one cannot be embarrassed or humiliated or shamed without actually being seen. Our later self can play the role of the other to our earlier selves. One often experiences

embarrassment, shame, and humiliation by reading one's old diaries, love letters, or published work. Cf., however, Silver et al., "Embarrassment," 53, who fail to recognize that we can play the other to ourselves.

32. Empirical studies of similarity among the emotion words connected with shame/shyness show that English speakers associate shame, humiliation, and embarrassment together as against other emotion words in the same field such as guilty, penitent, repentant, anxious, afraid, bashful, timid, shy, and self-conscious. See Crozier, "Social Psychological Perspectives on Shyness, Embarrassment, and Shame," 39–48.

33. I am accepting here Harré's notion of embarrassment as "occasioned by the realisation that others have become aware that what one has been doing . . . has been a breach of convention and the code of manners, a judgement in which I, as actor, concur" ("Embarrassment," 199). Harré's definition opposes embarrassment to shame (humiliation does not figure in his construct). Shame replaces "breach of convention and the code of manners" of embarrassment with "moral infraction." Shame thus engages the moral, embarrassment the conventional. This distinction works rather well in a rough way. I say "rough" because its utility, clearly, depends on our being able to distinguish morals from manners with greater confidence than we can distinguish shame from embarrassment.

He also earlier distinguishes shame from embarrassment (1) by the seriousness of the breach and (2) by the degree of fault accorded the agent. Both these criteria overlap and reproduce some of the inputs of the other, a point Harré's grid ignores, while neither quite reproduces the distinction of shame and embarrassment as the difference between breaches in moral as opposed to conventional norms. In his scheme embarrassment occupies the trivial/no fault quadrant, shame the serious/fault quadrant.

34. He might have known that he had been introduced to me and still not have recognized me.

35. See Sabini and Silver, *Moralities of Everyday Life* 23n7, for nicely distinguishing being ignored from being snubbed: "The difference between being ignored and being snubbed hinges on the fact that the ignored cannot point to any special dereliction in the distribution of attention; being ignored is cumulative, not involving any overt violation of constitutive rules of social interaction. Hence, it is extremely difficult to deal with"; also Silver et al., "Humiliation," 282n10; Geller et al., "On Being Ignored"; and Goffman's discussion in *Behavior in Public Places* 114–23.

36. Silver et al., "Humiliation," 278–79, discuss the case of a woman who waits for the man who told her he would call Thursday night to call, but who never does. They use the case to show that although humiliation depends on meeting publicly available objective standards, the actual humiliation suffered can be quite private.

37. See the insightful discussions of self-deception and wishful thinking

and other means of belief-manipulation in Elster's *Ulysses and the Sirens* and *Sour Grapes*.

38. There are those, of course, who will tell of their humiliations in order to entertain but who only embarrass others and do not amuse them at all by so doing. The measure of discomfort raised in the audience by these "confessions" is a measure of the extent to which the norms of publicity and privacy have been violated by the narrator. Embarrassments can be told to entertain; it is only the rare humiliation that can. There is also a sense that time does not work very well to turn humiliations into embarrassments. Time works to make embarrassments amusing, but humiliations tend to stay painful even if eventually revealed to another.

39. A related problem received a lot of social psychological attention in the 1960s and 1970s in the aftermath of several highly publicized cases in which bystanders failed to come to the aid of crime victims who screamed for help. This work suggested that it was the presence of more than one bystander which inhibited all bystanders from offering aid. Diffusing the responsibility for action raised problems of coordination and cooperation, a kind of free-rider problem. See Latané, *The Unresponsive Bystander*, and the critique in Frank, *Passions within Reason* 218–19. Diffusion of responsibility explains only the reticence about initiating assistance; it does not account for the continuing awkwardness one feels while already helping the person in need.

40. My drift suggests the argument of Douglas, *Purity and Danger*.

41. See Goffman, "Embarrassment and Social Organization," 108; Edelmann, *The Psychology of Embarrassment* 93; Asendorph, "Shyness, Embarrassment, and Self-Presentation."

42. Goffman, "Embarrassment and Social Organization," 108n6.

43. See R. Miller, "Empathetic Embarrassment"; also Modigliani, "Embarrassment and Embarrassability."

44. See Harré, "Embarrassment," 202.

45. See the discussion in Bourdieu, *Distinction* 183, where this kind of conviviality is dealt with as a ritualized behavior.

46. Figure skating is gendered feminine. It is purely decorative; it cannot claim that its skills are a kind of training for warrior-like virtue as so much nondecorative sport can. The feminine is allowed less leeway for acts of awkwardness, acts that show lack of bodily control.

47. There is a rich sociology of falling. Falling is the stuff of slapstick and embarrassment. As noted earlier, when we fall on the ice walking down the street in the winter we might say that we suffer humiliation, but here we are using the word only in the strong sense of acute embarrassment, unless we fall while engaged in some kind of display of ourselves which supposes poise and self-control. Men or women who stumble while trying to cut a figure before the opposite sex more than embarrass themselves, they humiliate

themselves with a fall. A president tumbling out of an airplane humiliates himself, because presidents are never allowed not to be posing.

48. See Scheff and Retzinger, *Emotions and Violence*. The sagas couple shame and anger rather frequently. See above Chapter 3.

49. Katz, *Seductions of Crime* 22–43; Harré, "Embarrassment," 191.

50. One rather superficial psychoanalytic treatment of humiliation assumes that humiliation by definition depends on unjustified assaults on self-esteem. See Stamm, "The Meaning of Humiliation." The relation of humiliation to justice is more complexly nuanced. A good case could be made that the most acute sensations of humiliation occur precisely when we feel the same distaste for the figure we cut which we suppose the observer had. The humiliation in which we can feel indignant at our humiliator is not as painful as the humiliation in which we have no basis for indignation.

51. See Katz's wonderful description, which runs rather counter to this one (*Seductions of Crime* 27–28). Because anger and outrage can attend the emotions of humiliation and shame just as well as despair, the display of anger might quickly overlay or replace the displays of humiliation and shame.

52. See Taylor, *Pride, Shame, Guilt* 70, who makes the core of embarrassment the imposition of a demand on another to do something. It is this imposition that makes one feel in a quandary.

53. There are clear parallels with how one responds to dharna and the sensations elicited when one deals with the blind and handicapped. Both situations play on the awkwardnesses generated by requests (implicit in the case of the blind, explicit in dharna) for aid by people who are seen as lacking the completeness and autonomy that adult actors are expected to have.

54. See Baumgartner, "Social Control from Below," for a discussion of rituals of social control available to low-status persons.

55. See Miller, "Choosing the Avenger." For a view of the ordeal as a ritual of humiliation rather than as a mode of proof see my "Ordeal in Iceland."

56. The Hebraic ceremony involves putting on sackcloth and sometimes also covering one's head with ashes. One forgiveness ceremony has Ben-hadad the king of the Syrians going to the king of Israel with sackcloth on his loins and a rope on his head (*I Kings* 20:31). Mordecai rends his clothes and puts on sackcloth and ashes as the first step in his strategy to counter Haman's anti-Jewish policy (*Esther* 4.1). For an especially interesting medieval ritual involving the degradation of saintly relics see Geary, "Humiliation of Saints," and also Brown, "Society and the Supernatural."

57. See generally Koziol, *Begging Pardon*.

58. See Tavuchis, *Mea Culpa* 17.

59. There is, of course, no guarantee that even sincere and abject apology will be accepted no matter how humiliating it is to the apologizer. Rituals are

not foolproof strategies just because they are ritualized. Sincere and abject apology can work to move the wronged party to disgust and even greater rage, while refusal to abase oneself in apology might elicit the admiration and ultimate forgiveness of the wronged party. See Montaigne, "By Diverse Means We Arrive at the Same End," 3–5.

60. On rituals of status degradation see Garfinkel, "Conditions of Successful Degradation Ceremonies."

61. *The Body in Pain*. Scarry does not refer to humiliation in her discussion of torture. She speaks of the use of pain in unmaking or annihilating people's worlds. Scarry's points depend on physical pain, a dependence making her unmaking a matter different from a simple one of humiliation. Richard Rorty, however, reads her to be making claims about the *humiliation* of having one's world unmade. Rorty's misreading is a function of his own view that humiliation is what might happen to those who believe in the naturalness and universality of their own "final vocabularies" or world views if ironists like himself who delight in contingency and the particular aren't careful to be nice to these nonironic universalists. See *Contingency, Irony, and Solidarity* 89–92, 177–78.

Those scholars who see torture chambers and death camps as the archetypal setting of humiliation (see, e.g., Silver et al., "Humiliation," S. Miller, "Humiliation and Shame," and also Rorty, ibid.) understand powerlessness to be the defining characteristic of humiliation. But powerlessness is intimately an aspect of several other unpleasant emotions—fear, especially, but also depression, anxiety, grief, remorse, and regret—and so does not work to distinguish humiliation.

62. The humiliation of sexual rejection is probably equally painful to both men and women, but for women the matter is more complicated. It seems that women would greatly prefer not to be considered as sexual beings in so many settings where men take them only as such. The woman who expects to be treated as a colleague or an employee or as a functionary doing her job can experience, I imagine, great humiliation by not being taken seriously in that role simply because the man dealing with her finds her attractive, or because he does not find her attractive and blames her for that.

63. In response to a draft of this chapter a woman, who wished to remain anonymous, writes (personal communication): "I think the notion of 'pretension,' the predicate of humiliation, is somehow borne heavily by women. To wear lipstick pretends to sexuality, for example. For a woman, just smiling can be sexually pretentious. . . . Any makeup, anything other than baggy clothes, anything other than workboots, any sort of styled hair, and you are perceived as having the sort of pretension that humiliators want to explode. I would almost go so far as to say that the definition of femininity is the assumption of bodily marks or postures that are deflatable. . . . 'Pretension'

(in the sense you mean it) is the heart of femininity—that to be feminine in any normal sense of the term is to be pretentious in your sense of the term. It is the condition of the feminine."

64. See, e.g., MacKinnon, *Feminism Unmodified*.

65. See André Gide, *Dostoïevsky* 101–12.

66. *The Idiot* I chap. 13. Margaret Drabble describes a lighter variation of the same game, played on the field of embarrassment and amusement rather than on one of humiliation and mortification. "She instigated a playground game called Confessions . . . which consisted of forcing everyone present to recount the most embarrassing experience of the last twenty-four hours" (*The Middle Ground* 19).

67. *Notes from the Underground* pt. I.iv.

68. *Notes from the Underground* pt. I.iii.

69. What, however, if he were performing before judges as subtly sensitive as himself? In fact, much of the point of his narration is to instruct us in the art of being sensitive to ridicule. My guess is that he could never trust the other to be as sensitive as himself. Such skill in another is one of the things he must always deny in order to maintain his own sense of superiority.

70. Letter to J. H. Reynolds, 4–27–1818, quoted in Ricks, *Keats and Embarrassment* 21.

Chapter 5. Humiliation: Part II

1. I use the infinitive form to stand for all the words for which it serves as a root.

2. The *OED*'s first instance that unambiguously refers to the state we associate with the unpleasant emotion and could not also refer to the fact of simply being humbled is from Christina Rossetti in 1879: "When we ask to be humbled, we must not recoil from being humiliated." This example is rather late. Humiliation, in the sense of an unpleasant emotion but still not unambiguously distinct from a more neutral notion of being brought low, is occasionally found in the pages of Jane Austen, where we find it linked, as might be predicted, with the piercing of vanity and the deflating of pretension:

> "How despicably have I acted!" she cried. "I, who have prided myself on my discernment! I, who have valued myself on my abilities! who have often disdained the generous candor of my sister and gratified my vanity in useless or blamable distrust. How humiliating is this discovery! Yet how just a humiliation." (*Pride and Prejudice* chap. 36)

Note that "humiliating" seems to indicate a feeling, but "humiliation" only a state. But see *Emma* III.xi: "Every moment had brought a fresh surprise; and every surprise must be a matter of humiliation to her."

3. In its glosses for *humiliate* and its various forms the *OED* seems to prefer the state to the feeling. Yet under its entry for *mortification,* 6, and *mortify,* 8, the gloss is "the *feeling* of humiliation," "to *feel* humiliated," where humiliation is impliedly understood as an emotion.

4. Smith's use of *humiliating* is still consistent with seeing humiliation as a form of humbling, a simple objective lowering of status, but the coupling of it with calamity suggests this is humiliation as we now know it.

5. It may be worth noting that the nineteenth-century English editors of the *OED* still were unable to extend *embarrass* much outside the world of "difficulties" (mostly financial but also social), timidities, perplexities, confusions, and bashfulnesses to the more uncomfortable feeling of blundering and social ineptitude.

6. Sterne's use appears in *Sentimental Journey.* See Ricks (3) who makes this point about Sterne. It is somewhat remarkable that the word does not appear at all in the lengthy *Tristram Shandy,* for there are any number of situations in which one could imagine its appearing.

7. I do not have great confidence in this assertion, so let me supply the basis for the claim fairly quickly. The *OED,* as well as some 220 titles from English and American fiction, belles-lettres, and philosophical texts, is available as part of a computer data base. Nearly 120 of these texts predate 1800, although they are mostly short, including plays and verse by Shakespeare and Marlowe; there are also works by Milton, Sterne, Fielding, Dryden, Defoe, Swift, and others. This is hardly a perfect sample, but it cannot be without some significance that the collection gives no uses of *feel (felt) ashamed, feel (felt) shame, feel (felt) guilty, sad, aggrieved,* etc. prior to the mid-nineteenth century. Yet *feel* plus an emotion word was not an impossible collocation before then: the *OED* lists Tyrwhyt in 1634 (s.v. feel, v. 9a): "I have not at all felt the emotion I shewed"; the data base also yields "feel an emotion" from *Shamela,* while Pope writes of woes being felt (*Eloisa* 366). But the preferred mode, and almost exclusively so, of expressing the thought of having an emotion was with the *to be* construction. Even in the nineteenth century it is greatly preferred, and not until the twentieth century did "feeling" emotions come into its own.

8. See Elias, *The Civilizing Process.*

9. See *OED* s.v. mortification, 6; mortified, 7; and mortify, 8.

10. See Bosworth and Toller, *An Anglo-Saxon Dictionary,* s.v. sceamu and sceamian.

11. For what it is worth, the data base of English and American writings would seem to confirm the trend toward uncoupling shame and blushing. It shows fewer than one-fifth of the occurrences of shame in the proximity of blushing or reddening occurring in texts dating from after 1800, this without weighting for the greater proportion of post-1800 pages in the data base.

12. See Piers and Singer, *Shame and Guilt.*

13. Harré, "Embarrassment," 181–82.

14. See the entry for *anno* 1049 in the *Anglo-Saxon Chronicle*. Earl Swein Godwinesson through deceit and treachery slew his cousin Earl Beorn. King Edward and the whole army convened and declared Swein a *niðingr*.

15. For the turf incident see *Eyrbyggja saga* chap. 41.

16. The medieval Icelanders had a saying "everything is compensable"; see *Bloodtaking and Peacemaking* 189–190.

17. I am painting a complicated story in very broad strokes. I am, for example, making my claims by recourse to the history of English and the moves made in English texts. These moves had already been anticipated in French by Chrétien's romances in the late twelfth century and by the fabliaux of the thirteenth. In Chrétien, the complications the new style of love give to shame is the central theme of *Le chevalier de la charette*. Yet Chrétien's psychological subtlety is focused more on love than on shame, and he does not give the peculiarly explicit attention to delineating various aspects of shame which the *Gawain* poet does, as we will see.

18. I am referring to the sumptuary legislation of the late Middle Ages and early Renaissance, for which see Hughes, "Sumptuary Law."

19. For the solution to the problem of how to divide a fart into twelve equal parts see Chaucer's *Summoner's Tale*, which brilliantly reveals that the art of deflating the pretentious had already achieved a very sophisticated form by the end of the fourteenth century.

20. For an engaging intellectual and cultural history of hypocrisy see Shklar, *Ordinary Vices*.

21. I am following the edition of *Sir Gawain* edited by J. R. R. Tolkien and E. V. Gordon, 2d ed. by Norman Davis. *Gawain* is written in a northwest midlands dialect and in a poetic style that presents some difficulty for modern readers, in a way that Chaucer, whose dialect had the fortune to survive for the most part as our modern standard, does not. I make use of several translation strategies here. In those passages in which enough words have passed into Modern English to make it possible to do so, I have simply modernized the spelling and supplied a ModE gloss for those words that have not made it into ModE. This is less a translation then than a transcription, although I have also on occasion altered word order. Other passages in which this practice is less feasible I have rendered into a kind of prose, but I still retain as many of the poet's constructions as readability will suffer. In some passages I have mixed paraphrase with translation, and I have indicated when I do so in the text. But I have not been altogether consistent either, and by design. Take for instance *gyng*, which though cognate with *gang* is not from the Old English that produced our *gang* but from Old Norse. Its meaning is clear, so I keep it, and it also gives more flavor of the original. The risk of modernizing the spellings of Middle English words is that the reader will be tempted to think the words meant precisely the same

thing then as now; the risk of retaining the Middle English spellings is that the reader then tends to trivialize the content of the text, taking it to be cute or quaint, and even denying the capacity for intellectual sophistication to people who so "misspell" their words. This sophisticated poem more than repays the efforts of reading it in the original, but for those who wish to capture its flavor see Marie Borroff's admirable rendition of it into Modern English verse, which retains all the metrical features of the original.

22. See Ricks's aperçu about the embarrassment generated by sleeping in public or by watching someone sleeping in public (13).

23. Notice how this scene rehearses nearly the entire politics of gift exchange and the demands of reciprocity that is my subject in Chapter 1.

24. Gawain may have felt some guilt for not handing over the girdle to the host, for he went to confession immediately after hiding the girdle away. Yet the poem suggests that he would have confessed anyway prior to what seemed like certain death the next day.

25. Ricks, *Keats and Embarrassment* 5–6. Harré ("Embarrassment," 186) notes the difficulty of translating embarrassment into Spanish: "In Spain, one might guess, embarrassment is not a separate category from shame, because, through *dignidad*, character is always 'on the line.'" In Italian *embarrassment* subsumes all of *imbarazzo* but also some of the range of *vergogna* according to Castelfranchi and Poggi, "Blushing as a Discourse."

26. See Rorty, *Contingency, Irony, and Solidarity* 91.

27. See Descartes, *The Passions of the Soul* (1649); Hobbes, *Leviathan*, pt. I (1651); Hume, *A Treatise of Human Nature*, bk. II (1740); and Adam Smith, *The Theory of Moral Sentiments* (1759).

28 A rich discussion of this literature and especially how it relates to styles of acting and to the expression of the emotions on stage can be found in Roach, *The Player's Passion*, esp. chaps. 1–3.

Epilogue

1. It is important, however, to recall that having specifically dedicated emotion words makes a difference: See Chapter 3 for the notion that emotion words can act as evaluative magnets.

2. See Chapter 5, n.26.

3. "Dans l'adversité de nos meilleurs amis, nous trouvons toujours quelque chose qui ne nous déplaît pas" (Maximes Suprimées #18). (In the misfortune of our best friends we always find something that does not displease us.)

Works Cited

Améry, Jean. *At the Mind's Limits: Contemplations by a Survivor on Auschwitz and Its Realities*. Translated by Sidney and Stella P. Rosenfeld. New York: Schocken, 1986. First published 1966.

Anderson, Benedict. *Imagined Communities*. 2d ed. London: Verso, 1991.

Andersson, Theodore, and William Ian Miller. *Law and Literature in Medieval Iceland*. Stanford: Stanford University Press, 1989.

Arasse, Daniel. *The Guillotine and the Terror*. Translated by Christopher Miller. London: Penguin, 1989. First published 1987.

Archer, Dane, and Rosemary Gartner. *Violence and Crime in Cross-National Perspective*. New Haven: Yale University Press, 1984.

Arendt, Hannah. *Eichmann in Jerusalem: A Report on the Banality of Evil*. Rev. ed. New York: Viking, 1965.

Aristotle. *The "Art" of Rhetoric*. Translated by John Henry Freese. Loeb Classical Library, 1926. Cambridge: Harvard University Press, 1982.

——. *The Ethics of Aristotle: The Nicomachean Ethics*. Translated by J. A. K. Thomson. Harmondsworth: Penguin, 1955.

Armstrong, Nancy, and Leonard Tennenhouse, eds. *The Violence of Representation: Literature and the History of Violence*. New York: Routledge, 1989.

Asendorph, Jens. "Shyness, Embarrassment, and Self-Presentation: A Control Theory Approach." In *The Self in Anxiety, Stress, and Depression*, edited by Ralf Schwarzer, 109–14. Amsterdam: North Holland, 1984.

Auðunar þáttr Vestfirzka. In *Vestfirðinga sögur*, edited by Björn K. Þórólfsson and Guðni Jónsson. Íslenzk Fornrit, vol. 6: 359–68. Reykjavík: Hið Íslenzka Fornritafélag, 1943. (Trans. Hermann Pálsson. "Audun's Story." In *Hrafnkel's Saga and Other Stories*. Harmondsworth: Penguin, 1971.)

Bakhtin, Mikhail. *Rabelais and His World*. Translated by Helene Iswolsky. Bloomington: Indiana University Press, 1984. First published 1965.

Bandamanna saga. In *Grettis saga Ásmundarsonar*, edited by Guðni Jóns-

son. Íslenzk Fornrit, vol. 7: 293–363. Reykjavík: Hið Íslenzka Fornritafélag, 1936. (Trans. Hermann Pálsson. *The Confederates and Hen-
Thorir*. Edinburgh: Southside, 1975.)

Bartlett, Robert. "The Impact of Royal Government in the French Ardennes:
The Evidence of the 1247 enquête." *Journal of Medieval History* 7
(1981): 83–96.

Bauman, Richard. "Performance and Honor in 13th-Century Iceland." *Journal of American Folklore* 99 (1986): 131–50.

Baumgartner, M. P. "Social Control from Below." In *Toward a General
Theory of Social Control*, 2 vols., edited by Donald Black, 1: 303–45.
New York: Academic Press, 1984.

Bell, Rudolf M. *Holy Anorexia*. Chicago: University of Chicago Press, 1985.

Benedict, Ruth. *The Chrysanthemum and the Sword*. Boston: Houghton
Mifflin, 1946.

Bersani, Leo, and Ulysse Dutoit. *The Forms of Violence: Narrative in As-
syrian Art and Modern Culture*. New York: Schocken, 1985.

Betzig, Laura. "On Reconsidering Violence in Simple Human Societies."
Current Anthropology 29 (1988): 624–25.

Bjarnar saga Hítdælakappa. In *Borgfirðinga sögur*, edited by Sigurður Nordal and Guðni Jónsson. Íslenzk Fornrit, vol. 3: 109–211. Reykjavík: Hið
Íslenzka Fornritafélag, 1938. (No English translation.)

Black, Donald. "Crime as Social Control." In *Toward a General Theory of
Social Control*, 2 vols., edited by D. Black, 2: 1–27. New York: Academic Press, 1984.

Black-Michaud, Jacob. *Feuding Societies*. Oxford: Basil Blackwell. Also published as *Cohesive Force: Feud in the Mediterranean and the Middle
East*. New York: St. Martin's Press, 1975.

Bloch, Marc. *Feudal Society*, 2 vols. Translated by L. A. Manyon. Chicago:
University of Chicago Press, 1961.

Blok, Anton. "Rams and Billy-Goats: A Key to the Mediterranean Code of
Honour." *Man* 16 (1981): 427–40.

Boehm, Christopher. *Blood Revenge: The Anthropology of Feuding in Mon-
tenegro and Other Tribal Societies*. Lawrence: University Press of Kan-
sas, 1984.

Borroff, Marie. *Sir Gawain and the Green Knight*. New York: Norton, 1967.

Bosworth, Joseph, and T. Northcote Toller, eds. *An Anglo-Saxon Dictionary*.
Oxford: Oxford University Press, 1898.

Boulding, Kenneth E. "Perspectives on Violence." *Zygon* 18 (1983): 425–37.

Bourdieu, Pierre. *Distinction: A Social Critique of the Judgment of Taste*.
Translated by Richard Nice. Cambridge: Harvard University Press,
1984. First published 1979.

——. *Outline of a Theory of Practice*. Translated by Richard Nice. Cambridge: Cambridge University Press, 1977. First published 1972.

——. *Le sens pratique*. Paris: Minuit, 1980.

——. "The Sentiment of Honor in Kabyle Society." In *Honour and Shame*, edited by J. G. Peristiany, 191–241. Chicago: University of Chicago Press, 1966.

Brandes, Stanley. "Reflections on Honor and Shame in the Mediterranean." In *Honor and Shame and the Unity of the Mediterranean*, edited by David D. Gilmore, 121–34. 1987.

Brennu-Njáls saga. See *Njáls saga*.

Briggs, Jean L. *Never in Anger: Portrait of an Eskimo Family*. New York: Knopf, 1970.

Broucek, Francis J. *Shame and the Self*. New York: Guilford Press, 1991.

Brown, Peter. "Society and the Supernatural: A Medieval Change." *Dædalus* 104 (1975): 133–51.

Burns, Robert. *The Poetical Works of Robert Burns*. Edited by J. Logie Robertson. London: Frowde, 1906.

Burton, Robert. *The Anatomy of Melancholy*. Edited by Floyd Dell and Paul Jordan-Smith. New York: Tudor, 1938.

Campbell, J. K. *Honour, Family, and Patronage: A Study of Institutions and Moral Values in a Greek Mountain Community*. Oxford: Oxford University Press, 1964.

Caplow, Theodore. "Christmas Gifts and Kin Networks." *American Sociological Review* 47 (1982): 383–92.

——. "Rule Enforcement without Visible Means: Christmas Gift Giving in Middletown." *American Journal of Sociology* 89 (1984): 1306–28.

Castelfranchi, Christiano, and Isabella Poggi. "Blushing as a Discourse: Was Darwin Wrong?" In *Shyness and Embarrassment*, edited by W. Ray Crozier, 230–51. Cambridge: Cambridge University Press, 1990.

Chaucer, Geoffrey. *The Works of Geoffrey Chaucer*. 2d ed. Edited by F. N. Robinson. Boston: Houghton Mifflin, 1957.

Cheal, David. *The Gift Economy*. London: Routledge, 1988.

Cleasby, Richard, and Gudbrand Vigfússon. *An Old-Icelandic Dictionary*. 2d ed. William A. Craigie. Oxford: Clarendon Press, 1957.

Clifford, James. "On Ethnographic Allegory." In *Writing Culture: The Poetics and Politics of Ethnography*, edited by James Clifford and George E. Marcus, 98–121. Berkeley: University of California Press, 1986.

Clover, Carol J. "The Eternal Effeminate: Sex and Gender in Early Northern Europe." *Speculum* (forthcoming 1993).

——."Hildigunnr's Lament." In *Structure and Meaning in Old Norse Literature: New Approaches to Textual Analysis and Literary Criticism*, edited by John Lindow, Lars Lönnroth, and Gerd Wolfgang Weber, 141–83. Odense: Odense University Press, 1986.

——. *Men, Women, and Chain Saws: Gender in the Modern Horror Film.* Princeton: Princeton University Press, 1992.

Cockburn, J. S. "The Patterns of Violence in English Society: Homicide in Kent, 1560–1985." *Past and Present* 130 (1991): 70–106.

Cohen, David. *Law, Sexuality, and Society: The Enforcement of Morals in Classical Athens.* Cambridge: Cambridge University Press, 1991.

Collins, Randall. "Three Faces of Cruelty: Towards a Comparative Sociology of Violence." *Theory and Society* 1 (1974): 415–40.

Copet-Rougier, Elisabeth. "'Le Mal Court': Visible and Invisible Violence in an Acephalous Society—Mkako of Cameroon." In *The Anthropology of Violence*, edited by David Riches, 50–69. Oxford: Basil Blackwell, 1986.

Cover, Robert M. "Violence and the Word." *Yale Law Journal* 95 (1986): 1601–29.

Crozier, W. Ray, ed. *Shyness and Embarrassment: Perspectives from Social Psychology.* Cambridge: Cambridge University Press, 1990.

——. "Social Psychological Perspectives on Shyness, Embarrassment, and Shame." In *Shyness and Embarrassment*, edited by W. Ray Crozier, 19–58. Cambridge: Cambridge University Press, 1990.

Darnton, Robert. *The Great Cat Massacre and Other Episodes in French Cultural History.* New York: Basic Books, 1984.

Darwin, Charles. *The Expression of the Emotions in Man and Animals.* Chicago: University of Chicago Press, 1965.

Davis, John. "Family and State in the Mediterranean." In *Honor and Shame and the Unity of the Mediterranean*, edited by David D. Gilmore, 22–34. 1987.

Davis, Natalie Zemon. *Fiction in the Archives: Pardon Tales and Their Tellers in Sixteenth-Century France.* Stanford: Stanford University Press, 1987.

——. "The Rites of Violence." In *Society and Culture in Early Modern France*, 152–87. Stanford: Stanford University Press, 1975.

Delaney, Carol. "Seeds of Honor, Fields of Shame." In *Honor and Shame and the Unity of the Mediterranean*, edited by David D. Gilmore, 35–48. 1987.

Dentan, Robert Knox. "On Reconsidering Violence in Simple Human Societies." *Current Anthropology* 29 (1988): 625–29.

——. *The Semai: A Non-violent People of Malaya.* New York: Holt, Rinehart, Winston, 1979.

Desan, Suzanne. "Crowds, Community, and Ritual in the Work of E. P.

Thompson and Natalie Davis." In *The New Cultural History*, edited by Lynn Hunt, 47–71. Berkeley: University of California Press, 1989.

Dodds, E. R. *The Greeks and the Irrational*. Berkeley: University of California Press, 1951.

Dostoyevsky, Fyodor. *The Idiot*. Translated by Constance Garnett. New York: Bantam, 1958.

——. *Notes from the Underground*. In *Three Short Novels of Dostoevsky*. Translated by Constance Garnett. Garden City, N.Y.: Anchor, 1960.

Douglas, Mary. *Purity and Danger: An Analysis of the Concepts of Pollution and Taboo*. London: Routledge and Kegan Paul, 1966.

Droplaugarsona saga. In *Austfirðinga sögur*, edited by Jón Jóhannesson. Íslenzk Fornrit, vol. 11: 135–80. Reykjavík: Hið Íslenzka Fornritafélag, 1950. (Trans. Margaret Schlauch. In *Three Icelandic Sagas*, translated by M. H. Scargill and Margaret Schlauch, 102–35. Princeton: Princeton University Press, 1950.)

Edelmann, Robert J. "Embarrassment and Blushing: A Component-Process Model, Some Initial Descriptive and Cross-Cultural Data." In *Shyness and Embarrassment*, edited by W. Ray Crozier, 205–29. Cambridge: Cambridge University Press, 1990.

——. *The Psychology of Embarrassment*. Chichester: Wiley, 1987.

Egils saga Skalla-Grímssonar. Edited by Sigurður Nordal. Íslenzk Fornrit, vol. 2. Reykjavík: Hið Íslenzka Fornritafélag, 1933. (Trans. Hermann Pálsson and Paul Edwards. *Egil's Saga*. Harmondsworth: Penguin, 1976.)

Ekman, Paul. "Biological and Cultural Contributions to Body and Facial Movement in the Expression of Emotions." In *Explaining Emotions*, edited by Amélie O. Rorty, 73–102. Berkeley: University of California Press, 1980.

Elias, Norbert. "An Essay on Sport and Violence." In Norbert Elias and Eric Dunning, *Quest for Excitement: Sport and Leisure in the Civilizing Process*, 150–74. Oxford: Basil Blackwell, 1986.

——. *History of Manners*. Translated by Edmund Jephcott, vol. 1 of *The Civilizing Process*. New York: Urizen, 1978. First published 1939.

——. *Power and Civility*. Translated by Edmund Jephcott, vol. 2 of *The Civilizing Process*. New York: Pantheon, 1982. First published 1939.

Ellsworth, Phoebe C. "Some Implications of Cognitive Appraisal Theories of Emotion." *International Review of Studies on Emotion* 1 (1991): 143–61.

Elster, Jon. *The Cement of Society: A Study of Social Order*. Cambridge: Cambridge University Press, 1989.

——. "The Norms of Revenge." *Ethics* 100 (1990): 862–85.

——. *Sour Grapes: Studies in the Subversion of Rationality*. Cambridge: Cambridge University Press, 1983.

——. *Ulysses and the Sirens: Studies in Rationality and Irrationality*. Cambridge: Cambridge University Press, 1979.

Evans-Pritchard, E. E. *The Nuer: A Description of the Modes of Livelihood and Political Institutions of a Nilotic People*. Oxford: Oxford University Press, 1940.

Eyrbyggja saga. Edited by Einar Ól. Sveinsson and Matthías Þórðarson. Íslenzk Fornrit, vol. 4. Reykjavík: Hið Íslenzka Fornritafélag, 1935. (Trans. Hermann Pálsson and Paul Edwards. *Eyrbyggja Saga*. Toronto: University of Toronto Press, 1973.)

Fairchilds, Cissie C. *Domestic Enemies: Servants and Their Masters in Old Regime France*. Baltimore: Johns Hopkins University Press, 1984.

Finnboga saga. In *Kjalnesinga saga*, edited by Jóhannes Halldórsson. Íslenzk Fornrit, vol. 14: 253–340. Reykjavík: Hið Íslenzka Fornritafélag, 1959. (No English translation.)

Foucault, Michel. "About the Concept of the 'Dangerous Individual' in 19th-Century Legal Psychiatry." Translated by Alain Baudot and Jane Couchman. *International Journal of Law and Psychiatry* 1 (1978): 1–18.

——. *Discipline and Punish: The Birth of the Prison*. Translated by Alan Sheridan. New York: Vintage, 1979. First published 1975.

——. *Language, Counter-Memory, Practice: Selected Essays and Interviews*. Edited by Donald F. Bouchard. Translated by Bouchard and Sherry Simon. Ithaca: Cornell University Press, 1977.

Frank, Robert H. *Passions within Reason: The Strategic Role of the Emotions*. New York: Norton, 1988.

Franklin, Benjamin. *The Autobiography*. New York: Vintage Books, Library of America, 1990.

Freud, Sigmund. "The Antithetical Sense of Primal Words." In *Character and Culture*, edited by Philip Rieff, 44–50. New York: Collier, 1963.

Garfinkel, Harold. "Conditions of Successful Degradation Ceremonies." *American Journal of Sociology* 61 (1956): 420–24.

Geary, Patrick. "Échange et relations entre les vivants et les morts dans la société du Haut Moyen Age." *Droits et Cultures* 12 (1986): 3–17.

——. *Furta Sacra*. Princeton: Princeton University Press, 1978.

——. "Humiliation of Saints." In *Saints and their Cults: Studies in Religious Sociology, Folklore, and History*, edited by Stephen Wilson, 123–40. Cambridge: Cambridge University Press, 1983. (Rpt. with some revisions and translated from "L'humiliation des saints." *Annales, E.S.C.* 34 [1979]: 27–42.)

Geller, Daniel M., Lynne Goodstein, Maury Silver, and Wendy C. Sternberg. "On Being Ignored: The Effects of the Violation of Implicit Rules of Social Interaction." *Sociometry* 37 (1974): 541–56.

Gibbard, Allan. *Wise Choices, Apt Feelings: A Theory of Normative Judgment.* Cambridge: Harvard University Press, 1990.

Giddens, Anthony. *The Nation-State and Violence.* Vol. 2 of *A Contemporary Critique of Historical Materialism.* Berkeley: University of California Press, 1987.

Gide, André. *Dostoïevsky.* Paris: Plon, 1923.

Gilmore, David D., ed. *Honor and Shame and the Unity of the Mediterranean.* A special publication of the American Anthropological Association, no. 22. Washington, D.C.: American Anthropological Association, 1987.

———. "Honor, Honesty, Shame: Male Status in Contemporary Andalusia." In *Honor and Shame and the Unity of the Mediterranean,* edited by David D. Gilmore, 90–103.

———. "The Shame of Dishonor." In *Honor and Shame and the Unity of the Mediterranean,* edited by David D. Gilmore, 2–21.

Girard, René. *Violence and the Sacred.* Translated by Patrick Gregory. Baltimore: The Johns Hopkins Press, 1977. First published 1972.

Gísla saga Súrssonar. In *Vestfirðinga sögur,* edited by Björn K. Þórólfsson and Guðni Jónsson. Íslenzk Fornrit, vol. 6: 1–118. Reykjavík: Hið Íslenzka Fornritafélag, 1943. (Trans. George Johnston. *The Saga of Gisli.* Toronto: University of Toronto Press, 1963.)

Gluckman, Max. *Custom and Conflict in Africa.* Oxford: Basil Blackwell, 1956.

Goffman, Erving. *Behavior in Public Places: Notes on the Social Organization of Gatherings.* New York: Free Press, 1963.

———. "Embarrassment and Social Organization." In Goffman, *Interaction Ritual: Essays in Face-to-Face Behavior,* 97–112. Chicago: Aldine, 1967.

———. "The Nature of Deference and Demeanor." In Goffman, *Interaction Ritual: Essays in Face-to-Face Behavior,* 47–95. Chicago: Aldine, 1967.

———. "On Face Work." In Goffman, *Interaction Ritual: Essays in Face-to-Face Behavior,* 5–45. Chicago: Aldine, 1967.

———. *Relations in Public.* New York: Basic Books, 1971.

Gouldner, Alvin W. *Enter Plato: Classical Greece and the Origins of Social Theory.* New York: Basic Books, 1965.

———. "The Norm of Reciprocity." *American Sociological Review* 25 (1960): 161–78.

Grænlendinga saga. In *Eyrbyggja saga,* edited by Einar Ól. Sveinsson and

Matthías Þórðarson. Íslenzk Fornrit, vol. 4: 239–70. Reykjavík: Hið Íslenzka Fornritafélag, 1935. (Trans. Magnus Magnusson and Hermann Pálsson. *The Vinland Sagas*, 47–72. Harmondsworth: Penguin, 1965.)

Greenblatt, Stephen J. *Learning to Curse: Essays in Early Modern Culture.* New York: Routledge, 1990.

Greenhouse, Carol J. "Reading Violence." In *Law's Violence*, edited by Austin Sarat and Thomas R. Kearns, 105–39. Ann Arbor: University of Michigan Press, 1992.

Gregory, C. A. "A Conceptual Analysis of a Non-Capitalist Gift Economy with Particular Reference to Papua New Guinea." *Cambridge Journal of Economics* 5 (1981): 119–35.

———. *Gifts and Commodities.* London: Academic Press, 1982.

———. "Gifts to Men and Gifts to God: Gift Exchange and Capital Accumulation in Contemporary Papua." *Man* 15 (1980): 626–52.

Grettis saga Ásmundarsonar. Edited by Guðni Jónsson. Íslenzk Fornrit, vol. 7. Reykjavík: Hið Íslenzka Fornritafélag, 1936. (Trans. Denton Fox and Hermann Pálsson. *Grettir's Saga.* Toronto: University of Toronto Press, 1974.)

Guðmundar saga dýra. In *Sturlunga saga*, 2 vols., edited by Jón Jóhannesson, Magnús Finnbogason, and Kristján Eldjárn, 1: 160–212. Reykjavík: Sturlunguútgáfan, 1946. (Trans. Julia H. McGrew and R. George Thomas. *Sturlunga saga*, 2 vols., 1: 147–206. New York: Twayne, 1970–74.)

Gurevich, A. Ya. "Wealth and Gift-Bestowal among the Ancient Scandinavians." *Scandinavica* 7 (1968): 126–38.

Gurr, Ted Robert. "War, Revolution, and the Growth of the Coercive State." *Comparative Political Studies* 21 (1988): 45–65.

Hallfreðar saga. In *Vatnsdæla saga*, edited by Einar Ól. Sveinsson. Íslenzk Fornrit, vol. 8: 135–200. Reykjavík: Hið Íslenzka Fornritafélag, 1939. (Trans. Alan Boucher. *The Saga of Hallfred the Troublesome Scald.* Reykjavík: Iceland Review, 1981.)

Harré, Rom. "Embarrassment: A Conceptual Analysis." In *Shyness and Embarrassment*, edited by W. Ray Crozier, 181–204. Cambridge: Cambridge University Press, 1990.

———. "Rules in the Explanation of Social Behaviour." In *Social Rules and Social Behaviour*, edited by Peter Collett, 28–41. Totowa, N.J.: Rowman and Littlefield, 1977.

Hávamál. In *Edda*, edited by Hans Kuhn. Heidelberg: Carl Winter, 1962.

Hávarðar saga Ísfirðings. In *Vestfirðinga sögur*, edited by Björn K. Þórólfsson and Guðni Jónsson. Íslenzk Fornrit, vol. 6: 291–358. Reykjavík: Hið Íslenzka Fornritafélag, 1943. (Trans. Guðbrandur Vigfússon and F. York Powell. *Origines Islandicae*, vol. 2: 213–328. Oxford: Clarendon Press, 1905.)

Hay, Douglas. "Time, Inequality, and Law's Violence." In *Law's Violence*, edited by Austin Sarat and Thomas R. Kearns, 141–73. Ann Arbor: University of Michigan Press, 1992.

Hay, Douglas, et al. *Albion's Fatal Tree: Crime and Society in Eighteenth-Century England*. New York: Pantheon, 1975.

Heath, Anthony. *Rational Choice and Social Exchange*. New York: Cambridge University Press, 1976.

Heelas, Paul. "Anthropological Perspectives on Violence: Universals and Particulars." Zygon 18 (1983): 375–404.

———. "Anthropology, Violence, and Catharsis." In *Aggression and Violence*, edited by Peter Marsh and Anne Campbell, 47–61. New York: St. Martin's Press, 1982.

Heiðarvíga saga. In *Borgfirðinga sögur*, edited by Sigurður Nordal and Guðni Jónsson. Íslenzk Fornrit, vol. 3: 213–328. Reykjavík: Hið Íslenzka Fornritafélag, 1938. (Trans. in part William Morris and Eirikr Magnússon. *The Story of the Ere-Dwellers with the Story of the Heath-Slayings as Appendix*, 191–259. London: Quaritch, 1892.)

Herdt, Gilbert. "Sambia Nosebleeding Rites and Male Proximity to Women." In *Cultural Psychology: Essays on Comparative Human Development*, edited by James W. Stigler, Richard A. Shweder, and Gilbert Herdt, 366–400. Cambridge: Cambridge University Press, 1990.

Herzfeld, Michael. "'As in Your Own House': Hospitality, Ethnography, and the Stereotype of Mediterranean Society." In *Honor and Shame and the Unity of the Mediterranean*, edited by David D. Gilmore, 75–89. 1987.

———. "Honour and Shame: Problems in the Comparative Analysis of Moral Systems." *Man* 15 (1980): 339–52.

Hiatt, L. R. "Classifications of the Emotions." *Australian Aboriginal Concepts*, edited by Hiatt, 182–87. Canberra: Australian Institute for Aboriginal Studies, 1978.

Hobbes, Thomas. *Leviathan*. London: Dent, Everyman, 1914.

Hochschild, Arlie Russell. *The Managed Heart: Commercialization of Human Feeling*. Berkeley: University of California Press, 1983.

Holmes, Stephen. "The Secret History of Self-Interest." In *Beyond Self-Interest*, edited by Jane J. Mansbridge, 267–86. Chicago: University of Chicago Press, 1990.

Hrafnkels saga Freysgoða. In *Austfirðinga sögur*, edited by Jón Jóhannesson. Íslenzk Fornrit, vol. 11: 95–133. Reykjavík: Hið Íslenzka Fornritafélag,

1950. (Trans. Hermann Pálsson. *Hrafnkel's Saga and Other Stories*. Harmondsworth: Penguin, 1971.)

Hughes, Diane Owen. "Sumptuary Law and Social Relations in Renaissance Italy." In *Disputes and Settlements: Law and Human Relations in the West*, edited by John Bossy, 69–99. Cambridge: Cambridge University Press, 1983.

Huizinga, J. *The Waning of the Middle Ages*. Garden City, N.Y.: Anchor, 1954. First published 1927.

Hultberg, Peer. "Shame—A Hidden Emotion." *Journal of Analytical Psychology* 33 (1988): 109–26.

Hume, David. *A Treatise of Human Nature*. Harmondsworth: Penguin, 1984.

Hyde, Lewis. *The Gift: Imagination and the Erotic Life of Property*. New York: Random House, 1983.

Ine. In Felix Liebermann. *Die Gesetze der Angelsachsen* 1: 88–123. Halle: Max Niemeyer, 1903.

Izard, Carroll E. *The Face of Emotion*. New York: Appleton-Century-Crofts, 1971.

———. *Human Emotions*. New York: Plenum, 1977.

Izard, Carroll E., and Marion C. Hyson. "Shyness as a Discrete Emotion." In *Shyness: Perspectives on Research and Treatment*, edited by Warren H. Jones, Jonathan M. Cheek, and Stephen R. Briggs, 147–60. New York: Plenum Press, 1986.

Jochens, Jenny M. "The Medieval Icelandic Heroine: Fact or Fiction?" *Viator* 17 (1986): 35–50.

Jones, George Fenwick. *The Ethos of the Song of Roland*. Baltimore: The Johns Hopkins Press, 1963.

Kagan, Jerome. "The Idea of Emotion in Human Development." In *Emotions, Cognition, and Behavior*, edited by Carroll E. Izard, Jerome Kagan, and Robert B. Zajonc, 38–72. Cambridge: Cambridge University Press, 1984.

Karen, Robert. "Shame." *Atlantic Monthly*, February 1992: 40–70.

Katz, Jack. *Seductions of Crime: Moral and Sensual Attractions in Doing Evil*. New York: Basic Books, 1988.

Ker, W. P. *Epic and Romance: Essays on Medieval Literature*. 2d ed., 1908. Reprint: New York: Dover, 1957.

Knauft, Bruce M. "Reconsidering Violence in Simple Human Societies: Homicide among the Gebusi of New Guinea." *Current Anthropology* 28 (1987): 457–82.

Kormáks saga. In *Vatnsdæla saga*, edited by Einar Ól. Sveinsson. Íslenzk

Fornrit, vol. 8: 203–302. Reykjavík: Hið Íslenzka Fornritafélag, 1939. (Trans. Lee M. Hollander. *The Sagas of Kormak and the Sworn Brothers*, 13–72. Princeton: Princeton University Press, 1949.)

Koziol, Geoffrey. *Begging Pardon and Favor: Ritual and Political Order in Early Medieval France*. Ithaca: Cornell University Press, 1991.

Krieken, Robert van. "Violence, Self-discipline, and Modernity: Beyond the 'Civilizing Process.'" *Sociological Review* 37 (1989): 193–218.

Landnámabók. Edited by Jakob Benediktsson. Íslenzk Fornrit, vol. 1. Reykjavík: Hið Íslenzka Fornritafélag, 1968. (Trans. Hermann Pálsson and Paul Edwards. *The Book of Settlements: Landnámabók*. University of Manitoba Icelandic Studies 1. Winnipeg: University of Manitoba Press, 1972.)

La Rochefoucauld. *Maximes et réflexions diverses*. Edited by Jacques Truchet. Paris: Flammarion, 1977.

Lasch, Christopher. "For Shame." *New Republic*, August 10, 1992: 29–34.

Latané, Bibb. *The Unresponsive Bystander: Why Doesn't He Help?* New York: Appleton-Century-Crofts, 1970.

Laxdæla saga. Edited by Einar Ól. Sveinsson. Íslenzk Fornrit, vol. 5. Reykjavík: Hið Íslenzka Fornritafélag, 1934. (Trans. Magnus Magnusson and Hermann Pálsson. *Laxdæla Saga*. Harmondsworth: Penguin, 1969.)

Levi, Primo. *The Drowned and the Saved*. Translated by Raymond Rosenthal. New York: Vintage, 1989. First published 1986.

Levinson, David. *Family Violence in Cross-cultural Perspective*. Frontiers of Anthropology, vol. 1. Newbury Park, Calif.: Sage, 1989.

Lewis, Michael. *Shame: The Exposed Self*. New York: Free Press, 1992.

Ljósvetninga saga, edited by Björn Sigfússon. Íslenzk Fornrit, vol. 10. Reykjavík: Hið Íslenzka Fornritafélag, 1940. (Trans. Theodore Andersson and William Ian Miller, in *Law and Literature*, listed fully above.)

Lofland, John. *State Executions*. Montclair, N.J.: Patterson Smith, 1977.

Lutz, Catherine. "The Domain of Emotion Words on Ifaluk." *American Ethnologist* 9 (1982): 113–28.

Lutz, Catherine, and Geoffrey M. White. "The Anthropology of Emotions." *Annual Review of Anthropology* 15 (1986): 405–36.

Lyons, William. *Emotions*. Cambridge: Cambridge University Press, 1980.

McGowan, Randall. "Punishing Violence, Sentencing Crime." In *The Violence of Representation: Literature and the History of Violence*, edited by Nancy Armstrong and Leonard Tennenhouse, 140–56. New York: Routledge, 1989.

MacKinnon, Catharine A. *Feminism Unmodified*. Cambridge: Harvard University Press, 1987.

Malinowski, B. *Argonauts of the Western Pacific*. 1922. New York: Dutton, 1961.

——. *Crime and Custom in Savage Society*. London: Routledge, 1925.

Marder, Dianna. "The Young and the Ruthless: A New Generation of Killers, Feeling No Blame and No Shame." *Philadelphia Inquirer* 6 December 1992: A1.

Martin, Judith. *Miss Manners' Guide for the Turn-of-the-Millennium*. New York: Simon and Schuster, 1990.

Massaro, Toni M. "Shame, Culture, and American Criminal Law." *Michigan Law Review* 89 (1991): 1880–1944.

Mauss, Marcel. *The Gift: Forms and Functions of Exchange in Archaic Societies*. Translated by Ian Cunnison. New York: Norton, 1967.

Meredith, George. "An Essay on Comedy." In *Comedy*, with introduction by Wylie Sypher, 1–57. Garden City, N.Y.: Anchor, 1956.

Milgram, Stanley. *Obedience to Authority*. New York: Harper and Row, 1974.

Miller, Rowland S. "Empathetic Embarrassment: Situational and Personal Determinants of Reactions to the Embarrassment of Another." *Journal of Personality and Social Psychology* 53 (1987): 1061–69.

Miller, Susan. "Humiliation and Shame: Comparing Two Affect States as Indicators of Narcissistic Stress." *Bulletin of the Menninger Clinic* 52 (1988): 40–51.

——. *The Shame Experience*. Hillsdale, N.J.: Analytic Press, 1985.

Miller, William Ian. "Beating Up on Women and Old Men and Other Enormities: A Social Historical Inquiry into Literary Sources." *Mercer Law Review* 39 (1988): 753–66.

——. *Bloodtaking and Peacemaking: Feud, Law, and Society in Saga Iceland*. Chicago: University of Chicago Press, 1990.

——. "Choosing the Avenger: Some Aspects of the Bloodfeud in Medieval Iceland and England." *Law and History Review* 1 (1983): 159–204.

——. "Justifying Skarpheðinn: Of Pretext and Politics in the Icelandic Bloodfeud." *Scandinavian Studies* 55 (1983): 316–44.

——. "Ordeal in Iceland." *Scandinavian Studies* 60 (1988): 189–218.

Modigliani, André. "Embarrassment and Embarrassability." *Sociometry* 31 (1968): 313–26.

Montaigne, Michel de. *The Complete Essays of Montaigne*. Translated by Donald M. Frame. Stanford: Stanford University Press, 1958.

Needham, Rodney. *Belief, Language, and Experience*. Oxford: Basil Blackwell, 1972.

Neu, Jerome. "Jealous Thoughts." In *Explaining Emotions*, edited by Amélie O. Rorty, 425–63. Berkeley: University of California Press, 1980.

Nietzsche, Friedrich. *Daybreak: Thoughts on the Prejudices of Morality*. Translated by R. J. Hollingdale. Cambridge: Cambridge University Press, 1982.

———. "Homer's Contest." In *Early Greek Philosophy and Other Essays*, translated by Maximilian A. Mügge. *The Complete Works of Friedrich Nietzsche*, vol. 2, 49–62. New York: Russell and Russell, 1964.

———. *On the Genealogy of Morals*. Translated by Walter Kaufmann. New York: Vintage, 1969.

Njáls saga. Brennu-Njáls saga. Edited by Einar Ól. Sveinsson. Íslenzk Fornrit, vol. 12. Reykjavík: Hið Íslenzka Fornritafélag, 1954. (Trans. Magnus Magnusson and Hermann Pálsson. *Njal's Saga*. Harmondsworth: Penguin, 1960.)

Nozick, Robert. *Anarchy, State, and Utopia*. New York: Basic Books, 1974.

Otterbein, Keith F. "On Reconsidering Violence in Simple Human Societies." *Current Anthropology* 29 (1988): 633–35.

Parry, Jonathan. "*The Gift*, the Indian Gift, and the 'Indian Gift.'" *Man* 21 (1986): 453–73.

———. "On the Moral Perils of Exchange." In *Money and the Morality of Exchange*, edited by J. Parry and M. Bloch, 64–93. Cambridge: Cambridge University Press, 1989.

Parry, Jonathan, and Maurice Bloch. "Introduction: Money and the Morality of Exchange." In *Money and the Morality of Exchange*, edited by Parry and Bloch, 1–32. Cambridge: Cambridge University Press, 1989.

Peristiany, J. G., ed. *Honour and Shame: The Values of Mediterranean Society*. Chicago: University of Chicago Press, 1966.

Pernick, Martin S. *A Calculus of Suffering: Pain, Professionalism, and Anesthesia in Nineteenth Century America*. New York: Columbia University Press, 1985.

Piers, Gerhart, and Milton B. Singer. *Shame and Guilt: A Psychoanalytic and a Cultural Study*. 1953. New York: Norton, 1971.

Piers Plowman: The B Version. Edited by George Kane and E. Talbot Donaldson. London: Athlone Press, 1975.

Pitt-Rivers, Julian. *The Fate of Shechem or the Politics of Sex: Essays in the Anthropology of the Mediterranean*. Cambridge: Cambridge University Press, 1977.

Prestssaga Guðmundar góða. In *Sturlunga saga*, 2 vols., edited by Jón Jóhannesson, Magnús Finnbogason, and Kristján Eldjárn, 1: 116–59. Reykjavík: Sturlunguútgáfan, 1946. (Trans. Julia H. McGrew and R. George Thomas. *Sturlunga saga*, 2 vols., 1: 93–143. New York: Twayne, 1970–74.)

Rawls, John. *A Theory of Justice*. Cambridge: Harvard University Press, 1971.

Riches, David. "The Phenomenon of Violence." In *The Anthropology of Violence*, edited by David Riches, 1–28. Oxford: Basil Blackwell, 1986.

Ricks, Christopher. *Keats and Embarrassment*. Oxford: Clarendon Press, 1974.

Roach, Joseph R. *The Player's Passion: Studies in the Science of Acting*. Newark: University of Delaware Press, 1985.

Rorty, Richard. *Contingency, Irony, and Solidarity*. Cambridge: Cambridge University Press, 1989.

Rosaldo, Michelle Z. *Knowledge and Passion: Ilongot Notions of Self and Social Life*. Cambridge: Cambridge University Press, 1980.

——. "The Shame of Headhunters and the Autonomy of Self." *Ethos* 11 (1983): 135–51.

Rosaldo, Renato. *Culture and Truth: The Remaking of Social Analysis*. Boston: Beacon Press, 1989.

Rosenwein, Barbara H. *To Be the Neighbor of Saint Peter: The Social Meaning of Cluny's Property, 909–1049*. Ithaca: Cornell University Press, 1989.

Ross, Marc Howard. "Internal and External Conflict and Violence: Cross-cultural Evidence and a New Analysis." *Journal of Conflict Resolution* 29 (1985): 547–79.

——. "The Limits to Social Structure: Social Structural and Psychocultural Explanations for Political Conflict and Violence." *Anthropological Quarterly* 59 (1986): 171–76.

Rule, James B. *Theories of Civil Violence*. Berkeley: University of California Press, 1988.

Sabini, John, and Maury Silver. *Moralities of Everyday Life*. New York: Oxford University Press, 1982.

Sahlins, Marshall. *Stone Age Economics*. New York: Aldine, 1972.

Sarat, Austin, and Thomas R. Kearns, eds. *Law's Violence*. Ann Arbor: University of Michigan Press, 1992.

Scarry, Elaine. *The Body in Pain: The Making and Unmaking of the World*. New York: Oxford University Press, 1985.

Scheff, Thomas J., and Suzanne M. Retzinger. *Emotions and Violence: Shame and Rage in Destructive Conflicts*. Lexington, Mass.: Lexington Books, 1991.

Schneider, Carl D. *Shame, Exposure, and Privacy*. Boston: Beacon Press, 1977.

Schoeck, Helmut. *Envy: A Theory of Social Behaviour.* Translated by Michael Glenny and Betty Ross. New York: Harcourt, Brace, 1970.

Sharpe, J. A. "The History of Violence in England: Some Observations." *Past and Present* 108 (1985): 206–15.

Shklar, Judith. *The Faces of Injustice.* New Haven: Yale University Press, 1990.

———. *Ordinary Vices.* Cambridge: Harvard University Press, 1984.

Shweder, Richard A., and Edmund J. Bourne, "Does the Concept of the Person Vary Cross-Culturally?" In *Thinking Through Cultures: Expeditions in Cultural Psychology*, edited by Richard A. Shweder, 113–55. Cambridge: Harvard University Press, 1991.

Shweder, Richard A., Manamohan Mahapatra, and Joan G. Miller. "Culture and Moral Development." In *Cultural Psychology: Essays on Comparative Human Development*, edited by James W. Stigler, Richard A. Shweder, and Gilbert Herdt, 130–204. Cambridge: Cambridge University Press, 1990.

Shweder, Richard A., and Joan G. Miller, "The Social Construction of the Person: How Is It Possible?" In *Thinking Through Cultures: Expeditions in Cultural Psychology*, edited by Richard A. Shweder, 156–85. Cambridge: Harvard University Press, 1991.

Silver, Maury, Rosaria Conte, Maria Miceli, and Isabella Poggi. "Humiliation: Feeling, Social Control, and the Construction of Identity." *Journal for the Theory of Social Behaviour* 16 (1986): 269–83.

Silver, Maury, John Sabini, and W. Gerrod Parrott. "Embarrassment: A Dramaturgic Account." *Journal for the Theory of Social Behaviour* 17 (1987): 47–61.

Simmel, Georg. *Conflict.* In *Conflict and the Web of Group-Affiliations*, translated by Kurt H. Wolff and Reinhard Bendix, 11–123. New York: Free Press, 1955.

———. "Faithfulness and Gratitude." In *The Sociology of Georg Simmel*, translated by Kurt H. Wolff, 379–95. New York: Free Press, 1950.

Sir Gawain and the Green Knight. Edited by J. R. R. Tolkien and E. V. Gordon; 2d edition edited by Norman Davis. Oxford: Clarendon Press, 1967.

Smith, Adam. *The Theory of Moral Sentiments.* Edited by D. D. Raphael and A. L. Macfie. Oxford: Clarendon Press, 1976.

Smith, Craig, and Phoebe C. Ellsworth. "Patterns of Cognitive Appraisal in Emotion." *Journal of Personality and Social Psychology* 48 (1985): 813–38.

Smith, Jean. "Self and Experience in Maori Culture." In *Indigenous Psychologies: The Anthropology of the Self*, edited by Paul Heelas and Andrew Locke, 145–59. London: Academic Press, 1981.

Solomon, Robert C. *The Passions: The Myth and Nature of Human Emotion*. 1976. Notre Dame, Ind.: University of Notre Dame Press, 1983.

Spierenburg, Pieter. *The Spectacle of Suffering: Executions and the Evolution of Repression*. Cambridge: Cambridge University Press, 1984.

Stamm, Julian L. "The Meaning of Humiliation and Its Relationship to Fluctuations in Self-esteem." *International Review of Psycho-Analysis* 5 (1978): 425–33.

Steblin-Kamenskij, M. I. *The Saga Mind*. Translated by Kenneth H. Ober. Odense: Odense University Press, 1973.

Stendhal. *Le rouge et le noir*. Paris: Gallimard, 1958.

Stone, Lawrence. "Interpersonal Violence in English Society, 1300–1980." *Past and Present* 101 (1983): 22–33.

——. "A Rejoinder." *Past and Present* 108 (1985): 216–24.

Strathern, Andrew. *The Rope of Moka: Big Men and Ceremonial Exchange in Mount Hagan New Guinea*. Cambridge: Cambridge University Press, 1971.

Sturlu saga. In *Sturlunga saga*, 2 vols., edited by Jón Jóhannesson, Magnús Finnbogason, and Kristján Eldjárn, 2: 104–226. Reykjavík: Sturlunguútgáfan, 1946. (Trans. Julia H. McGrew and R. George Thomas. *Sturlunga saga*, 2 vols., 1: 59–113. New York: Twayne, 1970–74.)

Svarfdæla saga. In *Eyfirðinga sögur*, edited by Jónas Kristjánsson. Íslenzk Fornrit, vol. 9: 129–211. Reykjavík: Hið Íslenzka Fornritafélag, 1956. (No English translation.)

Sveinsson, Einar Ól. *The Age of the Sturlungs: Icelandic Civilization in the Thirteenth Century*. Translated by Jóhann S. Hanneson. Ithaca: Cornell University Press, 1953.

Swift, Jonathan. *Swift: Poetical Works*. Edited by Herbert Davis. London: Oxford University Press, 1967.

Tavuchis, Nicholas. *Mea Culpa: A Sociology of Apology and Reconciliation*. Stanford: Stanford University Press, 1991.

Taylor, Gabriele. "Envy and Jealousy: Emotions and Vices." *Midwest Studies in Philosophy* 13 (1988): 233–49.

——. *Pride, Shame, and Guilt: Emotions of Self-assessment*. Oxford: Clarendon Press, 1985.

Thucydides. *History of the Peloponnesian War*. Translated by Rex Warner. Harmondsworth: Penguin, 1972.

Tilly, Charles. *From Mobilization to Revolution*. Reading, Mass.: Addison-Wesley, 1978.

Tocqueville, Alexis de. *Democracy in America*. Translated by George Lawrence, edited by J. P. Mayer. Garden City, N.Y.: Anchor, 1969.

Twitchell, James B. *Preposterous Violence: Fables of Aggression in Modern Culture*. New York: Oxford University Press, 1989.

Vatnsdæla saga. Edited by Einar Ól. Sveinsson. Íslenzk Fornrit, vol. 8. Reykjavík: Hið Íslenzka Fornritafélag, 1939. (Trans. Gwyn Jones. *The Vatnsdalers' Saga*. Princeton: Princeton University Press, 1944.)

Víga-Glúms saga. In *Eyfirðinga sögur*, edited by Jónas Kristjánsson. Íslenzk Fornrit, vol. 9: 1–98. Reykjavík: Hið Íslenzka Fornritafélag, 1956. (Trans. John McKinnell. *Víga-Glúm's Saga*. Edinburgh: Canongate, 1987.)

Weiner, Annette B. *Inalienable Possessions: The Paradox of Keeping-While-Giving*. Berkeley: University of California Press, 1992.

Weisberg, Robert. "Private Violence as Moral Action: The Law as Inspiration and Example." In *Law's Violence*, edited by Austin Sarat and Thomas R. Kearns, 175–210. Ann Arbor: University of Michigan Press, 1992.

Werbner, Pnina. "Economic Rationality and Hierarchical Gift Economies: Value and Ranking among British Pakistanis." *Man* 25 (1990): 266–85.

White, Stephen D. *Custom, Kinship, and Gifts to Saints*. Chapel Hill: University of North Carolina Press, 1988.

Wierzbicka, Anna. "Human Emotions: Universal or Culture-Specific?" *American Anthropologist* 88 (1986): 584–94.

Williams, Bernard. *Shame and Necessity*. Berkeley: University of California Press, 1993.

Wilson, Stephen. *Feuding, Conflict, and Banditry in Nineteenth-Century Corsica*. Cambridge: Cambridge University Press, 1988.

Wolff, Robert Paul. *The Rule of Law*. New York: Simon and Schuster, 1971.

Wormald, Jenny. "Bloodfeud, Kindred, and Government in Early Modern Scotland." *Past and Present* 87 (1980): 54–97.

Wurmser, Léon. *The Mask of Shame*. Baltimore: The Johns Hopkins University Press, 1981.

Þorgils saga skarða. In *Sturlunga saga*, 2 vols., edited by Jón Jóhannesson, Magnús Finnbogason, and Kristján Eldjárn, 2: 104–226. Reykjavík: Sturlunguútgáfan, 1946. (Trans. Julia H. McGrew and R. George Thomas. *Sturlunga saga*, 2 vols., 2: 347–485. New York: Twayne, 1970–74.)

Þorsteins þáttr stangarhöggs. In *Austfirðinga sögur*, edited by Jón Jóhannesson. Íslenzk Fornrit, vol. 11: 67–79. Reykjavík: Hið Íslenzka Fornritafélag, 1950. (Trans. Hermann Pálsson. *Hrafnkel's Saga and Other Stories*. Harmondsworth: Penguin, 1971.)

Index

Age: appropriateness of emotional expression and, 107; assumed willingness of gift recipient and, 28; embarrassment at good deeds and, 154; victimizers and, 62–63, 217n18
Aggressiveness, 209n1, 216n4
American culture: envy in, 204–5; fixity of character in, 109–10; gift exchange practices in, 20–25; honor ethic in, 9, 113–14, 204; morality vs. manners in, 200; perception of emotions in sagas and, 94–98
Amusement: and embarrassment, 148–49, 152, 158–59, 168. *See also* Comedy; Laughter; *Schadenfreude*
Anger: consciousness and, 99; convergence of emotions and, 225n21; revenge and, 226n23; in saga narrative, 104–5; vocabulary for, 100–101
Apology, 163
Arendt, Hannah, 62
Aristotle, 128, 226n23
Audun's Story, 211n8
Austen, Jane, 240n2
Ax killers, 65, 68

Banter, 157–58
Birthday gifts, 28
Bloodiness: and violence, 65, 68
Bluntness, 34–35
Body language, 101–8
Boorishness, 5. *See also* Mr. X anecdote
Boredom: in heroic society, 129–30
Bourdieu, Pierre, 19–20, 91
Bridal registry, 44–47
Burns, Robert, 136–37

Character: in sagas, 108–14
Charity: gift of money as, 42–43; gifts to, in another's name, 43n
Chaucer, Geoffrey, 181–83, 199, 230n61
Christmas gifts, 21, 28, 43, 212n26
Civilization: and violence, 73–83, 90–92
Comedy: embarrassment and, 148–49, 152, 158–59, 193; of fabliaux, 181–83; as genre, 210n7; humiliation and, 137, 148, 199, 204, 206–7; manners vs. morality and, 200; perception of violence and, 88–89; suicide of Chinese couple as, 40. *See also*

Library of Congress Cataloging-in-Publication Data

Miller, William Ian, 1946–
  Humiliation / William Ian Miller.
     p.   cm.
  Includes bibliographical references and index.
  ISBN 0-8014-2881-5
  1. Humiliation.   2. Shame.   3. Honor.   I. Title.
  BF575.H85M55   1993
  152.4—dc20
  93-1273